Helping Your Child
Develop His Potentialities

BY RUTH STRANG

Helping Your Gifted Child
Helping Your Child Improve His Reading
Helping Your Child Develop His Potentialities

The Adolescent Views Himself: A Psychology of Adolescence
The Administrator and the Improvement of Reading
(*with* Donald M. Lindquist)
Counseling Technics in College and Secondary School
Diagnostic Teaching of Reading
Group Work in Education
Exploration in Reading Patterns
An Introduction to Child Study
Making Better Readers
(*with* Dorothy K. Bracken)
Role of the Teacher in Personnel Work
Teen-Age Tales
Study Type of Reading Exercises

Helping Your Child
Develop His Potentialities

By RUTH STRANG

University of Arizona

E. P. DUTTON & CO., INC.

NEW YORK, 1965

FIRST EDITION

COPYRIGHTS FROM WHICH PERMISSION TO QUOTE HAS BEEN GRANTED:

Allport, Gordon W. "Psychological Models for Guidance," *Harvard Educational Review*, Vol. 32: (Fall, 1962), p. 379.

Ashton-Warner, Sylvia. *Teacher*, pp. 27–62. New York: Simon and Schuster, 1963.

Barber, Bernard. "Social-class Differences in Educational Life-chances," *Teachers College Record*, Vol. 63: (November 1961), pp. 103, 107.

Blanding, Sarah Gibson. "The Day I Spoke Off the Cuff to the Girls of Vassar," *McCall's*, Vol. 90: (November 1962), pp. 91, 162.

Children's Hospital Medical Center and Child Study Association of America. *Helping Parents of Handicapped Children: Group Approaches*, p. 18. Proceedings of Conference held in Boston, Mass., October 15–16, 1959. New York 28: The Child Study Association of America, 1959.

Coleman, James S. "Teen-agers and Their Crowd," *The PTA Magazine*, Vol. 56: (March 1962), pp. 4–7.

Craig, Marjorie L. and Frances U. Everett. "Developing Health Potentialities," *Teachers College Record*, Vol. 61: (May 1960), pp. 430–431.

Demonstration Guidance Project 1957–1962; Pilot Program for Higher Horizons. George Washington High School, Henry T. Tillson, Principal; Florence C. Myers, Administrative Assistant. Board of Education, New York City, May 1963.

Doll, Edgar. Quoted in Doris D. Klaussen, "The Physically Different," *Childhood Education*, Vol. 32, No. 5: (January 1956), p. 211. Reprinted by permission of the Association for Childhood Education International, 3615 Wisconsin Avenue, N.W., Washington, D.C.

Eisenberg, Leon. "Treatment of the Emotionally Disturbed Pre-adolescent Child," in *The Pre-adolescent Exceptional Child*, p. 39. Proceedings of the 35th Conference of the Child Research Clinic, held in Philadelphia, May 23, 1953, The Woods Schools, Langhorne, Pennsylvania.

Escalone, Sibylle. Summary of parts of *Children and the Threat of Nuclear War*. 9 East 89th Street, New York 28, New York: Child Study Association of America, Inc. 1962.

Gardner, John W. *Self-renewal: The Individual and the Innovative Society*, pp. 10–12. New York: Harper & Row, 1964. Reprinted with permission of the author and publisher.

Hinds, Gloria Jean. "Adolescents Gifted in the Performing Arts: A Study of Self Reports." Unpublished Doctoral Project, Teachers College, Columbia University, 1963.

Kanner, Leo. "The Emotional Quandaries of Exceptional Children," in *Helping Parents Understand the Exceptional Child*, p. 23. Proceedings of the Annual Spring Conference on Education and the Exceptional Child, Child Research Clinic of the Woods Schools, Langhorne, Pennsylvania, May 1952.

Kough, Jack and Robert F. DeHaan. *Teachers Guidance Handbook*, Part I, Identifying Children with Special Needs, pp. 76, 82, 88. Chicago: Science Research Associates, 1955.

Krogman, Wilton M. "How Your Children Grow," *Saturday Evening Post*, Vol. 235 (July 14–21, 1962), p. 50.

"On Telling Parents about Test Results," *Test Service Bulletin*, No. 54. New York: The Psychological Corporation (December 1959), pp. 1–4. (No author given.)

Penty, Ruth C. *Reading Ability and High School Dropouts*, pp. 43–50. New York: Bureau of Publications, Teachers College, Columbia University, 1956.

Repplier, Agnes. *Eight Decades*, p. 88. Boston: Houghton Mifflin Company, 1937.

Rosten, Leo. "The Real Reason for Being Alive," *This Week Magazine* (January 20, 1963), p. 2. Reprinted from *This Week Magazine*. Copyrighted 1963 by the United Newspapers Magazine Corporation.

Strang, Ruth. "Intellectual Differences," *Childhood Education*, Vol. 32: (January 1956), pp. 211–214. Reprinted by permission of the Association for Childhood Education International, 3615 Wisconsin Avenue, N.W., Washington, D.C.

Symonds, John Addington. *The Life of Michelangelo Buonarroti*, p. 543. New York: Modern Library (Random House), n.d.

Torrance, E. Paul. "Cultural Discontinuities and the Development of Originality of Thinking," *Exceptional Children*, Vol. 29: (September 1962), pp. 2–13.

———. "Who Is the Underachiever?" *The NEA Journal*, Vol. 51: (November 1962), pp. 15–17.

Warburton, Amber Arthur. *Stimulating Guidance in Rural Schools; Influence of the National Defense Education Act*. Title V-A on Guidance in Rural Schools, p. 25. Washington, D.C. 20009: American Personnel and Guidance Association, 1964.

Wray, Beulah K. Ephron. "The Good Mother," *Journal of the National Association of Women Deans and Counselors*, Vol. 24: (January 1961), p. 75.

FABLE

The mountain and the squirrel
Had a quarrel,
And the former called the latter "Little Prig";
Bun replied,
"You are doubtless very big;
But all sorts of things and weather
Must be taken in together,
To make up a year
And a sphere.
And I think it no disgrace
To occupy my place.
If I'm not so large as you,
You are not so small as I,
And not half so spry.
I'll not deny you make
A very pretty squirrel track;
Talents differ; all is well and wisely put;
If I cannot carry forests on my back,
Neither can you crack a nut."

RALPH WALDO EMERSON

Contents

Preface

"POTENTIALITIES" is one of the most frequently used words in education today. It is used in discussions of the gifted and of the culturally deprived, in discussions in connection with "the pursuit of excellence" and the fostering of creativity. It is used in defining democracy and in describing moral and religious ideals.

Helping every child develop his best potentialities is the central task of parents and teachers. It is natural for adults to focus their attention on the high achievement of the intellectually gifted child; on the child with special musical, mathematical, or mechanical talent; and on the socially gifted. The cultivation of exceptionally high creative thinking and productivity is essential for pushing forward the frontiers of science, art, and human relations. We should also be concerned with the child of retarded mental development, the physically handicapped, and the emotionally unstable children. These children, too, have potentialities that are often not fully developed. However, in our concern for exceptional children, we should not neglect the large middle group. The cultivation of the abilities of the multitude of average individuals adds up to a large total contribution to society.

This book aims to help parents and teachers understand the many-sided aspects of children's development—their physical, intellectual, artistic, educational, vocational, emotional, social, moral, and spiritual potentialities. Such understanding involves a recognition of the hereditary basis of a child's potential abilities—his strengths and his limitations. His potentialities unfold from the beginning of his life in developmental stages. Each child develops unique patterns of potentialities in response to conditions in his environment—physical conditions and interpersonal relations. To prevent failure in self-fulfillment, we should help the child combat forces within himself and his environment that are self-defeating.

While recognizing the interrelationship among different aspects of an individual's development, I decided to organize this book around the child's physical, intellectual, creative, educational, vocational, emotional, social, moral, and spiritual potentialities. Each chapter aims to give an understanding of (a) ways to develop each of these potential abilities, and (b) ways of helping children who are handicapped in any of these respects.

Many concrete illustrations of parents' hopes and fears, expectations and disappointments about their children's potentialities have been included, for specific descriptions help to prevent generalizations from being misinterpreted. For example, the oft-repeated emphasis on the importance of parents loving their children often is misinterpreted. There are all kinds of love: unconditional love that is steadfast no matter what the child does; conditional love, dependent upon the child's behavior; possessive love that closes the door on other relationships; and a kind of love that is competently concerned with the child's welfare. Intellectual understanding is not enough. Good ideas must be reinforced by right feelings. Insights may stem from changes in a person's behavior as well as result in changed behavior.

Too often people go to extremes in carrying out the advice given to them. For example, they may feel that if a little permissiveness is a good thing, a lot is much better. Parents can be too permissive. Children and adolescents sometimes need someone or something to rebel against. "It is hard," Dr. Charles Frankel said, "to rebel when everyone understands." It is hard for children to know what behavior is acceptable when solicitous parents tell them to do whatever they want to do.

A book of this kind must be suggestive rather than prescriptive. In the last analysis, the child's response to the parent or teacher's words and actions determines the effectiveness of any procedure for that particular child.

I am indebted to the parents, children, and adolescents who have given me insight into their feelings and aspirations. From many published sources relating to child development, I have tried to select the most relevant ideas. Instead of a general bibliography, the references related to each chapter, given at the end of the book, should prove most helpful to the reader who is interested in exploring further the ideas presented. The purpose of the book is mainly to alert parents and teachers to the possibility of discovering and developing the potentialities, not only of the children for whom they are immediately responsible, but also of less fortunate children whom other parents and society have neglected.

RUTH STRANG

ONE

Potentialities Unlimited

I do not want to MAKE you anything: I want to know what Nature has made you, and to perfect you on her plan.[1]

THE above quotation expresses the theme of this book. You will hear it repeated over and over in different words: "Accentuate the positive." Build on the potentials for growth in each child. Focus attention on what the child *can* do, not on what he cannot do.

Children and young people appreciate parents and teachers who enable them to do their best. Despite surface indifference or apathy, almost everyone has a drive toward self-realization, a deep desire to make himself as "good" or complete as possible.

But—are we going too far in this emphasis on individual development? Man does not live by self-realization alone. He is also his brother's keeper; he has social responsibility. Is our culture too child-centered, too individualistic? Does it give children an inflated sense of their importance in the total scheme of things? Is there a danger that they will become obnoxious about demanding the center of the stage, like the seven-year-old constantly interrupting adult conversations with his insistent demands: "See me do this somersault." "Just watch me do this trick."

How can we combine these two points of view—the individualistic and the social? First, by acknowledging that the individual is a social being; he needs others for the realization of his best self—and others need him. Second, by recognizing that the world can be no better than the individuals in it. This idea was illustrated by the remark of a little boy. To keep him occupied, his father had cut up a map of the world into a jig-saw puzzle. The child came back with the puzzle completed much sooner than the father had expected. He explained, "There was a picture of a man on the other side, and when I got the man right, the world was right." The world will become better only if and when we develop the individual potentiality and social responsibility of every child.

13

"The purpose of life is not to be happy. The purpose of life is to matter, to be productive, to have it make some difference that you lived at all. Happiness, in the ancient, noble sense, means self-fulfillment—and is given to those who use to the fullest whatever talents God or luck or fate bestowed upon them.

"Happiness, to me, lies in stretching, to the farthest boundaries of which we are capable, the resources of the mind and heart." [2]

"Freedom is the power of man to realize the possibilities of his being," said Howard Mumford Jones.[3] He went on to say that we desperately need a revival of belief in man—in his powers and potentialities.

Concern for our own children is not enough. If our country's human resources are to be fully developed, we must be concerned with the less fortunate children—those whose development is limited by ignorance, neglect, poverty, and other blighting conditions. Through our support of sound social legislation, social work agencies, nursing services, nursery schools and kindergartens, better neighborhood schools, and parent education groups, we can help provide better home conditions for some of these disadvantaged children. In these and many other ways we can give handicapped children opportunities that would otherwise be denied to them.

UNREALIZED POTENTIALITIES

The sum of unrealized potential in the total population is enormous. Slow-learning children, as well as the gifted, are allowed to languish in idleness. Talents in art, music, and sports may lie dormant for lack of opportunities for their development. Potential poets may never be discovered. The socially gifted may go unrecognized.

All children have unrealized potentialities. Why do they not realize them? One reason is that adult standards often restrict rather than stimulate children's growth; they impose a ceiling rather than offering a challenge. Joanne could have read, with comprehension and enjoyment, fifty books instead of the ten required during the year. John would have done more work on his composition if the teacher had not seemed satisfied with it. David stopped trying to make his writing more legible when no one even noticed the effort he was making. Adult standards for these children were too low and the children were too dependent upon them; they were more concerned with the approval of adults than with work well done.

We can help children to set their own standards by asking them such questions as these: "What were you trying to accomplish?" "Were *you* satisfied with the result?" "In what ways could it have been done better?" "Was your goal too high or too low—too difficult or too easy to reach?" "Would a check list help you to see your progress?"

Another reason for unrealized potentialities is that children's abilities are not recognized early and offered opportunities for their development. Bright children have trouble in the first grade because they already know so much. They are bored by instruction and drill that they do not need, and by books that were written for average or slow learners. Teachers who recognize the momentum that is generated by a child's curiosity and eagerness to learn try to let each child progress at his own pace. They try to avoid slowing down a young mind by underestimating its ability.

One result of unrealized potentialities may be unhappiness and apathy; a life that is unfulfilled seems meaningless. Another result is frustration that may find outlets in aggression. Or the discrepancy between a high level of aspiration and a low level of performance may result in poor mental health or addiction to alcohol or drugs.

THE DESIRE FOR SELF-FULFILLMENT

The desire for self-fulfillment is a basic urge. It is a "will to health," an urge to grow. Rarely is anyone completely satisfied with himself. Even adolescents who at first express no desire to change usually mention some way in which they would like to improve.

The opposite extreme—complete dissatisfaction with oneself—is illustrated by the response of an overweight, unpopular girl:

I would like to have no appetite and be very graceful. I would like to be more of an athlete and less of a lazybones. I wish I had no desire to sit down with a book instead of study as I should. I wish I was always gentle and courteous, instead of being too often rough and rude. And I wish I could never draw a bad picture, or make a clumsy piece of pottery, or play a sour note on the piano.

I try to make my work better, but too often there is a temptation to let it go badly done and do something pleasant. And too often I yield.

Between these two extremes are many degrees and combinations of satisfaction and dissatisfaction, indicating the basic urge toward self-realization that makes improvement possible.

GENESIS OF POTENTIALITIES

Every child comes into this world with certain potentialities. We recognize the influence of heredity in plants and in animals. We speak of children as being "well-born." We can observe differences in infants at birth. Some are more alert than others. Some evoke, while others repel, friendly responses. Both assets and limitations are, at least in part, genetically determined.

Very soon we begin to notice differences that result from the interplay of genetic and environmental factors. The growth of a physically normal child may be stunted by an inadequate diet. A potentially bright child may become dull if he is deprived of affection and normal sensory stimulation—things to handle, touch, taste, smell, and manipulate. A socially responsive infant may become apathetic in a home or institution where no one cares for him.

In our country, malnutrition can be eliminated. It is often due to "secondary poverty"—spending money for unessentials. In many rural communities, land resources could be used to better advantage. For example, one miner used his yard, which was similar to the barren yards of his neighbors, to grow fruit and vegetables. He had a cow and some chickens. He had become interested in farming as a boy in the 4-H Club. His house was clean, sanitary, and beautiful in a simple way. His children were healthy and alert, in marked contrast to the thin, malnourished, sickly children of his neighbors. Individual parents with vision and "know-how" can do much to make better homes for their children. The public schools and other organizations can help them. Slum neighborhoods, both rural and urban, can be and are being transformed into healthful homes for children.

During the child's early years, each culture shapes its children, largely through the home. Early childhood experiences influence later development, though not in a specific cause-and-effect relation. Intense rivalry with brothers and sisters, severe discipline, overindulgence, and parental quarreling are some of the conditions detrimental to child development. Yet there are individuals from disadvantaged homes who have grown up to be capable, cooperative, conscientious, and responsible adults. It is the meaning of the situation to the child that determines its influence on his personality development. To an outsider, a home may seem sordid; however, if the child senses a strong underlying parental affection, this is his home and he does not want to leave it.

Of all the home influences, personal relationships are the most important. Parents are teachers. The ideal parent has the qualities that are characteristic of the great teacher—love and respect for children, insight, imagination, and ability to provide an environment in which the child can be himself. The adult tries to understand, without intruding upon the child's private world. He listens. He is skillful in channeling the child's destructiveness into creative activities. He does not hesitate to impose discipline when it is necessary. Like Sylvia Ashton-Warner, teacher extraordinary in New Zealand, he believes that "for the spirit to live its freest, the mind must acknowledge discipline." [4]

The parent-child relationship is more important than any specific child-care practices. Breast or bottle feeding, methods of toilet training, and scheduling are important, only insofar as they affect this relationship. This fact should relieve parents of overanxiety about doing the "right thing" and about mistakes they think they may have made.

There are many right ways of helping children to develop their potentialities. The most important is to be sensitive to the child's responses. Even before he can talk, the child gives us clues about whether we are doing what is best for him. Children are by nature active and insatiably curious; they are essentially self-motivated. A home environment that encourages the child's initiative and spontaneity helps him to make the best use of his inherited capacities.

PATTERNS OF POTENTIALITIES

Each individual has a unique pattern of potentials. He may be high in some traits and low in others. Because he is low in one, he will not necessarily be limited in all other respects.

To develop a child's potentialities, it is essential to know the kind of child that he is: What are his abilities and aspirations? How does he get along with other persons? Does the world seem hostile or friendly to him? What kind of help does he want and need?

What are his feelings? Does he feel loved? Does he feel understood and accepted?

How does he behave? What does his behavior mean to him? What is he trying to accomplish by his behavior? To what or to whom is he responding? [5]

What is his concept of himself? Does he feel inferior because of mental or physical handicaps? Is he self-satisfied—content with the way he is? Or does he want to become, as Shakespeare wrote, "like one more rich in hope"?

Patterns of potentialities are revealed most vividly by adolescents' self-descriptions. In anonymous essays they give us glimpses of thoughts and feelings, of hopes and fears, that they seldom communicate to parents and teachers. This inner world is often quite different from the one that we would infer from their outward behavior. The defiant youngster with his cocksure air may not actually feel superior or independent at all.

Let us first look at a brief self-description, written by a boy whom some might call the "All-American type":

I feel I am an average American boy that goes out for sports such as football, wrestling and skindiving. I collect guns and I feel this is a good hobby. The guns as they get older increase their value.

In my future I plan to go to college. I have hopes to go to Scripps School of Oceanography. I want to be an oceanographer because I am interested in the sea.

I think I am a capable young boy with a lot of responsibility. I work weekends trying to make money to go to college. I also coach younger boys playing basketball on Saturdays during the basketball season.

I expect to live as good as any middle class way of life or higher. I am looking forward to getting out of college and getting married. I worry about today—tomorrow will come. I dread the thought of war. But I think the possibility of a world war is very remote and I think each nation will be able to live in peace, but not at first. It will take time. *

* In these introspective reports, wording and spelling are unchanged.

Those of us who think of adolescents as moody and without chart or compass will find some support for our opinions in the following composition, written by a fourteen-year-old boy:

I don't know how I feel about myself. I don't always feel the same way. I often wonder what other people think about, as for instance I feel everybody has importance of his own. I never thought of what I'm good for, and I haven't decided what yet.

I don't know about my future yet, and I don't know what I'm going to do. I don't know how I expect to live unless I join the service. I wouldn't know what I'm looking forward to.

Turning to compositions by girls, here is a girl who recognizes how deeply models, or admired persons, affect her own self-concept. She first makes a keen and critical analysis of the kind of person she thinks she is:

Nowadays most people tend to pattern themselves after someone or several people they admire. Borrowing traits you consider desirable and discarding ones you dislike, you may not even recognize the end result. I am no exception. I think of myself as trustworthy, generous, kind and sweet. But I never can convince myself that one person can be quite so perfect. In truth I am probably not quite so trustworthy, a little stingy, and one who loses her temper a little too quickly. I say probably because I am not quite sure what I think of myself. People my age in particular, think of themselves as being very mature. I suppose it's really a sign of immaturity to think this way, as I and others do.

This gifted girl then writes an equally perceptive description of "The Kind of Person Other People Think I Am":

Sometimes I wonder how people can stand me at all and then I'll think that maybe I'm not as bad as what I think of myself. Oftentimes finding out what people think of you is like listening to yourself on a tape recorder. You'll say "Do I really sound like that?" because it isn't at all like what you sound like to yourself. It's really very hard to find out what people think of you. Your friends will always say such nice things about you when you are within hearing distance. I have year-books full of, "stay as sweet as you are," and "to a real nice girl." I guess a good test of friendship is what your friends say of you behind your back. Your enemies of course will never hesitate to tell you what they think of you. In fact, they are the only ones you can really be sure of.

Finally, she describes "The Kind of Person I Want to Be":

I want to be a person that people will admire, but more important than that, a person I can admire. When I die I want to be able to say, "I have fulfilled some purpose, someone benefited from the few years I lived on this earth."

Here is a teen-ager with an unusual facility in self-appraisal and a firm commitment to chosen values.

A pattern even less common is revealed by a fifteen-year-old girl shuttling between two cultures, and conscious also of the conflicting values of two generations. She writes as follows:

I am one of the new generations that is living under the threat of the Atomic Bomb—one of the post-war generation who is supposed to try and relieve the world of the problems it formed before I was born. Being in the higher section of my class scholastically and socially, I am a preordained leader of others.

Being socially and scholastically higher than those of my race in this region, I find myself a loner. They don't seemed to take interest in my interests, nor do I show interest in theirs. For example, I am alone in enthusiasm for reading books, listening to semi-classical and classical music, preferring creative dancing to the latest steps others are doing. Being an only child I do not like to be alone so I try to make friends in everything I do.

Other people of my race—I have heard—think of me as a "snob," "stuck up," and "unsociable." To them maybe I am, but if I were to venture into their world I would find myself at a complete loss. . . .

The following is a uniquely perceptive and poetical description of a teen-ager's search for self-knowledge and self-realization:

Who am I? I guess I'm nothing to most of the world. Like an uncounted pebble on a endless shore; like a lost star beyond some uncrossed horizon. . . .

To begin with, I've found that there is no one else like me, anywhere, like snowflakes. No one else feels completely the way I do. No one else sees things in the same scope as I do. So my first discovery about myself is that I'm me. Though there are many traits in other people which I relish more than my own, I'm still me.

To me the world is like a wonderful challenge. I want to run into it full force. I want to know everyone and everything, to travel, to discover. I hate being a girl at times because people say the world opens its gates only to boys. Well, I'll get in and to me this is a goal in life. Goals help to build strong character. . . .

I am a person troubled with doubts. I am always wondering about my faith, about my friends, about my beliefs. The only key to doubt I've found is faith. Faith has always found the way for me and somehow though today may bring me manifold sorrow such as I have never felt before, I will always remember that tomorrow it will be yesterday.

I always cry if I am touched by something. Tears are good, I believe. I suppose you might say I'm a bit sentimental. I never forget a friend, nor a special day. I hate to see the old traditions change so. I suppose I feel underneath that as they change, I, too must grow up. . . .

Discovering realism is part of becoming an adult, but I believe keeping a fertile, compassionate, imaginative mind is also part of growing up. We don't have to grow old in spirit.

Who am I? I'm a lost sparrow on the limb of life, afraid, alone, confused. Jump or fly?—I believe I shall fly—soar into the great frontiers yet to be opened in my life. Crazy? Perhaps I am, but at least I am myself. What else really matters?

What is the significance of these self-portraits, written spontaneously in English classes? Do they not give adults a deeper understanding of the personalities and aspirations of adolescents? Each pattern is unique. Each pattern is in the process of becoming.

The range of feelings and aspirations is shown still more clearly by a summary of the statements that young adolescents have written about themselves:

"I am good for nothing."

"I feel like an ant in a world full of giants."

"I think of myself as a young boy who means nothing to the world."

"I feel no one cares what happens to me."

"I fear I will not be good at my job."

"When I get a job and start work then I would feel I was good for something."

"I feel I'm not really as good as I think I am."

"I feel all confused; anything I do for someone doesn't seem to be right."

"I feel I could be better. I am not important to other people but I am important to myself."

"I think I am an unimportant individual in a crazy mixed-up world."

"I am a person who lives in dreams of what I want to be, but my grades won't get me there."

The following comments are quoted from compositions by

young adolescents who had achieved some degree of self-acceptance and self-confidence:

"I am all right, I guess."

"I don't think I am really important, but my real mother does."

"I don't think I am important. But I may seem important to my mother and father for they love me."

"I feel that I'm an average girl with wonderful parents who give me the things I need in life such as a good home, good food, and lots of love. Actually I'm a nobody to anyone except my family and some boys in our school. I like to help and comfort my parents. I'm not good for much except for giving and accepting love."

"About myself, I feel content."

"I feel that I am not very important right now, but I guess I will be when I get a little older."

"I am an ordinary girl who doesn't think I am better than anybody else."

"I feel I can do just as well as the other fellows."

"I feel that everyone in the world is important, at least to someone."

"I like myself. I like the way I am built. I like my color. And I like the way I live."

"I may one day be principal of a high school; that's how important I am."

"I can do what anyone else does or better."

"I feel that I and all other teen-agers in the world are very important, because we will be running the world in the future."

For a parent the most direct understanding is to be gained from his own children's casual communications. In moments of stress or at times when they want to confide in someone, they reveal glimpses of what they *are* and what they *want* to be.

These glimpses of the young person's hidden self-concepts and aspirations enable parents to answer questions, explain perplexities, make suggestions, or give criticism, if that is necessary, in a manner that is acceptable to the child. Thus the child feels that his parents are his allies, helping him to be the kind of person he wants to be. They are reinforcing his own drive toward self-realization.

To maintain an adequate understanding of the way their children view themselves, parents must try to keep the avenue of communication open.

A fourteen-year-old boy wrote: "Having someone to go to is most important to me. Life would be hard if I could not tell someone my problems."

A bright fourteen-year-old girl expressed great appreciation of her parents' willingness to listen to whatever she wanted to tell them and their reticence about imposing their decisions upon her. She felt free to confide in them. There is nothing more comforting to a troubled child or adolescent than the feeling that he can confide in his parents. Children who cannot talk freely with their parents are truly disadvantaged.

THE SELF-CONCEPT AND ITS SIGNIFICANCE

"Who do you think you are?" is a good question for young people to ask themselves. Adults can encourage them to find satisfactory, sincere answers to such questions as these:

Who am I?
What are my goals in life?
What kind of person will I be ten or fifteen years from now?

It is exhilarating for a child or an adolescent to discover that he has abilities and that there are resources for developing them.

The self-concept is a person's inner world of ideas, attitudes, values, and commitments—the way he sees himself and feels about himself. It is all the meanings which he has attached to the word "I." It is the nucleus or radix of personality. To build a self-image and to arrive at self-understanding are major tasks of children and adolescents. A realistic self-acceptance is a manifestation of maturity. During adolescence, the individual identifies himself with many groups whose values may be contradictory. He strives to find a common ground of agreement between his description of himself and the descriptions made by other people. If he fails to integrate the diverse values in his life, he may develop inner conflicts, become prey to excessive daydreaming and fantasy, or escape into self-defeating activities. A unified and harmonious self-concept is an achievement.

The self-concept deeply affects the person's attitudes and achievement. Most people feel happy when they have a sense of personal growth, when they feel they are good for something rather than "good for nothing." It seems likely that delinquency, extreme withdrawal, and other behavior disorders are related to deficiencies in the self-concept. Too low a level of aspiration is sometimes more destructive of self-esteem than too high a level. One group of young teen-age delinquent boys in an institution for delinquent boys showed a need for higher values. Their values were vague and materialistic. They needed more insight into their conflicting values. They also needed help in finding more socially acceptable methods of attaining their goals in life.

Self-understanding should lead to self-acceptance. Self-acceptance is not synonymous with smugness or conceit. The person who accepts himself does the best he can with his resources, and does not fret about his limitations. Self-acceptance contributes to the mental health of both parents and children. Self-acceptance is essential to acceptance of others. As a person learns to accept himself, he becomes more accepting of others.

Experience is the mirror in which individuals see themselves as well liked, wanted, successful; or disliked, unwanted, unworthy, unimportant. It is thus that the individual discovers who he is and what he may become. He learns which opportunities are open to him and which are closed.

The development of a child's self-concept is primarily in the hands of the people who are significant in his life. In early infancy he begins to form impressions of his world. Is it a harsh world that does not meet his needs, or a kind world in which he feels secure, comfortable, and loved? The child's earliest self-appraisal is based on his awareness of how others think and feel about him and his actions. If his parents value him for himself, he accepts their evaluation; it becomes the core of his self-concept.

Between two and three years of age he becomes aware of himself as a person. He uses the pronoun "I" as a symbol of his newly discovered self. He comes up against restraint. He reaches out to his new experiences of freedom. If he meets with approval and helpfulness, he is likely to become self-confident. If his efforts are belittled, he may build a depreciatory attitude toward himself and others.

At about three years of age children tend to become less self-assertive. They conform because they are anxious to please. Later, as they become more conscious of their power, they swing back toward self-assertiveness. This is an exuberant expression of increased self-confidence.

The child's first models are his parents. He catches their attitudes, takes over their values, imitates their behavior. This is especially true of children who are fond of their parents and identify strongly with them. A child who becomes antagonistic to one or both parents resists becoming like them. A man who is now a leader in his profession recalls that his parents were shiftless and degraded alcoholics. He says, "When I was quite young, I was determined not to be like my parents." Fortunately for him, a fine teacher not only helped him to discover his potentialities, but also gave him practical help in realizing them.

When the child enters school, his self-concept is subject to a number of new influences. Among these are the social-emotional atmosphere of the classroom, the teacher's ability to accept him and others, and the school's child study program. In one study of elementary school children, it was shown that teachers who had completed three years of child study had greater insight into children's self-concepts than teachers who had never participated in child study.[6]

THE PROCESS OF BECOMING

"There is no being, for all is becoming." This line from a Buddhist writing is developed in a recent book by Gordon W. Allport entitled *Becoming*.[7] Living is the striving to be and to become. Though influenced by the past and taking shape in the present, each person's life lies in the future.

Youth today has many justified anxieties about the years ahead. Faced with an unknown and threatening future, some young people say, "What's the use?" They feel they have no goal to strive toward. Others find strength for the future in the possibility of a better world. They face the worst, both in themselves and in the world, but at the same time find some worthwhile values. To these values they bring a firm commitment.[8] Your thoughtful, troubled adolescent boy or girl may be inspired by this ancient inscription found somewhere on the coast of Greece:

> A shipwrecked sailor buried on this coast
> Bids you set sail.

> Full many a bark, when we were lost,
> Weathered the gale.[9]

Ralph Waldo Emerson suffered from formidable handicaps. As a child, he was troubled by low physical vitality. As a youth, he was severely disadvantaged by defective vision. He was threatened by tuberculosis. Socially he often felt rejected and lonely. Death came to his father when Ralph was nine years old. Two of the younger children died in childhood. One brilliant brother became violently insane. Ralph had constantly to care for another brother who had the mind of a four-year-old and from time to time became mentally deranged. He was poor; his mother struggled to support her family by taking in boarders. When he was twenty-seven years old, his young wife died from tuberculosis after much suffering. Several years later death came to his five-year-old son. He underwent great agony of spirit over his decision to resign his pastorate of the Second Church of Boston. This ordeal affected him both physically and emotionally. Indeed, few men have suffered more genuine misery.

Yet in spite of all these personal tragedies, Emerson learned to transcend suffering. He attained serenity. His life was a continuous self-renewal.[10] Instead of trying to escape from life, he sought to master it. His self-development was not selfish or self-insistent. He surrendered his own petty ego and focused on his strength rather than his weakness. In essence, this is what any person has to do to realize his potentialities.

Potentialities are latent powers or abilities; they unfold gradually throughout one's life. For example, many children seem to have limitless good health in their early years. However, as they grow and develop, limitations may become apparent. Unfortunately, such limitations become more complex and difficult to correct the longer they remain unrecognized. In general, we would expect the child who shows the greatest progress at any one time to have the greatest potential for continued or future achievement.[11]

Insofar as the past has influenced the child's concept of himself, it is a potent influence on his present behavior. If a child thinks of himself as "dumb" or stupid, if he has absorbed this impression of himself from those around him, no *sudden* reversal of his feelings is possible or even desirable. Any change in his self-concept must come about gradually. For example, Tom had always been considered "the stupid one" by his family. His stepfather added beatings to insults. His brothers made fun of him. Even his mother seemed to go along with the family opinion. It was uphill work for the aunt who took him away from his home to modify even slightly Tom's deep-seated feelings of inferiority. A series of successful experiences eventually did this. His first achievement was in dancing; the next was in baseball. After a summer in a reading center, he could also see improvement in his ability to read.

"Nothing succeeds like success" is more than an old saying. It has psychological verification. After one has had a successful experience, his attitude toward himself tends to become more hopeful. It has been found that students who were already successful expected the most success. Those who had failed, and consequently had the strongest need for achievement, saw the least success in store for them. They planned to work harder, but their path, like the proverbial way to Hell, was paved with good intentions. If we want children—our own and other people's—to fulfill their potential, we should remind them of their successes rather than their failures. We should avoid making them feel inferior or worthless.

The way a child behaves at any moment is dependent upon how he views himself in the past, present, and future. A retarded reader often thinks of himself as "a boy who can't learn to read." A stutterer expects to stutter, even though in his unself-conscious moments he may speak without hesitation or blocking. The shy guy's image of himself intensifies his ineptitude in social situations. A child usually hesitates to learn anything that is not in accord with his concept of himself.

All of us experience a more or less constant tug of war between our tendency to cling to the security of the past and our desire to accept the challenge of new experiences. As a person grows older, he is likely to defend his self-concept, no matter whether it favors or hinders his best development. Even if he thinks he is weak, bad, or stupid, he will try to maintain self-consistency in order to avoid loss of self.[12] It is painful to change a deep-seated habit of thought.

In venturing forward, any child will experience some frustration. The course of an adventurous life, like the course of true love, does not run smooth. At times the child will have to face failure, and learn how to avoid similar failure in the future. He has taken a long stride toward maturity when he has learned to tolerate frustration and to find more satisfaction in overcoming new obstacles than in salvaging his former security.

Perhaps the most effective way to bring about change in our children is to change ourselves. If admired adults set a pattern of crime, youngsters will tend to follow it. If we are apathetic, our children will be likely to catch this attitude. If we are irresponsible, our young people will often be more so. But can adults change themselves?

There are two opposing points of view about whether a person can change his present character. According to one point of view, he is saddled with his predispositions and habits and must get along the best he can. It is true that each life has its share of unhappiness, misery, and failure. Some lives seem to have more than their share. But if a person accepts this fact, he will not have to carry the added burden of resentment or be unduly disturbed by the discrepancy between his hopes and his aspirations. Like Emerson, he will be thankful for moderate good fortune.

While recognizing that human beings have inherent weaknesses and that they tend to resist change, we have evidence that change is possible. Changes in attitudes and behavior may take place as a result of some moving experience, some change in one's life situation, or simply as a result of determined positive thinking. Desirable changes have been due to association with great men and women, either in person or through their works. Many people have testified that change can be accomplished through the power of prayer. A basic assumption of both education and guidance is that individuals can change. They are in the process of becoming. They can call upon both inner resources and outside help to change in desirable directions.[13]

WHAT PRICE INFLUENCE?

Should we try to change our children? In order to help them realize their potentialities, should we set the stage, give calculated approval at strategic times, or manipulate them in other subtle ways so that they will do what we think they ought to do? Is there anything wrong about this? Don't we want them to grow up in what we consider the right way? Yes, but we also want them to be themselves, to take initiative, become self-directive, and increasingly find motivations within themselves. Every young person should be free to chart the course that he thinks will give meaning to his life.

Although we may in principle want our children to be free, at the same time we fear that if we do not consciously influence them, unscrupulous persons may. We are afraid that if we do not make the boy study, he will fail in his school work. We are afraid that if we allow the girl to choose her own friends, she may team up with people who will lead her astray. We are afraid that unless we insist on the child's eating wholesome meals, his health will suffer.

Is there any resolution for our conflicting desires to make the child do what we think is good for him, and to leave him free to choose his own way, make his own choices, make mistakes and take the responsibility for them?

The ratio of control to permissiveness should vary somewhat with the child's age and ability. We take responsibility for the infant's behavior, we provide the loving care he needs, protect him from harm, stimulate him to look, to listen, to feel, and to handle things. But even the infant can be encouraged to take some initiative. As he grows older, his areas of freedom expand. If the child is mentally retarded, he establishes good habits. We help him to take short, easy steps toward each immediate goal.

Our own certainty about the rightness of the child's goal also influences our degree of permissiveness. We feel justified in influencing his decision if it clearly seems to be damaging.

We should more often share with children our understanding of the ways in which people learn. We may show them how to apply learning theory to achieve their own ends and so teach them to use certain techniques for changing themselves. Thus, instead of becoming rebellious, the self-reliant child or adolescent will make good use of his parents' and teacher's knowledge and be stimulated by their approval of his initiative.

DILEMMAS OF GUIDANCE

How often parents say, "My son [or daughter] seems to resent any help or advice I try to give." What are the reasons for this common rejection of parental counsel? It may be that the advice isn't sound, and the youngster knows it. Maybe it will not work because the parents do not understand his world. Or the child may have such a feeling of resentment toward the parent, for any one of a number of reasons, that he may reject any suggestions, good or bad. Or his natural desire for independence may take the form of resistance to any authority.

The manner in which the parent gives the help may make the difference between its acceptance and rejection. If the parent understands what his child is striving for and gears his suggestions to the child's own ongoing purposeful activity, his help will usually be gratefully received. For example, in criticizing a bridge of blocks that a preschool child was building, instead of saying, "The bridge is too low," the father said, "Dolly can't walk under the bridge." This suggestion was in keeping with the child's viewpoint.

When asked what kind of guidance they wanted, young adolescents made such comments as the following: [14]

"I would like my parents to tell me what they expect of me and how I can attain these goals."

"Whenever I've had a problem I've usually gone to my mother about it. Most of them have been about my social and personal life. She's also helped me with my school problems. If there's a subject that she can't help me with, I go to my father for advice. Between them most of my school problems are solved. I've never really thought of going to my teacher for help unless I know my parents can't work it out. I suppose that this is because the teachers had enough to do without solving each student's individual problems. Sometimes I'd rather talk to my sister or my friends about my troubles."

"My mother listens sympathetically, which is always a help, since telling what's wrong often straightens things out in my own mind."

"When I go to people for guidance it's usually after having thought and thought on the topic myself. Therefore, when I do go, I don't want the person whose aid I've requested to 'throw the ball back' to me again. I want a definite opinion."

"If your request is reasonable, I feel that the parent should not brush you off abruptly. Instead, he should explain what he thinks is wrong. Teacher and parents should show an interest in you and help you with all sincerity."

The following incident shows how parents, by explaining their view of a situation, may help the child accept their decision:

"This summer I was asked out on a date. I wanted to go but I didn't know the boy well. My parents didn't know the boy at all, and he didn't live in our town. When I found out that my father wouldn't let me go, I felt that my parents wanted me to become an old maid. That night my parents explained why they didn't want me to go. I felt better after the talk and didn't feel resentful towards my parents."

A severely disturbed boy whose parents had refused psychological help for him answered the question about the kind of guidance he would like to receive by simply stating, "I would like them to put themselves in my shoes."

Adolescents seem to fall into several categories with respect to their desire for adult guidance. There are those who want adult guidance. There are those who want adults to let them strictly alone. To teachers, these youngsters say, in effect, "Stick to your teaching and keep hands off our private lives." Some adolescents do not believe that age necessarily brings wisdom and understanding; they turn to their peers for help because, in their view, "young people know and understand better."

In discussion, counseling, or therapy groups, led by a skillful leader, youngsters often speak freely about teachers, parents, and themselves. Often their feeling of inadequacy and their fear of failure come out into the open. In one group, thirteen- and four-teen-year-old boys, underachievers who had been disrupting their classes, were given opportunities to explore and express their feelings on issues about which they were anxious or hostile. In this special group, they could suggest various methods of handling difficult situations without fear of disapproval or punishment.

They discussed many things, such as the need for more shop work in the school curriculum. They explained why they didn't like teachers and why teachers didn't like them. Although they tended to take the part of the pupil against the teacher, they were usually on the teacher's side when they thought the pupil was obviously wrong. They seemed to want to be friends with teachers, despite their resentment of teachers' authority. They especially resented being called "dumb." For them, this was an emotionally charged word that intensified their feelings of inferiority. They were sensitive to criticism, and resented being placed in the lowest section of their grade. The low marks on their report cards periodically confirmed their low estimate of their ability.

As a group, these underachievers complained that parents were inconsistent about discipline and lacked understanding of adolescents. They "seemed to be pleading for more warmth and acceptance, which they felt they could not get." [15] Their negative or annoying behavior often seemed to stem from their feeling of worthlessness and from the conviction that "no one cares anyway."

QUESTIONS AND ANSWERS

1. *Which is more important, to develop a well-rounded personality or to develop one's special competencies?*

An individual's potentialities are uneven. Rarely is a child equally good in everything. Is it better for him to develop some superior abilities than to be mediocre in everything? In some cases of high ability or genius, we may have to forget about the desirability of developing a happy, well-adjusted person and allow the individual to concentrate on the special abilities through which he may make his greatest contribution to society.

The age of the individual must be considered. During the preschool and elementary years, and even in the high school years, the student's education can be broad, with considerable emphasis on social relations. If we allow the student to specialize too early, we may prevent him from discovering and developing other potentialities that are equally or even more important. Later, he may spend an increasing amount of time on his specialty. In the professions and many other vocations, a socially-minded, outgoing person is likely to have greater success than one of equal ability who has specialized too early, too narrowly, or too intensively.

2. *Does the idea of the "Pursuit of Excellence" apply only to intellectual activities?*

Excellence in any socially useful endeavor should be developed and rewarded. J. B. Priestley, the English author, once remarked that he would be happy indeed if he could write as well as his friend, the stonemason, built his stone walls. John W. Gardner, who has written much on this subject, emphasizes excellence in the most humble as well as in the most exalted activities.

3. *How does a child gain faith in himself?*

There are many ways: by having successful experiences, by learning not to be afraid of making mistakes, by knowing that others like him, and that there is some special person who loves and understands him—even when he is at his worst. "If someone has faith in you, then you will have faith in yourself," was the way one boy expressed it.

4. *Are our children losing their identity? Will they, before long, be reduced to a series of social security numbers?*

Achieving identity is a developmental task of the teen-age years. Every adolescent must develop his own self-image, or self-concept. He needs encouragement in this lonely, private job of finding satisfactory answers to such questions as these: Who am I? What kind of person am I really and truly? Where do I fit into the scheme of things? What do I want to do with my life? What can I do to become more nearly the kind of person I want to be? Whom can I believe in? The person who has conviction of his uniqueness and a consistent self-image will maintain his individuality despite the mass methods that are used to produce widespread conformity.

5. *Do children need nursery school experience for their best development?*

The answer, of course, depends first on the quality of the nursery school and second on the needs of the child. Following are some of the characteristics of a good nursery school: [16]

(1) Opportunities for the children to feel, handle, and work with many things; experiment, observe, question and learn; acquire skill and develop their newly discovered abilities.

(2) An understanding teacher who is sensitive to the needs of each child, whether overaggressive or exceedingly shy, eager to participate or withdrawn. The skillful teacher makes provision for these individual differences in ability, personality, and previous experience.

(3) Safe and healthful physical facilities, with plenty of space for active play, and nooks and corners for undisturbed individual and small-group activities such as building with blocks or playing house.

(4) Provision for the children's needs for varied social experiences: they join the large group at lunch time, and at other times play or work in small, congenial groups.

(5) Suitable equipment and materials (see catalogue published by Creative Playthings, Inc., Princeton, New Jersey).

(6) Not more than twenty children for two teachers, or for one teacher and an assistant.

(7) Flexible orderliness in the daily routine so that the children will learn to move from one activity to another, e.g. from play to clean-up time, without feelings of frustration.

(8) Concern for the way children learn as well as what they learn. They should be encouraged to show spontaneity, to take responsibility for their playthings, to take turns, and to show more and more consideration for others as they grow older.

(9) Opportunities for the parents to observe how a skillful teacher works with preschool children, and to note how their own children respond to positive suggestions, approval, and constructive criticism.

How many of these favorable environmental factors can a parent provide in his own home? How might a group of parents, on a voluntary basis, provide some of the same opportunites for underprivileged children in a small neighborhood nursery school?

6. *What is the ideal parent-child relation?*

Either of two extreme parental approaches may hamper the growth of a child or adolescent. The first is over-control: telling him exactly what to do and when to do it, prying into his private affairs; choosing all his clothes, demanding more of him than it is reasonable to expect, and never being satisfied with his behavior. The other extreme is to allow oneself to be imposed upon and suffer in silence over the child's "lack of consideration." Dorothy Barclay suggests that parents treat the teen-ager as they would treat an adult friend.[17]

7. *What is the task of the teacher in helping each student develop his potentialities?*

The teacher's task is (a) to ascertain each pupil's potential abilities and note any ways in which his growth is being blocked and (b) to discover means of releasing his creative energies so that he will move forward on his proper path toward maturity. Ideally, the teacher, like the parent, should serve as a model by presenting the example of a developing personality.

TWO

Potentialities, Limited

EVERY child has some limitations. The highly gifted child may have special problems of getting along with other children of his own age. The child who is socially well-adjusted may become quite upset by heavy homework assignments. The poor little rich girl may feel an acute lack of the kind of affection that a mother in a one-room cabin bestows on each of her eight children.

There are also persons who, though they appear severely handicapped, transcend their physical limitations. Helen Keller immediately comes to mind. Or one may recall a radiant young person who seemed almost oblivious of her physical handicap. One speaker at an important conference was a spastic who could not control his bodily movements; nevertheless the brilliance of his thoughts so entranced a large audience that they forgot his physical limitations.

WHEN IS A CHILD HANDICAPPED?

Handicapped children may have many assets and admirable characteristics. A blind child may be as bright, as keen in hearing, as strong physically, as other children. He may talk fluently and be able to get along well with people. A physically handicapped child who is clumsy in sports may be able to write the sports news for his school paper. A mentally retarded child can solve practical problems within the limits of his experience. He can grasp explanations if the adult makes the problem clear and "doesn't go too fast." If parents expect the best of him, he tries not to "let them down." Of a teacher, one child said, "She didn't seem to know I was dumb, and I tried not to let her find out." When we study any handicapped child, we may find potentialities whose presence we did not even suspect. No child can be adequately described by a single characteristic, such as "blind," "deaf," or "mentally retarded."

There is no such thing as an "average" child. All children are exceptional in some respect. They vary widely in interests, in emotional stability, and in other aspects of development. Edgar Doll of Vineland, New Jersey, has summed it up this way: "Let us remember the paradox that the [so-called] *average child* is exceptional in some respects and that the exceptional child is average in most respects. This implies a double necessity for conserving what is normal as well as making the most of what is exceptional." [1]

Exceptional children are first of all children. We should not let a special handicap divert our attention from this fact. They have common basic needs: to be loved, respected, accepted, valued. They need success and recognition. They need to learn self-direction and to build self-esteem. In these respects handicapped children and normal children are more alike than different. [2]

WHAT ARE THE SPECIAL NEEDS OF THESE CHILDREN?

Because these children have special needs, we often speak of them as *exceptional children*. Some need crutches or wheel chairs; others, speech or reading lessons; the mentally retarded need vivid and concrete instruction at a slower than average pace. All need understanding.

We need much more understanding of what children's behavior means to them. An inexperienced person often interprets a child's anger as an attack on him rather than an expression of the child's frustration. He may label lack of effort as laziness, whereas it may actually stem from deep despair. A child's behavior is a sensitive indicator of the emotional climate that surrounds him. We still have much to learn about "the language of behavior."

The handicapped child is keenly aware of his parents' feelings toward him—their affection and acceptance or their rejection and disappointment. If they are ashamed of him, he senses this. Children in a fine institution for exceptional children often lose ground emotionally when they go home for a Christmas or summer vacation. The self-esteem and sense of status that they have built in the school is destroyed or altered in the home. Adults at the school have accepted and encouraged them, and shown affection for them. At home, the atmosphere may be different. Even though the parents try their best to give the child a happy vacation, they often fail to convey the affection the child so desperately needs. One child sobbed all the way back to the school after her Christmas vacation; she was only slightly consoled by her friend, the driver of the school bus. Handicapped children, even more than other children, "depend for their emotional security on the three A's of affection, acceptance, approval." [3]

The child's own personal and inner experiences are of the utmost importance in his adjustment. How does he feel about his handicap? How does he handle his feelings of frustration, inferiority, or despair? Is he really as disturbed about his condition as we think he might be? May it even be that he does not want to be different? What attitude does he bring to the treatments the doctor prescribes, and to his family's anxieties and expectations?

PARENTS' "PUZZLEMENTS AND PERPLEXITIES"

We must also recognize the "puzzlements and perplexities" of parents and their effect on the children. Parents may be so concerned with their own emotional problems and their efforts to adjust to having a handicapped child that they fail to inquire how the child himself feels. Parents might well ask themselves: "How do I think my child regards himself and his situation?"

Kanner described the case of a five-and-one-half-year-old boy whose mother brought him to the Children's Psychiatric Service of the Johns Hopkins Hospital,

because the school recommended that he be retained in kindergarten for another year. He had done well in nursery school in which he had spent two years. He presented no problem at home. The teacher complained that Kenneth was immature, cried much in the classroom, became frustrated when he was unable to keep within the lines while crayoning, and generally had poor motor coordination. At age five years and seven months, he tested at four years and two months. His IQ was 75. Whenever he was incapable of solving a test problem, he promptly tried to divert the examiner's attention by "talking a blue streak." He certainly had no idea that he was not equal to scholastic expectation. He had no knowledge of psychometry. But somehow he sensed that he was different from his classmates. He was not happy in his dealings with them. He came home often saying that they did not like him and that they laughed at him. However, his mother spoke of him as a perfectly secure child who did not have any misgivings. If he was uncomfortable in school, it must have been the fault of the teacher who did not know how to handle him. The notion that the child was struggling against heavy odds and, of necessity, must have been thwarted in his attempt to compete successfully, came as a great revelation to the mother. She had formerly seen his retardation simply as a blow to her own happiness, to her parental ambitions for him, to her prestige among her friends and inlaws. Now, for the first time, she became alert to her son's feelings in the matter.

Kenneth's behavior, like that of any other child, reflected his attitude toward himself and his world. He displayed no difficulties at home where, being an only child, he had no reason for self-comparison, where his parents did not push him and where his mother's projection of blame on the teacher gave him a comfortable feeling of being acquitted. He cooperated well at the clinic where he met with a friendly reception. But even there, stumped by some of the test items, he tried to make an impression by means of digressive chatter, which said, in essence, "I may not be able to answer your question, but don't think that I am stupid. There are many things which I do know and about which I can talk to you." In the classroom, however, he had no such handy safeguards. There, talking at random or out of turn interfered with instruction and was not tolerated. His work, even at kindergarten level, was inadequate, and he was forever deprived of the praise which the other children received. His pathetic helplessness, his clumsiness, the observation that *his* drawings were never put up on the wall for everybody to see, and the occasional taunts which came from some of his classmates resulted in a diffuse, painful feeling of being different, of falling short, of the futility of every effort on his part to do as well as the rest of the children.[4]

Kenneth's emotional problems were caused not by his below-average intelligence quotient per se, but by the school's failure to meet his emotional needs, and help him tolerate the necessary frustrations of school life.

PARENTS' ATTITUDES TOWARD THEIR EXCEPTIONAL CHILDREN

The range of possible parental attitudes toward an exceptional child is presented by Kanner with sympathy and understanding.[5] He recognizes the heartache associated with the realization of their child's social and intellectual incompetence. He does not expect the parents to show "unmitigated Pollyannish acquiescence." While not rejoicing over their child's handicap, some parents are able to maintain a warm relationship with him. "They neither reject nor overprotect him, but try to assess the extent of his abilities and limitations, and make realistic provision for his education and his future." They do not have false hopes of his outgrowing the handicap or catching up later. They do not subject the child to endless visits from one clinic to another, expecting psychiatric or medical miracles. Instead they provide an environment suited to his needs, in which the handicapped child can accept himself without shame and guilt.

It is natural for parents to overprotect a handicapped child—to make all kinds of allowances for him, to give him anything that will make him happy, to do things for him that he could do for himself.

The child who is used to this kind of treatment comes to school expecting similar treatment from his teacher and classmates. Johnny, for example, waited for the teacher to take off his coat and overshoes. He would make no effort to do it himself, although children who were more handicapped than he took care of themselves. The teacher is too busy to help the child who is able to help himself. The children in his class are often indifferent, unsympathetic, or even thoughtlessly cruel. The handicapped child who expects the same solicitude he has been shown at home has a difficult adjustment to make. His dependency and his expectation that people will always do things for him and give things to him make it still more difficult for him to adjust to life as it is.

Parents who are aware of this danger begin early to teach the child to help himself and to do the things that other children do, except as actually prevented by his handicap.

IDENTIFICATION OF EXCEPTIONAL CHILDREN

Since each child is special, he should receive education tailored to his unique personality. To do this, his special needs must be identified. Techniques of identifying and appraising children's abilities cover a wide range—all the way from casual conversation and daily observation to medical and psychological examinations.

The classroom teacher, trained in observation, has many opportunities for child study. School administrators, nurses, attendance officers and guidance staff should participate in the identification process. The specialist can describe the handicap more precisely, and suggest ways to remedy it. Some mental, emotional, and social problems are difficult to diagnose; they require expert study.

The family physician or pediatrician can generally identify mental retardation and physical impairments during the so-important first year of life.

The purpose of the periodic school medical examination is (a) to discover defects that may be interfering with the child's school achievement and general health, (b) to contribute to the pupil's knowledge of methods for protecting and improving his health, and (c) to establish a habit that will lead the individual to seek preventive checkups later on. School health examinations should be educational in nature.

In the course of a thorough examination, the physician and nurse obtain a detailed medical history. This kind of examination requires thirty to forty minutes. Parents should be present; they should be encouraged to express their concerns and ask questions about the health of their child.

Even in a superior school health examination program, it is difficult to fulfill completely the three objectives stated above. In many schools, the physician's or nurse's examination is much too hurried. For these and other reasons the trend is to discontinue routine health examinations for all students. It is better that the family physician examine the child in the family setting.

The purpose of the individual psychological examination is to appraise a child's intellectual and emotional development. If the psychologist tells you your child is a "slow learner," he probably means that the child has scored below average on one or more intelligence tests and is not making as much progress in school as other children of his chronological age. On an individual intelligence test, such as the Stanford-Binet, his IQ will probably fall between 75 and 90. On another test, such as the Wechsler Intelligence Test for children which yields two IQs—a verbal and a quantitative—he may be average or above average in facility with words and below average in facility with numbers and spatial relations, or *vice versa*. He may be learning to read at a more rapid rate than one would expect from his mental age, or his school achievement may be below expectancy. He may have a mental age of four on tests of memory, a mental age of twelve on reasoning ability, and a total mental age of eight. Two children who have the same total mental age may have quite different mental abilities. You can see how difficult it is to define a "slow learner"; he may be slow in learning some things but quick in learning others.

In addition to the mentally handicapped children who are commonly called "slow learners," there are children whose mental retardation is much more severe. They are described as mentally deficient. Some are untrainable; they are unable to care for themselves. Their mental age is no higher than that of a two-year-old baby. Other mentally deficient persons are trainable. They can learn to care for their physical needs, but they require close supervision either in an institution or by their families. They can learn to do simple routine work such as making beds and mopping floors. Their mental age does not exceed that of a seven-year-old child.

The mentally handicapped persons who are popularly called "morons" can learn the elements of reading and writing. As adults, they perform many routine jobs satisfactorily. Their adult mental age will equal that of the average child of seven to eleven years.

The description of a mentally retarded child should be functional; that is, it should indicate whether he is able to make adjustments under given conditions. According to this criterion, mentally handicapped children can be put into three groups:

1. Those who can be trained to work successfully under supervision as in a sheltered workshop.

2. Those who may initially appear to be of limited capacity, but improve under stimulating conditions.

3. Those who may have latent abilities and should be observed under optimum conditions before any important decision is made.

Border-line children are not easily identified; their retardation may not be apparent at first. Their limited ability to reason, to understand abstract concepts, and to see relevant relationships may not become evident until they are well into the third grade.

Mentally retarded children are often confused with the educationally retarded. The latter may be detected by group achievement tests, but these tests do not indicate whether the child is also mentally retarded.[6] The most dependable identification procedure includes a developmental history, psychometric and clinical, and, in some cases, a neurological examination.

Parents of an exceptional child often have difficulty in understanding and accepting the facts of the diagnosis. The psychologist can help parents understand (a) how the child feels about himself and his physical or mental limitations, (b) what he is capable of doing now, and (c) how he may change as his condition changes in the years ahead. Early detection of a handicap usually makes effective treatment easier.

"WHY DID THIS HAPPEN?"

Parents of handicapped children often wonder, "why did this happen?" This question is difficult to answer because there are two hundred specific causes of mental retardation alone. The greatest damage to the development of the unborn child—the embryo or fetus—is done by toxic influences, maternal infections, Rh incompatibility, and endocrine deficiencies. The toxic influences are most serious in the first months of pregnancy when growth is most rapid. The effects on the unborn child of dietary deficiencies have long been recognized. In laboratory experiments in 1940, a research pediatrician showed that a deficiency of vitamin B-2 in the mother may produce a severely deformed baby. In the same year an Australian eye specialist discovered the relation between German measles and infant blindness: if the mother caught German measles during the first through the third month of pregnancy, there was a great danger that the infant might be born with cataracts, or with heart defects, deafness, or mental retardation. The tragic effect that some of the new medicines and drugs may have on the unborn child at certain stages of his development has only recently been recognized (see Chapter Three). Oxygen deprivation at birth, even if it lasts only several minutes, may have a serious effect.

Great progress has been made in understanding certain causes of brain damage that originate during pregnancy and early infancy. The physical and mental retardation that is known as cretinism can often be prevented by supplying the mother's deficiency in iodine. By giving the thyroid hormone under the most careful medical supervision, a child's condition may be improved. New discoveries of biochemical causes of handicaps are constantly being made and tests, such as the PKU test, have been developed to detect these conditions.

Psychosocial causes, though probably more prevalent than biological, are not as definitely understood. These concern primarily the child's learning—the development of speech, interest, curiosity, emotion, and thinking.

Specific information about the probable causes of the child's condition often relieves the parents' feelings of guilt, and prevents their blaming themselves or accusing each other. It also gives them a basis either for expecting improvement or accepting characteristics that cannot be changed.

WHAT DOES THE HANDICAPPED CHILD NEED TO LEARN?

To minimize the disadvantages of an unattractive appearance, handicapped children should be taught to care for their hair and skin, and to be attentive to other aspects of grooming. Their clothes should be becoming and appropriate.

They need to learn good manners and all the little amenities that evoke social acceptance by peers, friends, and strangers. Knowing "the thing to do" in specific social situations gives them confidence and a feeling of success; without this knowledge they are more likely to feel inferior or resentful.

Additional training in specific health and safety practices will help to make their lives more pleasant for them and less burdensome to others. Good posture in sitting, standing, and walking, chological as well as physical efficiency. habits of cleanliness, a well balanced diet—all contribute to psy-

Attention to nutrition is especially important in caring for the exceptional child. Lack of certain food elements such as vitamins may affect his mental functioning as well as his physical condition. Some children may be underfed because of ignorance, neglect, or poverty. Others overeat to compensate for their lack of other satisfactions. It is far better to provide good nutrition from birth than to try to correct malnutrition later on.

The child should be patiently taught proper habits of eating. Such training will increase the child's self-esteem and make meal-time more pleasant for all concerned. One episode in the film, *The Miracle Worker* (The Helen Keller Story), illustrated drastic methods of changing the bad table manners of a handicapped child. Her parents had allowed her to grab and gobble her food, and to spill it all over the table. The teacher was firm. The better habits were rewarded and eventually established.

Listening to music and drama, looking at pictures, playing games, viewing spectator sports, and taking trips will enrich the leisure of these children. The mentally retarded can understand things that come within their experience, but they have difficulty with abstractions and with subtle relationships. They learn by doing and by being shown *and* told.

The need of the handicapped child for communication skills is obvious. These skills may be acquired through varied drills and through participation in real and in imagined situations. Mealtime is an opportunity for conversation about their interesting experiences. By dramatizing various social situations, these youngsters prepare themselves to join in conversations with friends and visitors. They learn to write in response to the need to send a letter to a friend, to fill out an application for a job, to keep a diary, to take notes of things they see and hear.

The occupational training given to the special child as he grows older can include many more skills than the usual woodworking, weaving, sewing, and laundry and kitchen work. Before applying for a job, the young person may dramatize a job interview and certain occupational routines.

We should not neglect the religious education of exceptional children. More than most children, perhaps, they may find solace and security in the sense of a power beyond themselves. Membership in church groups may assist them to gain acceptance in the community, as well as help them to do the right thing. The church school teacher should avoid causing them embarrassment because of their handicap. For example, one adolescent stopped going to Sunday School because he was ashamed to read aloud.

The education of all children should emphasize the three H's— a trained *hand*, a thinking *head*, and a kind *heart*.

WHAT EDUCATIONAL AND TRAINING OPPORTUNITIES
ARE AVAILABLE?

The provision made for handicapped children in the public schools varies greatly in different parts of the country. At one extreme, exceptional children are placed in regular classrooms; at the other extreme, they are assigned to special classes within a school or to special schools.* Some public trade schools meet the needs of mentally retarded youth.

Children who are not too severely handicapped to profit by the usual school instruction and are not a danger to others can be taught in ordinary classrooms all or part of the day. With the help of specialists on the school staff, children who are hard of hearing can be taught to read lips; blind children can be given instruction in Braille; and mentally retarded children can be helped to acquire reading ability up to their capacity. The present policy is to meet the needs of exceptional children within the regular classes whenever possible.

Being with normal children helps the handicapped accept their differences and prepares them for the adult world into which they will go. It is also good for the normal children to learn to accept children who are unlike them in certain ways. The more severely handicapped the child is, the harder it is for the other children to treat him as a friend. In time, however, almost any class will begin to reflect the teacher's attitude; children tend to follow the teacher's lead. They accept the slow learner's limitations without comment and praise him for any progress he shows. To one slow learner who was discouraged over his low mark on an arithmetic test, a kindly classmate said, "But think how much better you did today than yesterday."

If the needs of exceptional children are to be effectively met in regular classrooms, the classes must be smaller than they are at present. The teachers must be alert to individual differences and skillful in providing for them. They must have suitable instructional materials for them. They must have suitable equipment to accommodate a wide range of interests and abilities.

Because these conditions have not prevailed in many schools,

* A *Directory for Exceptional Children,* published by Porter Sargent, Publishers, 11 Beacon Street, Boston, Massachusetts, is a guide for finding suitable facilities for various types of exceptional children.

special classes for exceptional children have been formed. Even these special classes have sometimes lacked the essential special materials and procedures. For example, children who have impaired vision should have books that are printed in large type, large pencils with which to write, relief maps, and the like. Since blind children can begin early to learn to read and write Braille, they should have directions and books in Braille. They learn arithmetic by means of objects—little sticks and circles, familiar objects in miniature. They need most of the same prereading experiences that other children need—opportunities to explore and talk about their environment, to ask questions, to distinguish the different sounds in words, to learn to anticipate meaning by supplying missing words in sentences.

Educable mentally retarded children are not ready to read at the usual age of entrance to school. Accordingly, the skillful teacher provides these children with the kind of work in which they can make the greatest progress—usually handwork, music, and art. But he also helps them to achieve in some of the areas that they have previously avoided because of fear of failure. The mentally retarded child wants to succeed in the things that other children are doing; he wants to do the same kind of work and contribute to the class discussion as the other children do. And he can, if the teacher provides simpler tasks in short single steps, gives him individual attention, and helps him at points where he cannot succeed alone. Genuine success that results from his best efforts expended on worthwhile tasks will gradually increase his self-confidence. Morale-building experiences are essential to the growth of all children, at every stage of development, but they are especially necessary for the mentally handicapped child.

Special teachers in art, music, and physical education can be of great assistance to the teacher of slow learners. When some mentally retarded junior high school students were having difficulty in acquiring muscular coordination, the gym teacher taught them games and exercises, to improve eye-hand and general coordination. The music teacher taught them songs, rhythms, and singing games. The art teacher used craft work to help them gain control of the smaller muscles.

If there is no special class for mentally handicapped children in your school system, the parents need not be too disappointed.

Research has failed to show that the special class has decided advantage over regular classes.[7] Several possible explanations have been suggested. The mentally handicapped child in a special class lacks the stimulation that he might get from association with normal children; this reduces his motivation to achieve. Probably more important is the possibility that the special teacher, in the effort to avoid undue pressure, may underemphasize the child's ability and expect too little progress of him. Like other children he needs a goal that he can reach—a goal that is raised slightly as he makes progress toward it.

The decision about whether to place the child in a special class or in a regular class requires time and thought. There must also be continued study of the child's adjustment after the initial decision has been made. The following steps are important in deciding whether to place a handicapped child in a regular or a special class:

1. Consider the child's probable ability to make a social adjustment in a larger, more competitive group.

2. Appraise the child's physical condition: his need for rest periods and for assistance in going to the toilet, and the effect of his handicap on his acceptance by the other children. Check on whether the classroom is on the first floor, near an exit, and large enough for a special desk or chair, if needed.

3. Be sure that the group will make provision for special learning problems.

4. Take into consideration the prospective teacher's friendliness and patience, her ability to plan and carry out an appropriate program for the handicapped child, and her skill in helping the other children to understand, accept, and assist him. The pupil-teacher and the parent-child relationship is of the utmost importance; it determines whether the child will want to learn or will resist learning.

We should be cautious about assigning children to special classes. Assignment to an inappropriate class or school is disturbing to both parent and child.

A few children with multiple handicaps are taken care of in private residential schools. Among the best of these are the Woods Schools in Langhorne, Pennsylvania. One program is on a nine-month basis for pupils who require emphasis on academic, educational, and/or occupational instruction plus a well rounded social experience. The other is a full-year residential-care program for long-term socialization training with less academic work. The schools maintain a large staff of highly trained psychologists, psychiatrists, social workers, physicians, and remedial reading teachers. There is a residence director in each of the units, all of which are situated in a beautiful physical setting. The cost of sending a child to a school like this is about four to five thousand dollars a year.

The most severely handicapped children and young people are institutionalized, most of them in state institutions. There the mentally retarded and mentally deficient learn to do useful work that is within their capacities.

In recent years more responsibility for the care and education of mentally retarded children has been placed on the community school workers who are now employed in the more progressive school systems to visit homes and advise with parents. In the last thirty years the system of Family Care has spread to many states. This involves boarding children in private homes at state expense. If they are of school age, they enroll in special classes; where there are no special classes, they are fitted into the grades that seem best suited to them. The state pays for board and clothing, medical care, and faithful supervision. It is good for these children to be members of a normal family. In one home, for example, the foster father, who had had little education himself, often struggled over the arithmetic lesson along with the two little boys. They were all happily learning together.

In some states there is a supervisor who goes into the homes to help parents understand their child's condition, think through their immediate problems, and anticipate problems that may come up in the future.

The home supervisor starts training the child on an appropriate level and encourages him to help himself and to acquire any skill he is able to learn. The supervisor comes once a week or once every two weeks. He expects the mother to continue the training between visits. However, it is hard for some mothers to adopt the teacher's role; they find it difficult to avoid being impatient and annoyed when the child learns slowly.

If the child needs to be referred to a clinic, the home supervisor prepares the parent to accept the clinic's diagnosis. If institutional care is needed, the supervisor gives the parents information about different kinds of institutions and helps them develop a constructive attitude toward taking this step. Recognizing that the mother has many things to do and cannot constantly be the child's playmate, the supervisor may help several parents to organize a play group or bring several children together in one home.

Day-care centers for children with IQs of under 50 are designed to take over some of the parents' responsibility for training these children. It is a relief to know that one's child, as he grows up, will have social contacts with others and an opportunity to be useful in some way. The low-cost training program of the day-care centers should reduce the number of children who will eventually require institutional care, costing from two to ten times more.

If the child does not respond to the day-care program, he probably needs institutional care. If parents look upon the institution as a resource designed to meet the needs of their child and not as an evidence of their own failure, they will be able to accept institutional care for their child and help him to accept it.

WILL HE BE ABLE TO GET A JOB?

What will happen to a severely handicapped child when his parents die or are no longer able to take care of him? This is a matter of deep concern to both parents and child. As children approach adolescence, they tend to become more fearful of the future. Their very anxiety may prevent their learning the things they most need.

There is useful work that handicapped people can do. Each person has a pattern of abilities that may be useful in certain kinds of work. Young people of very low mentality can be placed in suitable routine jobs, if they are well adjusted socially and emotionally. Some positions that require a minimum of judgment and social maturity can be held successfully by people who simply do what they are told. They are able to contribute to their self-support in sheltered workshops or at home, where they are given work that they can do at their own pace. One sheltered workshop, using a simulated hospital room, trained a small group of young women as nurses' aids. The girls learned to make a hospital bed, bring fresh water to the patient, and perform other simple duties that encroach on the time of a trained nurse. An important part of their training consisted in learning that they were *not* to do things for which they had not been specifically trained. Every one of these girls obtained and held jobs in public or private hospitals and were happy in their work.

Other handicapped adolescents may be helped by guidance, appropriate training, and vocational placement, to enter the world of work with every likelihood of success. They are no longer automatically excluded from most vocations. Rehabilitation and other community agencies help handicapped people to obtain new earning power, new skills, new friends, and new confidence. Parents, who are fortunate enough not to have handicapped children of their own, can help others by contributing to organizations that are giving services of this kind.

However, we must face two facts. The first is that some handicapped children are placed at a social and vocational disadvantage by their very appearance. A Mongoloid boy, who had been in the regular special class in public school, had made progress in reading and number work. His speech was good. He could coordinate his movements well. He was able to get along with other people. But when he reached the age of sixteen, the combined efforts of school and rehabilitation counselors were unsuccessful in getting him a job. He was ready for employment, but his physical appearance made him unacceptable to employers. The second fact that must be faced is that the repetitive, manual jobs that mentally retarded young people can do are becoming fewer and fewer as machines replace unskilled workers.

GUIDANCE OF PARENTS

Parents of handicapped children are often burdened with many fears—fear that some accident will befall the blind or mentally retarded or crippled child; fear that he will not be able to succeed in school; fear that he will always be dependent upon them; and fear of what will become of him when they die. In addition, parents sometimes have feelings of guilt which may lead them to overprotect or overindulge the handicapped child, often to the detriment of other children in the family. They may also feel bitterly disappointed in their hopes, expectations, and ambitions for the child.

Periodically the teacher, the child, and the parents all confer together. The teacher shows the parents samples of the child's work at the beginning and at the end of the school year. Charts, graphs, dated worksheets, and test scores help to give these children and their parents a sense of progress. One of their greatest sources of happiness is the feeling that they are growing.

During the parent-teacher conference the teachers should listen to the parents and try to see the situation through the parents' eyes. The teacher may then tell them about some of the ways in which she has been able to help the child in school—if they seem ready for suggestions.

The school counselor and psychologist have important responsibilities in any educational program for exceptional children. By means of interviews, other tests, and other measurements, they help make the initial identification. They secure additional social, psychological, and psychiatric appraisal when it is needed. They suggest the best grade placement of these children, taking into consideration all available information about their physical, social, intellectual, and emotional characteristics. Counseling also helps these children to develop confidence in themselves and their ability to get along with their classmates.

The pastor, priest, or rabbi is in a strategic position because he is in contact with the whole family and has known the children from their earliest years. Working with the family physician or pediatrician, he can do much to prevent the development of detrimental attitudes during the preschool years. The pastor continues this supporting relationship with the family during the child's school years. The parents find it a relief just to be able to talk about their fears and anxieties to a sympathetic, understanding person. In such conferences they often clarify their confused thoughts and feelings, and get a sense of direction. The pastor's role is to reinforce their positive insights, help them to obtain a more hopeful and realistic picture of the child, and suggest resources to which they may have access. Both the parents and the child should feel: Here is someone who is sincere, who is concerned about us, who understands how we feel, and who will do all he can to provide the experiences in the church and in the community that the child needs for his best development.

HOW DO PARENT GROUPS HELP?

More and more discussion groups are being formed by parents of exceptional children. Each group needs the services of a professionally trained leader who has both technical knowledge and skill in interpreting it. The leader must be able to reinforce the members' constructive contributions and supply additional ideas. Equally important are the insights that the parents gain from one another. As they exchange experiences, each finds support and comfort in the realization that he is not alone in his struggle to do right by his handicapped child. As they share the methods that they have found successful, all may acquire new approaches to their problems and alternate ways of helping their child.

The members gain insights into their own feelings and behavior as well as those of their children. In these groups parents often feel free to express fears, anxieties, and expectations that they can then check against reality. They sometimes become aware of feelings that they had concealed even from themselves. As a result, they begin to perceive their child in a different light; this change in perception may produce changes in their behavior toward the child, which may cause the child to respond more favorably to his parents. The parents' changed image of the child influences the child's concept of himself.

A summary of a series of discussion meetings for parents of pre-school, mentally retarded children conducted by a skillful leader will illustrate some of the points made above.[8] The group discussed in more or less detail a broad range of problems including discipline, toilet training, the causes of mental retardation, their feelings of disappointment and guilt, the relationship of the mentally retarded child to normal children in the family and in the community, and a review of community resources. They were very much concerned with ways to establish expectations for the child at different ages and to help him best use his abilities.

The group was troubled about the dangers of pushing the child too hard and expecting more than he could reasonably accomplish. The parents were also aware of the dangers of overprotection and of the need to help a child to capitalize on his eagerness and readiness to grow up. They began to show a greater willingness to experiment and to try new approaches in helping children to help themselves. They shared their disappointment in having retarded children and the effect of their own feelings on the child.

It has been noted by many leaders of such groups that parents of disabled or handicapped children usually proceed very quickly to enter into significant discussion, even in a first meeting. There seems to be an immediate sense of identification from one parent to another that enables the group process to become effective more quickly than in other kinds of groups. It is often in the early meetings of these groups that parents "spill over" with their resentments against the outside world and the community.[9]

Parent groups have also taken responsibility for publicizing the need for studying handicapped children and making provisions for them in the local community. Some groups have initiated vocational training classes for handicapped adolescents. In the case of younger children, they have organized play groups to give them opportunities for social contact.

QUESTIONS AND ANSWERS

1. *What do parents desire from professional workers?*

Most parents say they want physicians, psychologists, teachers, and other professional persons to be honest with them. If a child is mentally retarded, for example, they want to know it as soon as possible, so that they can provide the experiences he needs. They want to know about the child's potentialities as well as his limitations. They want to know specifically what opportunities are available for his education, and how to gain access to these resources. However, they do not want the professional person to make the decisions for them; that must be left to the family.

2. *What do parents expect of the community?*

They want their exceptional child to be treated as other children are treated, except as his limitations require special provisions. They want the respect and understanding of people in the community. They want a chance for their child to lead as useful a life as possible, doing whatever work he has been trained to do.

3. *When should a mentally retarded child be sent to an institution?*

Ordinarily an institution should be the last resort. It seldom provides opportunities for the kind of personal relationships that are possible in a good home. It often fails to furnish all the experiences that are necessary for full mental growth. It may tend to foster irresponsibility. On the other hand, a good institution enables many handicapped children to learn how to return to the community as self-sustaining citizens. For severely handicapped children, the institution provides perpetual care—a refuge against the indifference and disdain of the outside world.

However, there are parents who are incapable of coping with a subnormal child. The child deteriorates; the parents are miserable. The retarded child has a harmful effect on the other children in the family and, perhaps, on the community as a whole. Under these conditions, placement in an institution is necessary. Putting a child in an institution does not necessarily mean that the home is inadequate or that the parents are heartless.

4. *What is the state's responsibility for the mentally retarded child?*

The state has a number of important responsibilities:

(1) To certify and supervise foster homes and placement homes.

(2) To regulate schools for handicapped children.

(3) To maintain certain standards in health services.

(4) To see that public school superintendents and teachers have an understanding of handicapped pupils and their education.

(5) To provide financial aid for the support of programs that are needed for these children, and to determine experimentally the value of different methods of educating them.

(6) To counsel parents, school systems, institutions, and health clinics in their responsibilities for the retarded.

(7) To provide institutional care for handicapped people who cannot be cared for in a home.

5. *What is the ideal parental attitude toward the handicapped child?*

Realizing how much their attitude affects the child, parents should try to overcome their feelings of disappointment and concentrate on helping the child develop his strengths and accept his unalterable limitation.

THREE

Physical Potentialities and Limitations

EVERY parent would like his child to be "the picture of health": a rosy-cheeked, red-lipped, bright-eyed, happy baby, child, or adolescent, full of vim, vigor, and vitality.

Actually, good health may have a variety of appearances. Some children who seem to be lacking in energy have naturally low energy levels; they simply need more rest than the average child. Some children are naturally scrawny rather than brawny. The father who was a college athlete should not be too disappointed if Junior does not follow in his footsteps. The mother who was a beauty in her day cannot expect that her daughter will necessarily have similar physical attractiveness. A child may have good health without conforming to any stereotype.

GROWTH POTENTIAL

The relation between heredity and environment has been clearly and effectively stated by Craig and Everett:

Each child is born with individual and unique potentialities for healthy growth and development depending on his hereditary pattern. Body stature, facial features, eye and hair color—these and other distinguishing characteristics are given each child at birth and become more clearly apparent as he grows. Other hereditary factors, such as rate of growth, are less apparent but also of importance in understanding individual differences among children. Recent studies of children's growth corroborate much previous knowledge on the individuality of the rate of growth and the fact that children do not grow alike. We now know, too, that children in the United States are taller than they used to be, with boys in California, for example, about one inch taller than their fathers, and girls 1.4 inches taller than their mothers. We know that girls outpace boys in their growth after the early years and by the age of seventeen are usually as tall as they will be, while boys do not reach their height potential until around nineteen. In the early years growth is determined by genes, but later the sex hormones begin to be the major factor. However, there is still much to be learned about hereditary traits and qualities. Geneticists now suspect that resistance or susceptibility to disease, susceptibility to psychosis, longevity, body endurance, mechanical talent, and some other human characteristics are, at least in part, attributable to heredity.[1]

One mother took her seven-year-old son to the doctor to see what could be done about his small size. "He's the runt of his class," she said, "and we want to know if there is something you can do to make him grow." This statement, made in the boy's hearing, may have hurt and embarrassed him more than being short for his age. The doctor reassured the boy, sympathetically, and fairly accurately. He told the youngster that a puppy with big paws will grow up to be a big dog. Then he said, "You know what? When you grow up, you're going to be a fairly big man—because your feet are fairly big for your size right now. And one thing's for sure, boys and puppies grow up to their feet."[2]

A more scientific indication of potential growth is obtained from X-rays of the child's hands and knees. For example, a ten-year-old boy had the bone development of an eight-year-old. This was good news to the boy and his parents because it showed that he had two more years of growth coming to him. This growth potential would help him to catch up with bigger classmates of the same age whose hand and knee X-rays were already characteristic of ten-year-olds. Another boy began to grow rapidly between his eleventh and twelfth birthdays. At fourteen, his hand and knee X-rays showed that he was a year ahead in bone growth. He will probably not grow much after he reaches the age of seventeen.

Each child grows in his own way, according to his own time-table. Each has his own characteristic growth pattern. No medicines or vitamins or stretching exercises will enable a child to grow beyond the limits nature has set for him.

This does not mean that diet and other environmental conditions are unimportant. A poor environment can prevent a child from reaching his growth potential, especially an environment with deficiencies in food, clothing, shelter, exercise, rest, and an unfavorable home and neighborhood atmosphere. On the other hand, the child who has favorable environmental conditions is likely to achieve his full growth potential. Largely because of better diet and improved child care practices, children are growing faster than in the past. They are not only taller but fatter!

Overweight is becoming more prevalent in the United States. Recruits in the Armed Forces in 1957-58 were, on the average, seven pounds heavier than inductees of World War II and eighteen pounds heavier than those of World War I. Many were rejected because of overweight. But obesity is not solely a problem of adults. About 10 per cent of American children were found to be overweight. Nutritional problems among children in the United States today are more often due to overabundance and unwise choice of foods than to food shortage. Overweight is likely to be a social disadvantage to both boys and girls.

Girls who are naturally tall, or who suddenly grow taller than their age mates, have their special problems of adjustment. Carol described hers in this way:

"The only thing that took my mind off this problem was that in the upper grades—the seventh and eighth—the other kids were finally growing taller, too.

"Now I don't even feel different, because some of the kids are almost as tall or even taller than I."

The physical education teachers might have convinced Carol that her growth was not abnormal by showing her pictures that illustrate the wide variations in children's growth. If they had also helped her to gain recognition in games like volleyball where height is an advantage, Carol might have had fewer worries in her early years. Fortunately for the naturally short boy and the naturally tall girl, size is not necessarily a determinant to happiness or success.

Claire, too, was helped to solve her problem. She was the only child of indulgent parents. In the seventh grade she was taller and heavier than her classmates, and less skillful in physical activities. Their ridicule frequently brought tears to her eyes. Her inadequacy in games and sports spread to other events and areas of her school work. When her parents requested that she be excused from taking gym, the principal invited them to the school for a conference with the physical education teacher and the counselor. Together with Claire, they worked out a plan for less indulgence at home and a more suitable physical education program in school.

Physical characteristics or body build, do not, as is commonly thought, determine the nature of one's personality, although there may be some relation between body-type and personality traits. We sometimes find overweight associated with an easygoing, sociable personality, and a lean, muscular development with an adventurous, energetic personality.

During adolescence, individual physical idiosyncrasies, or even the common irregularities in growth that are found at this period, undoubtedly do disturb some teen-agers. They are embarrassed by acne, wonder whether their nose will grow still longer, and become disturbed by the physiological changes that mark the transition from childhood to adulthood. It is reassuring for them to know that these are signs of approaching maturity.

DYNAMIC HEALTH AND PHYSICAL FITNESS

Dynamic health has been defined as "optimal personal fitness for full, fruitful, creative living." [3] This implies a sense of well-being. One not only feels fit, but is confident of an ability to live at the top of his powers.

Physical fitness is a complex thing. It cannot be appraised by a single simple test. However, physical performance tests can measure agility, muscular strength, endurance, flexibility, and motor coordination. One of the best known tests of physical fitness was developed by the American Association for Health, Physical Education, and Recreation. It is known as the *AAHPER Youth Fitness Test*, a battery of seven measures of physical performance. [4] By means of such tests, relationships have been found between body build, strength, and scores on motor-performance tests. The early maturing boy has an advantage over the late maturing boy, both in strength and in skill in sports.

Proficiency in motor performance during the child's growing years can be increased by daily physical education. A required program of physical education increased the scores of Yale freshmen on six fitness tests from 41 to 80 per cent after 12–14 weeks of instruction. Extreme inactivity, on the other hand, decreases physical efficiency even in such exercise as slow, relaxed walking.

In an international experiment using tests of physical fitness with children ten to seventeen years old, investigators found that British and Danish children were superior to American children on almost all measures. There is other evidence of the unsatisfactory physical condition of today's American youth. Such facts indicate that something is wrong with our children's way of life.

Many other factors have a bearing on children's health. Childhood diseases come first to mind. It is encouraging to know that, according to data reported by the Metropolitan Life Insurance Company, deaths from communicable diseases became far less frequent in the decade from 1948–1949 to 1958–1959.[5] Accomplishments in tuberculosis prevention have been phenomenal. The marked decrease in this disease may be attributed to health education, chest X-rays, further examination and appropriate treatment of the cases detected.

During the same decade, deaths from poliomyelitis have also decreased approximately 90 per cent; deaths from the common communicable diseases of childhood, 75 per cent; from appendicitis and heart diseases, 75 per cent; and from pneumonia, approximately 33 per cent. However, the decade showed an increase in deaths from cancer and similar diseases, and from congenital malformations.

Although the mortality rate for school-age children was steadily decreasing, the incidence of acute illness, mostly from respiratory diseases, was high. Because of this, children lost, on the average, 5.3 school days per child per year.

Overfatigue is another factor that reduces physical efficiency. Signs of insufficient sleep are a tired feeling and an unwillingness to get up in the morning. The rested child appears alert and energetic. An overactive, restless child is usually a tired child or, sometimes, an ill child. Shortage of sleep also causes irritability. One experiment on children's sleep had to be discontinued because the children became so irritable the experimenters could not stand being with them!

The amount of sleep a child requires varies with his age and characteristics. Infants usually sleep from mealtime to mealtime. As the weeks pass they remain awake for longer intervals. Two-year-old children require, on the average, twelve hours of sleep at night and one or two hours in the daytime. The daytime naps become gradually shorter. Between the ages of six and eight, the night-time sleep can be shortened gradually to eleven hours; ten hours is usually sufficient by the age of twelve.

Many children come to school tired from staying up late to watch television. TV and other attractions that cause reluctance to go to bed present a real problem in this over-stimulating modern world. For the sake of the young child, parents must be firm. In the case of the older child, cooperative planning of his daily schedule will focus his attention on the most worthwhile programs that come at appropriate times.

Nutrition is another basic factor in health and growth. The poorest fed member of the American family is often the teen-age girl. Fearing to be overweight, she decides to diet in a haphazard fashion. Tired in the morning from staying up late the night before, she hurries off to school without breakfast. After school she joins the gang at the corner drug store or snack bar, where she indulges in cokes and candy bars that take away her appetite for a substantial evening meal. Studies of the nutritional status of adolescents have indicated that their intake of calcium, iron, ascorbic acid, and B-complex vitamins is below recommended levels.[6] They often need more milk, cheese, fruits, and vegetables.

If a few attractive, popular girls and boys were to set the style of sensible eating, they would have more influence than adults. Peer opinion is important to teen-agers; they do not want to be different. A group nutritional project in school may accomplish more than parental pleas.

In a seventh-grade class in California, it was found that approximately one-third of the pupils ate a poor breakfast or none at all. After a "Better Breakfast Week" campaign, carried on by means of posters, a parade, and short talks, more of the pupils reported that they were starting the day with an adequate meal. There was also a larger number who reported eating breakfast with one or both parents, or with the entire family.

Early adolescence should be a relatively healthy period—in fact, just about the healthiest of one's entire life. One should be at a peak of resistance to infectious diseases, and free as yet from various disabilities that may set in later. Why is it that so many adolescents fall short of their health potential? Why, as adolescents, have they become sallow, apathetic, and over- or underweight? How and why did they acquire their debutante slouch and their aversion to active outdoor exercise?

There are many reasons why children's health deteriorates from infancy to adolescence. Perhaps most important is that they fail to develop a sense of responsibility for their own health. They are cajoled, persuaded, threatened, or coerced, but to no avail. The health knowledge they are taught does not ring a bell with them; it does not fit into their pattern of attitudes and beliefs. Appeals focused on health per se leave them unmoved. Too seldom is health presented as a source of delight and "wholeness." Too seldom is it associated with adventure and happy social relations.

Smoking has become an important adolescent health problem, related to lung cancer, heart disease, and other serious illnesses. The Surgeon General's report in January, 1964, left no doubt about the health hazards of cigarettes.

An investigation of the smoking attitudes and habits of 22,000 high school students in the Portland, Oregon area showed that 26 per cent of the boys and 20 per cent of the girls were smokers.[7] Other surveys have shown an increase in the number of girls smoking from 4.4 per cent in the seventh grade to 40.5 per cent in the twelfth grade. For boys the figures were 22.2 per cent in the seventh grade and 56.4 per cent in the twelfth grade.[8] Two factors have been associated with teen-age smoking: the example of parents who smoke, and lack of success in school related to low academic goals.

Drinking is a still more serious problem. Estimates state that one out of five persons who drink is an alcoholic. Between five and seven million Americans are alcoholics. Drinking is becoming increasingly prevalent among teen-agers. National surveys have shown that the proportion of teen-agers who drink more or less regularly is from 50 to 66 per cent. In one state the figure for high school students was 90 per cent. A fifteen-year-old girl from a conservative suburban family, whose classmate got sick after drinking too much, tried to reassure her father by telling him that she "had only had two Scotches that night." [9]

Teen-age drinking is a psychological, social, and moral as well as a health and safety problem. Psychologically, according to one of the most insightful psychiatrists, alcohol "definitely poisons the self-system progressively." [10] The menace of young people who drive cars after drinking is clearly recognized. The vandalism so prevalent in many urban and suburban communities is usually perpetrated by hoodlums who have been drinking. Crimes of all kinds are commonly committed under the influence of alcohol. In all these serious social and personal problems, alcohol is a common factor. Young people associate drinking with a pseudo-maturity, and have not been schooled in social responsibility.

The Yale alcohol study at one time presented as a major conclusion that drunkenness was encouraged by an ambivalent, amused attitude toward drinking. It was pointed out that in Greece there was no drunkenness because it was definitely and unequivocably considered disgraceful. In our society, it is the subject of innumerable jokes. Until this attitude is changed, is there any chance that young people will have the conviction to resist the pressures to drink, to which they are subjected in our culture today?

Unfortunately, alcoholic beverages, tobacco, and other products and practices detrimental to health are being made irresistibly attractive to young people by association with social activities and outdoor sports that have high prestige values. This fact need not be illustrated here; it becomes apparent in countless advertisements and in movies, plays, TV programs, and stories in popular magazines. To a large degree, these influences neutralize the learning that takes place at home and at school.

Narcotic addiction, too, is becoming alarmingly prevalent. But it presents a somewhat different problem from alcoholic addiction. Its motivation is more pathological. Its horrors are vividly presented in films, television, books and magazines. But like alcoholic addiction, the consequences of the first steps are not vividly realized by the young persons. Some take narcotics for a thrill, others to gain status with their gang, still others for temporary relief from their feelings of emptiness, loneliness, and failure. Just as there are many causes of this problem, there should also be a many-sided attack on it. Awareness of the danger of addiction is only the first step. Adolescents' value systems need to be changed; they need something to live for—worthwhile work to do that demands health and strength. The school program should prevent academic failure more effectively. The social climate should provide opportunities for wholesome friendships. Persons who make available and push the sale of narcotics should obtain a court sentence commensurate with the crime.

Other negative social forces are at work. The incessant stimulation of the sex drive contributes to the increase in adolescent promiscuity with all its attendant health problems and moral tragedies.

Sometimes we have to face ugly facts. The American Social Health Association has reported that the rate of infectious syphilis among teen-agers fifteen to nineteen years of age more than doubled between 1956 and 1961. The rate of reported gonorrhea among teen-age boys and girls has been seen to rise in similar proportions. The total venereal rate for this age group is three times that for the population as a whole. Still more alarming is the fact that only about one venereal case in five is reported. Moreover, venereal disease, like delinquency, narcotics, and illegitimacy, is no longer confined to "the other side of the tracks." Its victims, according to Doctor Leona Baumgartner, Chairman of the United States Surgeon General's Task Force on Syphilis, are found in all social and economic groups; they include the most sheltered and privileged young people.[11]

What should boys and girls know about the venereal diseases? The following facts are most important: they are contagious diseases spread by sexual contact. Gonorrhea may show itself in burning or itching sensations or a discharge. The most common signs of syphilis are minor sores, rashes that do not itch, or insect-like bites. However, either disease may occur without warning signs: only a doctor can be sure. Syphilis is especially serious because of its possible long-term after-effects—blindness, deafness, insanity, and deformed offspring. In its early stages, it usually responds to penicillin shots. Hence it is important to consult a doctor or health clinic at once if there is any possibility of infection. Being cured of either of these diseases does not make one immune; reinfection is possible.

There is also an increasing incidence among children of psychological tension, anxiety, and mental illness. Something is wrong when young children begin to develop psychosomatic complaints such as peptic ulcer and ulcerative colitis. These are diseases that used to be characteristic of the harried executive. What is causing these disorders in children? Is it their reaction to what has been

called the "junior rat race?" [12] Are these physical symptoms oc-
curring because parents forget that young children and adolescents
need time to explore, to be idle, to dream, to follow their own
fancies? Is it because adults insist that youngsters, as Kipling
wrote, "fill each unforgiving minute with sixty seconds' worth of
distance run?" Are we confusing what the adult considers "constructive" with what is really "constructive" from the child's point
of view? Many children are frustrated by imposed schedules. They
have no satisfactory way of coping with this kind of pressure from
parents who do not realize that they may be satisfying their own
needs for status, instead of considering the child's developmental
needs.

THE ROLE OF OUTDOOR RECREATION

Outdoor recreation is an antidote for many of the ills of our urban-
technological society, which is rapidly losing contact with the
natural world. Walking, swimming, skating, boating, fishing, bird-
watching, mountain climbing, camping—all of these offer opportunities for contemplation, adventure, dependence upon natural
forces, vigorous activity, and appreciation of what A.E., the Irish
poet, has called "the quietude of earth."

On a canoe trip, emotionally disturbed youngsters who were
characteristically uncooperative, inconsiderate of others, and un-
communicative, smiled, laughed, shared the work, and tolerated
the natural vicissitudes of outdoor life. They ate and slept as never
before. During this outdoor experience they found satisfactions
that they had rarely known before.

As parents and citizens, we should promote and support conservation projects that will enable our citizens to have the outdoor
recreation that they need for optimum health and well-being.

"Little Leagues" are a good idea if fathers do not introduce an
overcompetitive element that takes the joy out of the activity itself.
When Junior feels practically obliged to hit a home-run, then
striking out becomes a disaster rather than an incident in playing
for fun.

The typical playground with its heavy metal swings and slides
and its asphalt pavements does not appeal to many children. Playgrounds can be made safer and at the same time more appealing
to adventurous and imaginative children. Many new types of

equipment have been designed. There are colorful concrete and metal dragons to crawl over and through, spiraling tunnel slides, large building blocks, and tools for making and doing things one-self. In one playground there is a wigwam village for small cow-boys and Indians. A wading pool invites happy splashing in hot weather. A corner of good earth for growing things keeps city children in touch with nature. These and many other kinds of equipment stimulate imagination, encourage large muscle activity, give children a sense of adventure without exposing them to undue hazards.

Neighborhood groups in both urban and rural areas are improving present playgrounds. One group of mothers raised $2,500 for new-type apparatus, which the Park Department installed. Another groups of mothers, dissatisfied with the danger and dull-ness of their neighborhood playground, studied the situation, made a report, and persuaded the Park Department to put new per-manent rubber matting under all equipment.

Better playgrounds should not mean more regimented play; they should encourage more free play, creative activity, and initiative. This kind of play contributes to the development of a child's phys-ical, mental, and emotional potentialities.

PHYSICAL LIMITATIONS

Many children have physical handicaps and defects. Some are crip-pled, some are blind or partially-seeing, some deaf or hard of hear-ing. They fall short of the optimum of health and physical fitness that has just been described.

Some of these children with physical impairment are confident, cheerful, friendly; others have feelings of inferiority; still others constantly seek attention or withdraw from difficult situations. What makes the difference?

Crippled Children

One five-year-old with no left hand, only a stub at the wrist, was an unusually attractive child. He had been in a group of eight children for half an hour before the teacher even noticed that he was handicapped. He used his arm in buttoning his coat and in pulling on his cap. Who could say he was handicapped? He was limited in very few activities. He was mentally alert and well accepted socially. It must have been a wise, accepting mother who helped him remain so unself-conscious about his physical handicap.

A woman who was born without arms and with only one leg now occupies a prominent position in the field of education. Ever since she can remember, her mother expected her to share household responsibilities with the other children in the family. "It will take you longer and you'll have to try harder," her mother told her, "but you have your chores just like the other children." She would go on errands, mind children, and do many other tasks that lay within the limits of her physical ability. Consider, in contrast, the overprotected child, much less seriously handicapped, who at nine years of age makes no effort to put on his outside clothing or help himself in other ways.

Changes in attitude sometimes explain apparent miracles of healing. In the course of play therapy, an eight-year-old child, who was confined to a wheelchair, discarded the wheelchair and began to walk with ease. He abandoned his sullen behavior, and improved in his school work. Apparently much of his physical disability had been due to emotional attitudes.[13] Older boys, similarly handicapped, when they were given encouragement and when they engaged in independent activities that were within their capabilities, showed greater interest and self-reliance. Their achievement also was higher than their intelligence test scores would lead one to expect. They seemed happier, less aggressive, and more cooperative both at home and at school.

Three factors may seriously affect the adjustment of the crippled child: (a) the social prejudice that makes the parents and the other children in the family feel ashamed of him; (b) the wishful thinking and unrealistic expectations and hopes of parents; the futile courses of action that are insisted on by other relatives; the tendency to emphasize the slowness of the child's progress rather than his actual gains, however small; and (c) the parents' personal attitudes. They could be of most help to the child by accepting him as he is, living their own lives in their accustomed way, and meeting the needs of their other children.

If a crippled child accepts himself as he is, other children are likely to accept him. A teacher heard this conversation between Dick, a child born without a left arm, and another boy:

Other boy: what happened to your arm?

Dick: Oh, I was just born that way.

Other boy: OK, let's get going (and they went off to play).

It is especially difficult for a father to face the facts about his son's physical limitations. Most fathers want a real boy—a masculine type. An athletic father, who was very much concerned with his own prestige, refused to admit that he had a physically handicapped son. Although the boy's coordination was very poor, the father rejected the corrective treatment offered by the school. Later, he refused to send the boy to a special school where he could have obtained the guidance and training he needed for a suitable occupation. Without this preparation, the boy was unable to obtain a job commensurate with his real capacity.

As parents learn more about the causes of physical impairments, they become more accepting of their child and often realize that they are not to blame. Of 340,000 cases of crippled persons under twenty years of age, 25 per cent were due to congenital malformation, 20 per cent to diseases of muscle and bone, 8 per cent to cerebral palsy, and 7 per cent to after-effects of poliomyelitis.

In 1962, accounts of a new hazard to unborn children filled pages in newspapers and magazines.[14] More than five thousand babies in Germany and England, and a smaller number in the United States, had been born deformed because their mothers had taken thalidomide tranquilizers and sleeping pills at a critical stage in their child's prenatal development—in the second month of pregnancy. These tablets had been selling in Germany at a rate of 20,000,000 a month before their effect on unborn babies was discovered.

Fortunately the drug's effect does not persist from one pregnancy to the next; a number of the unfortunate mothers have since had a second child who was normal.

New drugs, not yet adequately tested for long-term effects, may be found to cause malformation in infants. To be on the safe side, pregnant women should avoid taking, except on a competent doctor's orders, any of the numerous tranquilizers, sleeping pills, and headache medicines that are being presented so persuasively in advertisements and television commercials.

The most common causes of crippling and deaths are accidents.[15] Many of these injuries result in permanent disfigurement, as well as occasioning great expense to the family, and an enormous loss of school time for the child.

There are three factors to be considered here: children's varied susceptibility to accidents, injurious agents, and unsafe environments. Boys, especially those who are bold and courageous, are more susceptible to accidents than girls. The emotionally excitable child; the impulsive, rude child; the child who is rejected by his playmates; and the child who feels insecure at home are also especially susceptible.[16]

Injurious agents include motor vehicles, firearms, and equipment that causes burns or falls. Add water (drownings) to these four, and you have the five most common causes of accidental death among school children. In the fifteen-to-nineteen-year-old group, the death rate almost doubles—the cause, automobile accidents.

The environment in which accidents occur varies somewhat with the age of the child. Accidents to young children naturally occur most frequently in the home. Accidents to the older elementary school children occur most often on the playground and in unsupervised activities in the school. With children in the seventh to ninth grades, many accidents occur in connection with organized sports; some take place in classes such as chemistry and manual training. From the tenth grade until college, organized sports and motor vehicles are the major sources of accidents.

Most accidents are unnecessary. They can be prevented. If teachers and student safety patrols know which areas of the school program are potentially dangerous, they can supervise these areas with particular care. If parents know the danger spots at home and in the neighborhood, they can instruct children in appropriate safety measures. Habits of caution, not feelings of fear, with respect to streets, fire, water, and firearms are best established before the age of five. Parent study groups might well work out practical suggestions for making their neighborhoods safer, and for teaching children caution without squelching their sense of adventure. We still need to know more about why accidents happen. We need to know how to create a sense of responsibility in the reckless teen-agers who are involved in so many accidents.

In driver education classes, the students learn the actual mechanics of driving before they reach legal driving age. They also become familiar with motor vehicle laws and with common dangers. Emphasis on courteous driving habits appeals more to al-truistic adolescents than the slogan, "The life you save may be your own."

Another way to reduce auto accidents is to limit teen-agers' use of cars. Parents are often lax about this. Studies of teen-agers have shown a positive relation between frequent use of family cars and failing grades, and also between car ownership and lack of achievement in school.

Injuries occur quite commonly during athletic events, especially in football and basketball games. Good coaches train their players to handle themselves skillfully, and make sure that all their players are in the best physical condition. Proper equipment and strict enforcement of game rules help to prevent accidents. The American Academy of Pediatrics has recommended that students under age of fourteen should not engage in competitive sports.

It was especially shocking to note from a report of the American Medical Association that severe beatings were found to be almost on a par with accidents as a cause of deaths among children.

The majority of colleges accept physically handicapped students. Those who are intellectually able to can succeed in college if their disability is not too severe, if the college provides for their special needs, and if the faculty members are understanding and helpful. In planning new buildings, college administrators are becoming increasingly concerned about providing for students who must use wheel chairs or need other special facilities. Some colleges recognize the needs of handicapped students by making adjustments in their program—providing, for example, for limited laboratory work. These adaptations should be made as inconspicuously as possible. College faculty members who have the essential facts about the physically handicapped students in their classes should be able to help them with both academic and nonacademic problems.[17]

Children Who Are Partially-sighted or Blind

In the case of a blind child, as with other handicapped children, the parents are naturally much concerned. They are afraid he will get hurt. They worry about whether he will be accepted by other children. They wonder how he can get an education and whether he will ever become self-supporting. As the child grows older, parents become more concerned with his social welfare, and less with his physical safety.

It is reassuring to know that there are relatively fewer accidents to blind children than to normal children of the same age. Parents are more careful to remove dangerous objects from the blind child's environment and to give more effective instruction in common safety practices and precautions. On the street, people are quick to guide a blind person. Since he is more sensitive than the average child to sounds and movements, the visually handicapped child learns to move with greater caution than his heedless brother or sister.

One way to promote the acceptance and understanding of visually handicapped children is to emphasize the ways in which they are like other children. They engage in many of the same school activities. Both blind and sighted children learn the same subject matter. Both enjoy listening to stories and class discussions. In fact, all pupils in the elementary school spend more than half their time in listening—much more in the first grades.

It is well to encourage blind children to report their own sense impressions rather than repeat other children's descriptions. For example, after a boat trip, the teacher asked the children to tell what they had seen. Blind Tommy said, "The flag on the boat waving in the breeze." "You're teasing me," the teacher said, "Tell me what *you* saw on the trip." Tommy laughed and said, "When I was walking on the gangplank, I felt the vibration of the engine. I smelled the diesel engine oil. I heard the waves splashing against the side of the boat." "Good!" said the teacher, "Those were the things *you* saw on the trip." Such reports from blind children enrich the sensory experiences of the others. Helen Keller once said that the worst calamity that could befall a person was "to have eyes and fail to see."

Blind or partially-seeing children are not necessarily poorly adjusted.[18] Cowen and others found no evidence that visually disabled adolescents were less well adjusted than adolescents who could see.[19] In fact, the visually handicapped adolescents who lived at home seemed better adjusted; apparently they had enjoyed a constructive relationship with patient and perceptive parents.

In addition to a favorable home environment, the blind urgently need more suitable school facilities, more qualified teachers, and more effective instructional materials. They need to experience the joys that they could gain from Braille reading and recorded "Talking Books." These recordings are furnished free of charge by the Library of Congress and by private organizations such as Recordings for the Blind, Inc., New York City. This organization records educational material on request for blind students.

Parents can cooperate more fully in the education of their visually limited children if they know what the schools are doing. Though different school systems have different programs, all programs should include some of the following features:

Braille classes of ten or twelve children whose corrected vision is less than 20/200. They have tape recordings or "talking books" with embossed diagrams. The new "compressed speech" tape recordings that are graded to increase in speed enable pupils to comprehend four times as fast as the usual Braille material. Pupils read Braille at sixty words per minute and compressed speech at 240 words per minute—equal to the average rate for seeing children on the same kind of material.

Sight conservation classes for children whose vision prevents them from doing well in regular classes. Teachers of regular classes refer children who have corrected vision of 20/70 or less in both eyes, and who have difficulty in using their eyes in daily school work.

In these classes children with limited vision participate in activities similar to those in the regular classrooms. In addition, they should have specially trained teachers to give them instruction, whenever it is needed, in writing Braille. They need special instructional materials such as Braille writers and slates; pencils with thick, soft leads; files of large pictures, unglazed writing paper, tests and books printed in large, clear type (18–24 point); tape recordings and typewriters with large size type (see booklet of the National Society for the Prevention of Blindness, 16 East 40th Street, New York 16, New York, *The Case for the Partially Seeing Child* and publications of American Foundation for the Blind, Inc., 15 West 16th Street, New York 11, New York). These children should be seated where they have a clear view of chalkboards and charts. Their schedule should provide alternate periods of reading and of less visually demanding activities. They should have frequent eye examinations. Although it is best that they refrain from physical activities such as jumping, tumbling, diving, and body-contact sports, there are many other games they can play.

Regular classes adjusted to their needs. When a child with limited vision is put in a regular class, the special teacher holds a conference with the child's parents. He then gives the regular teacher information about the child's home and family background, personality, social maturity, and special health needs, in addition to facts about his eye condition and suggestions for his safety, health, and education. The regular teacher may train pupil assistants to serve as "buddies" for the partially-sighted children. Thus they can take part in the regular class activities, trips, and excursions.

A brief description of one case will illustrate the cooperation that should prevail among special teacher, regular teacher, and parents:

Stanley, in the fifth grade, has visual acuity with glasses of 20/70–20/100. He has a Binet IQ of 122. When his grade teacher suggested that he make a study of a trail blazer in connection with the class unit on Westward Expansion, Stanley's sight conservation teacher helped him to choose the pioneer who interested him most—Daniel Boone. She also secured two sets of talking book records to give him background in the period. He listened to these during reading periods. In the picture files, they found illustrations of pioneer clothing, log cabins, and wild animals, as well as a picture of Daniel Boone. His parents found other related books, which they read to him at home.

He shared his information with his committee and invited them to look at the special picture file in the sight conservation room.

Before giving his report to the regular class, Stanley had a chance to give it in the sight conservation class, where he gained both confidence and helpful suggestions. His report was so interesting that he won the recognition of pupils in his regular class and the praise of his parents.

The transition from a neighborhood elementary school where the pupil has had one teacher most of the day, to a departmentalized high school at some distance from home, is difficult enough for the most normal child; it is especially difficult for the child who is visually handicapped. He and his parents should have a chance to visit the high school in the spring, make a tour of the building, and obtain answers to their specific questions. Some teachers provide a leaflet of orientation suggestions, printed in 24-point type, that describe the student's responsibilities and opportunities.

Bright visually and environmentally handicapped children would profit by attendance at a special school such as The New York Academy for the Gifted Blind Child. This school, a division of the New York Institute for the Blind, offers special programs that prepare gifted blind children for college, the performing arts, and various skilled trades.

No charge is made to students who are residents of the staie of New York and who have received state appointments to the Academy. Non-residents of New York State are charged $2,000 a year for residence boarding and $1,400 for the day school program, including lunches. A scholarship fund makes attendance possible for a limited number of students who cannot afford the fee. Further information may be obtained from the principal of the New York Institute for the Education of the Blind, 999 Pelham Parkway, New York 69, New York.

The preschool and kindergarten years should provide many kinds of play that develop skills and provide pleasure. The children learn manual skills by handling and using a wide variety of materials. They develop a sense of direction, and acquire freedom and security in physical activities through marching, skipping, going up and down a little flight of stairs, swinging, and many other experiences in movement. The teacher introduces a reading readiness program as soon as the child is capable of profiting by it.

During the elementary school years, there are various provisions in school and at home for developing the potentialities of visually handicapped children. Among these are maps and globes, a variety of illustrative materials, and opportunities to develop coordination and dexterity, to foster the child's natural creative ability, and to encourage productive use of leisure time. A natural environment of trees, shrubs, and flowers provides opportunity for nature study. Access to many books and recordings helps him cultivate an interest in reading for both information and pleasure. Choral singing, piano instruction, and the reading of Braille music scores develop music appreciation. Teaching the child to eat a balanced diet, acquire good table manners, practice basic health rules, and overcome socially unacceptable mannerisms is also an important part of his education. The visual handicapped child can also engage in folk, social, and interpretive dancing. He enjoys games, puzzles, and other material for creative play. He likes to go to parties, picnics, and trips to interesting places.

During the junior and senior high school years, the adolescent develops greater independence and responsibility in personal, social, and academic activities. Classes in Braille, typewriting, and vocational and industrial arts are an important part of his program. School clubs offer social opportunities, as well as instruction in voice, piano, and other instruments, and participation in choral singing and music appreciation.

Guidance and counseling services help the student to make the best use of his present opportunities and to face the future with confidence.

Handwork, such as woodwork, ceramics, and weaving, may have vocational value, release tension, satisfy the desire to create, and develop dexterity and appreciation of craftsmanship.

Of about 360,000 blind persons in America of whom half are sixty-five or older, 1,100 were recently reported to be in college, and 1,000 in senior high school preparing for college. In May 1962, three scholastic achievement awards were presented at the White House to students who were blind, either from birth or from early childhood. Blindness itself is not a barrier to the pursuit of knowledge, even in the most complicated and technical studies.[20]

The intellectually able blind student can master even the most difficult subjects—advanced chemistry and physics, law and languages, higher mathematics. Thus he is able to prepare for a career in business or a profession, and to become an independent and productive member of society. Blind individuals are holding more than seven thousand kinds of jobs.

Children with Hearing Loss

It has been estimated that from ½ to 1 per cent of our children have hearing losses severe enough for them to be considered acoustically handicapped. About 125,000 are totally deaf. Children who cannot hear have difficulty in speaking and understanding the language.

The degree of difficulty in hearing is measured by audiometers in units called decibels. Hearing examinations are usually reported to parents in these units, too often without any explanation of their significance. Children with a hearing loss in the 20–30 decibel range should be seated where it will be easiest for them to hear. In addition, they should have auditory training and instruction in speech reading for a half hour period two or three times a week. Most children who have a loss of 30–35 decibels or more need carefully selected hearing aids, speech reading, and speech training. Children whose hearing loss is between 50 and 70 decibels will profit by being enrolled in special classes in regular schools where they will have some contact with hearing children. They will also have opportunities for speech improvement through playground activities, assembly programs, contacts in the halls, and special projects. It is usually best not to enroll them in a special school unless they fail to learn and adjust in the special class. Children with severe hearing losses—more than 70 decibels —are often placed in a separate school where they can develop means of communication such as lip reading.

It is important to identify preschool children who have a hearing loss. At two to three years of age they can be fitted with a hearing aid that will enable them to learn the language as normal children do. Otherwise they miss this language learning, which is so essential to further development in speaking, listening, writing, and reading. These children also need help in obtaining a broader experience through avenues of learning that do not involve language.

It is heartening to know that some youngsters who are hard of hearing take a constructive attitude toward their handicap, and do all they can to overcome or minimize it. Max, now in the eighth grade, tells how he overcame his hearing handicap:

"I can certainly say that I have a handicap: I need a hearing aid. I used to think of my hearing aid as a handicap, but not any more.

"When I began third grade, I started wearing my 'radio,' and I was pretty scared that the kids would laugh at me and the teacher wouldn't understand. But I quickly found that people aren't like that at all. My

Mom came to school with me one day, showed the hearing aid to my class, and answered their questions.

"Although the hearing aid does not bother me any more, when I start feeling sorry for myself, I think of the story of Roy Campanella. Here was a man sitting on the top of the world, the best catcher in baseball, when on the night of January 28, 1959, his car skidded on the ice and crashed into a telephone pole. Campy was paralyzed from the waist down. His fight back is one of the bravest stories the world has ever known.

"My Mom was always the person who helped me most in overcoming my handicap. She suggested that I write to Bernard Baruch, advisor to every president since Wilson. Mr. Baruch also wears a hearing aid, and his birthday is the same as mine. I first wrote to him four years ago, and we are still corresponding.

"People have got to learn that a hearing aid, like glasses or false teeth, is to help you, not hurt you. I learned this lesson so well that when my younger brother needed a hearing aid recently, I was able to talk him into it.

"I still have fun fooling people—making them think I'm wearing a radio. In fact, on the first day of school this year, my teacher looked at me, then wrote me this note: 'Hearing aid or transistor?' "

A serious hearing loss has motivated Mrs. Robert Ramsey of Short Hills, New Jersey, to help others who are deaf or hard of hearing. Her hearing defect, clearly recognized when she was thirteen, grew progressively worse. As a teen-ager she was excluded from many enjoyable social activities. She could understand the problems of deaf people because she had experienced them herself.

She determined to help them. Her plan was to get to the root of the problem—to discover the relationships among the many possible causes of deafness: damage to the pathway from the ear to the brain, infections, malformations, and diseases of the ear, and inability of the brain to interpret sounds. To throw light on the conditions that may cause deafness, Mrs. Ramsey established the Deafness Research Foundation. People with hearing problems often come to Mrs. Ramsey for advice about where to obtain the best medical help. This self-imposed task keeps Mrs. Ramsey working many hours a day without pay. Her favorite expression is: "If life hands you a lemon, make a lemonade." [21] She has helped many who bear handicaps to find them less bitter.

Children Who Have Epilepsy or Cerebral Palsy

Certain diseases have such disagreeable manifestations that the fear of an attack may be more detrimental to a child than the attack itself. Let us consider epilepsy as an example.[22] It is estimated that almost two million men, women, and children are subject to epileptic attacks, though you would never suspect that most of these persons have epilepsy.

An epileptic attack occurs when the brain cells, instead of firing off their electrical charges one at a time, all go off at once, many times a second. When the cells become fatigued, the seizure, or fit, comes to an end.

This malfunction of the brain may be due to many causes. It may be caused by a serious lack of sugar in the blood, by excessive amounts of alcohol in the blood, or by many kinds of brain damage such as a tumor, a severe blow on the head, an infection, etc. However, in about half of the cases of epilepsy no such specific causes have been discovered. The brain cells seem normal, but they behave somewhat like an automobile engine firing all its cylinders simultaneously.

Some children have few and very mild attacks; you might not even notice anything unusual in their behavior. Others may have frequent and violent attacks—contortions of the whole body that they cannot control. Some have warnings of oncoming attacks, which enable them to lie down in privacy. Others have no warning. When they come to, they wonder what happened to them. They should be told the truth; otherwise they may imagine worse things. Because of these variations, it is a mistake to treat all children who have the disease as though they had one of its severe forms.

In children, an attack that looks like epilepsy may occur in connection with a high fever. This kind of seizure may never recur. The majority of children "grow out of it"; they may never have another attack after they get to be eight or ten years old.

Wrong ideas about epilepsy have been very detrimental to children. It is true that some epileptics are mentally retarded; some have personality disorders; some may become progressively worse. But it is very wrong to jump to such conclusions about any child who has ever had an epileptic seizure. The majority of persons who are subject to seizures are otherwise normal; some have high intelligence: such a genius as Dostoevski, for example, was an epileptic.

If teachers are told that a certain child may possibly have a seizure, they will know what to do. They will handle the child sympathetically, and explain the attack to the other pupils. They will keep calm, remembering that the attack is not so serious as it appears; that it will come to an end of its own accord in a little while; and that the person is not in pain. They will put a pillow or something soft under the pupil's head and turn his head to one side, if that is possible. After the attack, they will see that he is put in a private place where he can rest quietly. Afterward they will treat the child in the usual friendly, matter-of-fact way. It is cruel to add social rejection to the epileptic's other problems of adjustment.

In the diagnosis of epilepsy, the parent can give much necessary information about the child's medical history, previous emotional upsets, and the exact nature of his seizures. This supplements such medical measures as urinalysis, blood-chemistry analysis, study of the brain waves (encephalogram), and, perhaps, X-rays.

Even children with severe epilepsy should try to lead normal lives, as far as possible. Overprotection deprives them of friends, causes frustration, and may lead them to think of themselves as invalids. They need psychological and spiritual encouragement.

The same principles apply to many other physical impairments. Knowledge of the causes helps the parents to understand the child and often relieves their feelings of guilt. For example, it is well to know that most cases of cerebral palsy occur about the time of birth, but that others develop in infancy. Premature or sudden birth, difficult or prolonged labor, and lack of oxygen at birth are some of the conditions that may cause cerebral palsy.

Cerebral palsy affects the parts of the brain that control the motor responses. This disease has many varieties. *Spastics* make up about 60 per cent of the cases. They cannot control their muscles. When the spastic attempts to move a joint, his muscles contract and block the motion. Mental retardation and disorders of speech, perception, hearing, or vision may also be part of the pattern.[23]

If the child is limited physically, the parents should lose no time in recognizing and accepting his special difficulty, and in making appropriate adjustments to it. Fear and fallacies should be replaced by faith and facts.

QUESTIONS AND ANSWERS

1. *Where may one obtain detailed authoritative information about various disabilities?*

The Committee on Child Health of the American Public Health Association has prepared a series of authoritative guides for public health personnel, which are also valuable to parents of handicapped children:

Services for Handicapped Children; a guide to general principles and practices for public health personnel.
> *Services for Children with Orthopedic Handicaps*
> *Services for Children with Emotional Handicaps*
> *Services for Children with Epilepsy*
> *Services for Children with Cerebral Palsy*
> *Services for Children with Cleft Lip and Cleft Palate*
> *Services for Children with Dentofacial Handicaps*
> *Services for Children with Heart Disease and Rheumatic Fever*
> *Services for Children with Hearing Impairment*
> *Services for Children with Vision and Eye Problems*

These are paper-bound books; each costs about $2.50.

2. *Should a child be told that he has epilepsy?*

Yes, if he is old enough to understand the nature of the disorder. He can then cooperate better with his physician and take more responsibility for his own care. Knowing what he can do for his own health and well-being will build confidence and decrease his fear and anxiety.

3. *Where can one obtain more information about accident prevention?*

The National Safety Council, Chicago, Illinois, publishes news of current *Accident Facts,* and reviews of safety measures. The Committee on Safety Education of the National Education Association, Washington, D.C., has concentrated on driver education. New York University's "Center of Safety Education" has published booklets on *Family Recreation and Safety* and *Safety Education.*

FOUR

Intellectual and Creative Potentialities

"I hope my child will be average in intelligence," one prospective mother said. "I don't want either a genius or a moron." Actually, there is no average child; every child is brighter in some respects than in others. We seldom find a child who is uniformly high or uniformly low in all mental abilities. Moreover, every child is in the process of becoming. Every child has potentialities for growth.

INTELLIGENCE IN THE MAKING

Children are born different; they have different hereditary constitutions. Some are equipped with a nervous system that is more than ordinarily sensitive. Some are born with an exceptional quality of mind—a quality that enables them to organize and see relationships between things they see, hear, taste, and feel.

This quality of mind affects the child's entire response to his environment. Have you ever noticed the differences between two babies in the same room? One will be alert and curious. He will try to reach out for nearby objects. He will notice new sounds. He will associate being held in his mother's arms with mealtime. He will connect putting on his wraps with going out for an airing. Another baby will show little interest in his surroundings. He will be slow to respond to anything; he will not be outgoing or interested. When mother approaches with his bottle, he will not associate her coming with his feeding time; he will be slow in putting two and two together.

Children differ in the way in which they use their environment. The bright child finds an opportunity to learn with a stick and a puddle of water. He learns that wood floats, that the wind moves a floating object through the water, that wood will not sink below the surface of the water, while a stone will. He learns many things from the simplest experience. The curious child learns as he lives. Some children make good use of a meager environment, while others profit little from a rich environment. Indeed, high ability helps a child create his own environment, so to speak.

What are the relative contributions of inheritable capacity and environmental influence? Estimates vary. Some scientists attribute about 80 per cent to heredity. Others think environment is all important. But one thing we know for sure: there is a constant interaction between the individual's capabilities and the opportunities presented by his environment. A child's potentials are not likely to be discovered or developed unless he has opportunities and the freedom to take advantage of them. The adult's role is first to provide the experiences and second, to know what to do or say when a teachable moment presents itself.

The mental capacity with which the child is endowed at birth is somewhat like a seed. It grows. It unfolds. As Piaget, the French psychologist, said, "Intelligence elaborates itself." From the moment of birth, the child's mind is in the making. He is constantly building the patterns of thought that affect his way of perceiving and responding to each new situation. He fits each impression that he gains from a new experience into the patterns that are already in his mind.

The loving mother contributes to the child's intellectual development. Her affection is not a passive thing; she responds to the infant's activities. She gives him opportunities to look, to listen, to feel, to take the initiative in his own learning. As a result he becomes increasingly eager to look and explore.

Most young children are stimulated intellectually to explore the ordinary home environment. Strings that ring bells when you pull them, knobs that open doors, buttons that turn lights off and on—these are all fascinating to the baby. The toddler sees Mother fill a pot with water, take a match from the box. He sees it burst into flame to light the gas stove. The water in the pot begins to bubble. Mother puts in the potatoes. If the child has helped scrub the potatoes, he knows they are hard. When they come out of the pot later, they are soft and mealy. In time, with a little help, the child comes to understand. Country children watch father plant seeds. Later they witness the miracle of growth. They are learning to perceive, to relate, to reason, to know. This is what we call "cognitive development." All they need is a wise person who can explain baffling things in a way that they can understand.

Early sensory experiences contribute to the development of the child's language and number concepts. As a prelude to learning to talk, the baby learns to distinguish many sounds. His world is full of sounds. The sound of running water means that he is going to take a bath. The quick footsteps down the hall mean mother is coming. He understands many words that mother speaks before he can say them himself. If mother talks to him about the things she is doing, words become more meaningful and memorable to him.

Learning to walk widens the child's world. Suddenly there are many more things to see, to handle, to listen to, to explore. To many children this expanding world is a challenge. But to others it is a threat; they are loath to leave the security of infancy.

FACETS OF INTELLIGENCE

Intelligence is difficult to define.[1] You may think of it, as the British psychologist Philip E. Vernon did, as a hierarchy of abilities which include the following: [2]

General Organizing Ability

Verbal-educational abilities		Quantitative-spacial abilities		
verbal comprehension	word fluency	the space factor	number	arithmetical reasoning
and others			and others	

Some psychologists have pictured intelligence as a complicated cluster of abilities. And there are still other views, too numerous to mention here. The view we have presented is perhaps the most useful in understanding our children's mental ability.

The overall general organizing factor involves the ability to remember relevant parts of one's past experiences, group these into concepts and patterns, and discover the underlying rule or principle. A high general ability can be turned on, as it were, for any kind of learning. It can be used to improve any specific performance. This means that a bright child can do a number of things well if he wants to.

The verbal-educational factor is evident in children's interest in words, and proficiency in their use. Some children, from their earliest years, delight in the sound of words. One baby would laugh gleefully when her father said a string of funny sounding words: "bunny, honey, shunny, munny." Some children are very fluent with words. When asked to name as many things of one kind as they can think of, they will quickly give a long list. Pre-school children often use words in a truly poetic way as they try to tell about the wonderful world that is unfolding to them. Later on, children with high verbal ability tend to do well on vocabulary tests and tests of ability to understand sentences and paragraphs. However, these two abilities—fluency and comprehension—do not always go together. We have all met glib children whose comprehension was shallow, and children with extensive vocabulary and ability to comprehend complicated prose, who lacked the ability to express themselves fluently in words.

Other children show an unusual interest in numbers. One mother described her little boy as "completely captivated by numbers." In this case, the child's special interest in numbers may have been partly hereditary; it may also have been due to the approval his parents expressed whenever he showed an interest in numbers.

Some children are very good at visualizing objects in space. They can steer a tricycle successfully in close quarters. They are quick to see where the parts of a jigsaw puzzle fit. Children with this ability are usually good at recognizing words in beginning reading by the "look-say" method.

Under these main categories are many specific abilities that constitute intelligent behavior.

INDIVIDUAL DIFFERENCES IN INTELLIGENCE

Differences in children's mental ability are easily recognized.[3] The parents of two boys noticed that Donald, a gifted child, learned to walk and to talk earlier than Stephen. He follows directions better. He remembers people he has seen and facts he has heard. When asked the meaning of certain words, Donald gave definitions such as these:

Skill: "Ease and grace in doing a thing."
Regard: "Can mean two different things—to look at something or to think well of someone."

Tolerate: "You may not like something but you bear it because you have to."

Perfunctory: "In an offhand manner; more from a sense of duty than because you want to do it."

Stephen, a year older than Donald but mentally retarded, made these inadequate attempts to define the same words:

Skill: "You do something with skill."
Regard: "Be careful."
Tolerate: "Be good and kind."
Perfunctory: "Perform your duties."

The two boys also showed marked differences on tests of reasoning and ability to see relations. When asked how he would look for a lost ball, the bright child drew a systematic plan for going round and round the field, coming closer and closer to its center, thus covering the area thoroughly. The less intelligent child made a few criss-cross lines, showing that he would run aimlessly here and there, often going over ground he had already covered.

When absurd statements were read to Donald, he immediately laughed and pointed out the absurdity. Stephen, on the other hand, saw nothing amusing or queer in the statements.

Day-by-day observation shows many other differences between bright and retarded children. Bright children, in general:

are quick to see relations.
are quick to learn—they do not need to have an explanation repeated; they get it the first time.

are good at solving problems.
like to read, and read more than the average child.
are accurate and fluent in their conversation.
are intellectually curious about many things.

However, some truly bright children do not show all these characteristics. Some do not read much because the available books are too childish or dull. Some have a meager vocabulary because they come from homes where a foreign language is spoken, or where no one bothers to talk with them. Some bright children try to conceal their real ability because they are afraid their classmates will call them "brains," "squares," or whatever term is fashionable for disparaging intellectual curiosity. However, if parents and teachers provide appropriate reading materials, frequent opportunities to explore and discover and create, and interesting and challenging projects, gifted children will usually show the characteristics we have listed.

A six-year-old boy had many of the characteristics usually associated with "genius." His mental age, according to the Stanford Binet Intelligence Test, was nine years, eight months. On the vocabulary test, he took his time and refused to give a definition unless he was certain that he was right. He scored low on the word-naming test because his superior ability to organize impelled him to classify each word and illustrate its use.

He became completely absorbed in any task—a common characteristic of genius. His memory was aided by his ability to associate each new idea with related clusters of ideas that he had already filed away in his mind.

He could also repeat strings of numbers either forward or backward after hearing them spoken only once. He had an intense interest in numbers. Every chance he got, he would play number games; when shopping with his mother at the supermarket, he liked to keep track of the price on each item she bought, and total them in his head. On the Achievement Test his grade score in arithmetic was 4.9—almost five years above his actual placement in the first grade. He understood multiplication and division, and added mixed fractions. He liked to spend his time with numbers.

Although his interest in reading was less intense, his reading grade level on the Wide Range Achievement Test was 5.1—fully five years above the grade he was in. Most of the errors he made were on words that are not pronounced according to phonetic rules. He wanted to classify words according to their letter sounds, and was annoyed by the inconsistencies of the English language.

Although he had some difficulty in understanding the directions for performing a physical task, his coordination in performing it was satisfactory.

His parents claimed that all they had done for the child was to respond to his initiative—answer his questions, play games with him when he asked them to, and provide him with intellectually stimulating things to see and do.

Naturally such a child would be bored by the usual kindergarten and first grade activities. His understanding teacher allowed him to keep a detailed record of everything that went on, to assist her in many ways, and to carry out advanced projects of his own.

INTERPRETATION AND USE OF INTELLIGENCE TESTS

When your child enters school, he will probably be given a reading readiness test. His performance on this test helps the teachers to decide whether he is ready to begin reading instruction and what kind of reading experiences he would need.

At the end of the third grade and again just before he enters junior high school, he may take intelligence tests and achievement tests to learn about any particular difficulties he may be having and to see whether he is progressing as well as might be expected.

In the first year of senior high school, tests are given as one basis for helping the student choose a suitable high school program. Other tests are given to tenth grade students to discover their levels of ability and special talents, and to help each student answer such questions as these: "Should I go to college? If so, which college? Which general fields of work do I seem to be best suited for?"

Persons untrained in psychology often have an erroneous impression of the significance of intelligence tests. They may still have the idea that intelligence as measured by tests is an unalterable hereditary characteristic, an infallible indication of success or failure in life. People who have this idea tend to take a fatalistic attitude toward a child's Intelligence Quotient (IQ).

The group tests given in schools are inadequate to measure fully anything as subtle and complex as intelligence. They do not measure originality, imagination, creativity, or insight. They favor the kind of mental ability that is quick and sharp, and can give the answers that most people agree are correct. These tests penalize the divergent thinker—the child who seeks to penetrate deeply or goes off on a tangent, instead of being content with a single, generally accepted answer.

Test results show how well a child performed certain tasks at a certain time. Something may have been bothering him when he was taking the test; consequently he did not give the test his full attention. His performance at a given time also depended partly on the opportunities he had had to develop his abilities. If a child is a poor reader, he will be handicapped on the parts of the test that require reading. Intelligence tests penalize children who have had ineffective school instruction, little intellectual stimulation at home, little encouragement along educational lines, and limited access to books. Thus they often underestimate the intelligence of children from poor homes, or homes where no English is spoken. The following exercise would probably be intelligible only to a child who has some background in art and classical music:

"An author is to a book as a composer is to: (a) a symphony; (b) a statue; (c) a building; (d) a bouquet."

The underprivileged child might be able to answer a question that called for the same kind of reasoning, but used words and ideas that were within his experience. Scores on intelligence tests should always be interpreted with reference to a child's environmental opportunities.

In the interpretation of a child's intelligence test score, we should also recognize the possible fluctuation from one testing to another. Although the IQs of some children maintain a high degree of consistency from infancy to twelve years, about half the school population undergo marked changes in IQ. One child scored 135 in September and 105 six months later. Only further testing and observation would show which figure represented the more accurate general measure of her mental ability. It is also true that a child may obtain a considerably higher IQ on one test than he would on another. The fact that scores are less precise than they seem makes interpretation still more difficult. An IQ of 90 does not mean exactly 90. It may represent a true score of anywhere from 80 to 100, or even from 75 to 105.

Despite their limitations, intelligence tests are useful. They may bring to light previously unrecognized potentialities that would be awakened and developed. They may call attention to deficiencies that could be minimized or corrected. Insofar as they measure previous achievement under favorable environmental conditions, they may predict future success in school.

However, human resources are not only discovered; they are

created and stimulated. One of the best ways to ascertain a child's potentiality is to provide learning experiences that encourage him to explore a wide range of abilities. Tests cannot take the place of the perceptive teacher who is alert to note the way each child develops and learns.[4]

The teacher who gives frequent informal tests and has the opportunity to observe children day after day can tell parents much about their child's abilities. Martin is a whiz with numbers. Patty writes imaginative stories and poems. Esther can solve concrete practical problems although she is bewildered by abstract ideas. Ann has a wealth of inner resources and is less dependent than most children on external stimulation. Teddy is socially gifted; he just naturally knows what to do in social situations; he makes everyone feel successful and happy.

Teachers and counselors may also help parents to understand the results of standardized tests and to be aware of four basic considerations:

1. No test gives a complete appraisal of the individual; each measures only a small sample of his total abilities.

2. A test score should not necessarily be accepted at its face value; errors do occur in computation and in the interpretation of scores.

3. A child is constantly changing and growing; he might score differently today if he were to retake the test.

4. A child's interests, goals, values, and motives affect his day-by-day accomplishment in ways that are not reflected in his test results.

For all these reasons, no important decision should be based on the results of a single test.

CHILDREN'S RESPONSE TO THE TEST SITUATION

Some children become confused in taking group tests, but do well on tests administered individually. In the fifth grade Helen did so poorly in her group intelligence aptitude test that the teacher thought she ought to be moved to a slower class. However, to all appearances, Helen was alert and bright; she read widely and showed an active mind at home and at school. When given an individual test at a private clinic, she scored above average.

How well a child does on a test depends partly on the way he perceives the testing situation, partly on how he utilizes the skills he has, and partly on his habitual response to difficulty. Whether he is by temperament exuberant or reticent, reflective or assertive, his total personality will assert itself in response to the challenge or stress of the test situation as he perceives it.[5] One child immediately surveys the overall operation and begins to concentrate on the first task. He is proud of his reading skill, and uses his previous experience confidently. He enjoys the tasks. Difficulty intrigues him. He rebounds from setbacks with renewed effort. A second child, who has a superior IQ, is afraid to think and feel spontaneously. He hesitates and fumbles, and shows no pleasure in the task. A third child, who has a much lower IQ, uses her resources more efficiently than the brighter child. She frequently uses trial-and-error methods, but is quick to grasp any clues the situation offers. While recognizing her limits, she is also conscious of the problems that she has handled well. A fourth child, who has an average IQ, handles the test material with hurried, aggressive movements. His excessive activity and intense need to please interfere with his performance. He often asks for help. However, when the tasks become difficult he tries to shift to something easier, or to escape frustration by saying he is thirsty or tired. He scores as high as he does because he keeps bouncing back to the tasks at hand.[6]

Parents who seek technical psychological appraisal of their child from a psychologist, psychiatrist, child guidance clinic, or some other special agencies should consider how the child himself feels about it. Does having a special examination suggest that something must be very wrong with him, or that his parents are disappointed or dissatisfied with him? Do the more difficult questions on the psychological tests make him feel more inferior and inadequate than he felt before?

WAYS TO FURTHER CHILD'S INTELLECTUAL GROWTH

Home conditions affect a child's intellectual potentialities. A warm, democratic family atmosphere is conducive to intellectual growth. It has been found that parents of children who developed high verbal ability bought storybooks for them, read to them, and encouraged them, even as preschool children, to participate in family conversation. They withheld help when they thought the child could solve a problem himself. Mothers of these children were especially interested in getting information about the best methods of child rearing.[7]

The child's native ability to organize and relate is developed through suitable experiences from early infancy. Things to handle —pegs to fit into holes, blocks to build with, picture puzzles to put together—all these stimulate thought. New sights and sounds encountered on a trip to the seashore, a farm, or a zoo give meaning to the words he uses to describe these experiences. By approval of his spontaneous efforts to find meaning in his environment, his intellectual development is stimulated. As children grow older, they profit by school experiences that will stimulate them to develop their abilities to the full.

THE CHILD WITH SPECIAL TALENT

How can a parent know whether his child is especially talented? Most young children like to draw and paint; they respond to music; they enjoy rhythms; they delight in being in plays. However, most great artists and musicians had demonstrated extraordinary ability before the age of ten.

Lorin Maazel achieved fame as a conductor at nine. His parents were musicians who were studying music in Paris when Lorin was born. They were naturally alert to early indications of exceptional musical ability, which other parents might have overlooked. Their child could identify the pitch of any tone as soon as he heard it. His memory for music was extraordinary; he could memorize entire scores at one reading, and could also write them from memory.

By the time Lorin had reached the age of five, in a home where his talent had every opportunity to manifest itself, he had become so intensely interested in the violin that his parents began to give him lessons. Two years later he was accepted as a pupil by the former musical director of the Moscow Art Theatre. When he was nine years old, he made his conducting debut at the New York World's Fair in Mendlessohn's "Italian" Symphony. This performance attracted the attention of authorities who unanimously acclaimed his extraordinary gifts.

Although his parents wanted to avoid exploiting their child, they were also afraid they would hold him back if they did not give him opportunities to develop his phenomenal gift. It was a problem. They finally decided to let him accept fifteen conducting engagements a year while he was attending public school. It was indeed an ordeal for a boy not yet in his teens to face initially defiant and sarcastic adult musicians. However, they soon realized that Lorin had "the entire score inside his head and would see to it that they performed it the way he wanted it." [8]

When he reached adolescence, his career as a conductor seemed to be at an end. "I was dropped flat as soon as I lost my market value as a monstrosity," he said.[9] He then, while still an adolescent, made his concert debut as a violinist, entered the University of Pittsburgh to study languages and philosophy, organized the Fine Arts String Quartet, and joined the violin section of the Pittsburgh Symphony. Later, as assistant conductor of this orchestra, he had the opportunity to resume his chosen work of conducting. At thirty-two, he returned to America to conduct France's *Orchestre Nationale* at the Lincoln Center in New York City.

In personality, Maazel seems somewhat distant. Intensely absorbed in music, he is unable to communicate with others on an ordinary everyday level of conversation. For one so young, he seems excessively austere. Although he does not seem to feel bitter or resentful about his upbringing, he wonders: "Why should any child be put through the unhealthy experience of 'performing' before a bunch of gushing adults?" [10]

Although the best way to identify talent is to have the child's performance judged by one or more persons who are highly competent in their special field, the following lists of characteristics may aid in the identification of children who have talent in one or more of three different areas:

Identifying Characteristics of Talent in the Dance
1. Responds to rhythm of music.
2. Is well coordinated, limber, light on feet.
3. Uses whole body to respond to feelings or experiences.

4. Responds to the sense of music; can tell whether to skip, run, or hop, by the mood of the music.

5. Can pantomime easily—using only motions; can depict emotional and dramatic situations.

6. Enjoys tapping out rhythms with fingers, sticks, or feet.

7. Enjoys some form of dancing.[11]

Identifying Characteristics of Talent in Drama

1. Readily shifts into the role of another character, animal, or object.

2. Shows interest in dramatic activities.

3. Uses voice to reflect changes of idea and mood.

4. Understands and portrays the conflict in the situation, when given the opportunity to act out a dramatic event.

5. Communicates feelings by means of facial expression, gestures, and bodily movements.

6. Enjoys evoking emotional responses from listeners.

7. Shows unusual ability to dramatize feelings and experiences.

8. Moves a dramatic situation to a climax and brings it to a well-timed conclusion when telling a story.

9. Gets a good deal of satisfaction and happiness from play-acting or dramatizing.

10. Writes original plays or makes up plays from stories.

11. Can imitate others; mimics people and animals.[12]

Identifying Characteristics of Talent in Music

1. Responds more than others to rhythm and melody.

2. Sings well.

3. Puts verve and vigor into his music.

4. Is interested in music; listens to music whenever possible.

5. Enjoys harmonizing with others or singing in groups.

6. Uses music to express his feelings and experiences.

7. Makes up original tunes.

8. Plays one or more musical instruments well.[13]

How important is superior mental ability, as measured by intelligence tests, in the development of special talents? This is an open question. Superior mental ability is almost always associated with outstanding talent. However, although a high IQ generally forecasts superior academic achievement, a relatively moderate intelligence rating may be sufficient to predict modest achievement in the arts—provided, of course, that it is combined with other necessary traits and special skills.

The students who were admitted, on the basis of auditions, to a special high school with programs in the dance, music, and drama had IQs that ranged from 90 to 159, with an average of 122. They all scored exceptionally high on a standardized test of educational achievement. The vocational histories, social relationships, and self-descriptions were studied by Gloria Jean Hinds.[14] There were sixty of these students, all in the eleventh grade.

The experience of being thus selected does not seem to make these students overconfident or lead them to regard themselves as exceptional. A surprisingly large number of the young people who were studied (31 per cent) reported that they were troubled by shyness. Others were struggling with supersensitiveness and overemotionality. They described these feelings in their own words:

"All my friends are good looking and sometimes when I come to school I get a sort of complex within me. . . . Sometimes I wish I was a smart boy that could do well on tests and not fail the tests that are so easy, as I am doing now. I know I try hard but it doesn't seem to work out. I'm ashamed to talk in class because I'm afraid I'll say the wrong thing and have the class laugh at me."

A girl in music (IQ 124) seemed to be afraid to put her abilities to the test:

"Musically I think I am finding evidence that in any other person would seem close to genius. I can hear almost anything and play it back. I can transpose almost any piece easily. I can play wonderfully when I dare let go, but I am always afraid to. . . . If I were giving advice to someone in a similar situation I would tell him to take the risk, but since I'm myself I'm unable to."

One youngster seemed to have a pervasive feeling of anxiety:

"I break out in tears for apparently no reason at all. I still don't know what is bothering me. The crying I usually do in private. My mother seems to get angry when I cry, so I don't do it where she can see it."

It is interesting to note that the average IQ of those who described themselves as oversensitive was somewhat lower than the IQ of the group as a whole. Shyness, while common among adolescents, would seem to be a handicap to persons who perform in public, unless, as one girl said, "on stage, it is so different."

Perhaps even more than most adolescents, talented youngsters want to be liked by others and to make a good impression on people, as the following quotations from their self-descriptions show:

"Having people like you is winning half the battle of facing life and its difficulties."

"I can't stand the thought of anyone disliking me."

"As to what people think about me, I become very upset if it isn't exactly in my favor."

"I think other people find that I'm fun to be with but that is only because I try my darndest to be that way."

"I am always striving for a more interesting and pleasing personality. I try to keep the motto, 'It doesn't cost anything to be nice.' I try my best to be as cooperative, cheerful, and useful as possible."

Establishing friendly relationships with both boys and girls is an important adolescent task. On a sociometric test on which each student was asked to choose the person he would like to have for his friend, the most chosen had, on the average, high IQs. Those chosen only as work partners had still higher IQs.

Parents often wonder what makes a child or adolescent popular. Some of these self-descriptions, supplemented by comments from other pupils and teachers, throw some light on this question. The students in this study who were much chosen were very different from those who were not chosen or neglected. They had IQs of around 130 and were in good standing academically. They were praised by their teachers. "They were characterized as mature leaders, serious, dependable, hardworking, cooperative, and resourceful. Their classmates stressed the same qualities, adding intelligent, enthusiastic, quick-to-see values in work assigned, and able to obtain effective cooperation. Occasionally these popular students were labeled conceited, overconscientious, and too unselfish for their own good by their more critical peers. . . . The superselected proved to be more efficient and better adjusted than the less popular boys and girls." [15]

Following is a description of the most chosen girl:

She was majoring in dance. Her IQ was 131 and her academic average 93 per cent. An honor student, she was chosen as a best friend four times, and as a workmate twenty-four times.

The most chosen girl, besides having the traits attributed to all the stars, was described by her teachers as alert and enthusiastic. She had a reputation for taking on difficult jobs and sparing herself nothing in completing them. Her classmates felt, in addition, that she was efficient and imaginative.

The girl herself said she realized that she was capable but not as bright as others thought. . . . Tenderhearted and sensitive, she was always on the side of the underdog. The idea of anyone disliking her pained her, so she tried to be a good and true friend. Wistfully she added that she wished she could find one as good. Carrying out her intention to be natural, forthright, and completely honest was, she confessed "a very difficult thing." In spite of this, she considered herself to be one of the luckiest girls in the world.[16]

Interestingly enough, this concern for others, this ability to help them feel successful and happy, was also characteristic of the most popular girl in a very different group—a group of neglected or delinquent adolescent girls. The most chosen girl in that group was not the one with the highest IQ nor the one with the most attractive personal appearance, but the one who made a habit of helping others to succeed.

Another developmental task of adolescence is to sharpen and define one's vocational preference. During these years, the adolescent weighs the fancied joys of his earlier choice of a glamorous career against the realistic demands of the world of work and his own more or less recognized limitations. In the following quotations various students express this readjustment as a result of their experience in a school that put their special talent to the test. A girl (IQ 128) in dance briefly summarized her viewpoint:

"I don't have talent. Not really. My nineteen-year-old sister and her friends tell me that I am bright and talented but they are overestimating me."

An excerpt from the essay of a sixteen-year-old girl (IQ 144):

"I doubt that I have talent in dramatics. The flare is ever so slight—definitely minimal. In my workshop I merely find amusement. Challenge of the intellect is the thing that attracts my attention; the theater is a secondary interest."

A girl (IQ 142) in music stated:

"I gave up becoming a professional musician soon after I entered this school. I do not think I have talent. I love to sing and act as well as play the piano and clarinet, and I try to improve these abilities, primarily for the enjoyment it brings to others."

The autobiography of a fifteen-year-old girl, who was already talented as an actress, shows us something about the way a highly gifted child develops a vocational interest:

"As far back as I can remember I wanted to be an actress. . . . In the fifth grade I had the lead in the Halloween play and that just about confirmed my ideas for an acting career. I thought it would be a wonderful profession for fame and fortune. Since coming to this school, I realize it is not all glamour but plenty of hard work.

"But I do want to be an actress—a good one. I love my family very much and want them to be proud of me. My family are always ready to encourage me. My mother thinks I'm perfect but I guess she's prejudiced. . . ."

Here we catch glimpses of a number of conditions that are conducive to the development of talent: a very early interest in a given vocation, initial success in following it, opportunity to get the special education it requires, the encouragement of family and friends, and a recognition that much hard work will be involved.

In the course of their high school experience, some highly gifted students who had thought they were interested in dancing, drama, or music, shifted their vocational choices to other fields such as writing, science, and linguistics. One of the problems of the gifted student is to choose among his many interests and the wide range of vocations that are open to him. One youngster expressed this dilemma as follows:

"I'm interested in nearly everything. I could be a pianist or teach. Musically, what I would like to do is either conduct or accompany. Academically, I would like to go into biology or physics or do something in English. I've always liked to write . . . make things funny on paper."

There are many ways in which talented high school students are like many other adolescents; in some ways they are like most adolescents; and in a few ways each is unique. They generally adhere to the behavior patterns of their peers; they want to be liked; they have their emotional upsets and periods of moodiness; they are concerned about their personal appearance; and they are often accused of being lazy. Like many other high school students, the talented group showed versatility, altruism, industry, desire for solitude, and a sense of humor. But they, too, "must face the unique cares and triumphs peculiar to each individual." [17]

POTENTIALITIES FOR CREATIVITY

Suppose we are dealing with a child who cannot draw exceptionally well, nor give pleasure to others through his unusual musical ability, nor take part in the ballet given at the school or community center, nor charm an audience as Shirley Temple once did, nor show great insight into science and mathematical problems. Suppose our child will never create a great work of art, a perfect sonnet, or a symphony such as the world has never heard before. Even though he lacks necessary originality and insight to create things of permanent interest and value, can he still be creative in another sense? Yes, he may create something or discover something that is original for him, though other people have created or discovered it before. As far as the child is concerned, his painting, or his imaginative play is a creative experience. It is his way of expressing his ideas and feelings. It is a creative process for the child and important from the standpoint of his development, even though it does not result in an original product. [18]

Children's drawings may reflect their intellectual and emotional development. Teachers have noted changes in a child's drawings during a single year. Parents, too, would be interested in keeping dated samples of their children's drawings over a period of time—their self-portraits, their drawings of members of the family, of a house, a tree; and their completely imaginative drawings. A series of paintings made by emotionally disturbed adolescents showed marked changes during the period in which they were undergoing psychiatric treatment. As their adjustment im-

proved, their drawings tended to become more free, less stereotyped, more original, less bizarre.

Young children are naturally curious, creative, and experi-
mental. They are always asking "Why?" They want to know how
something "got that way" and "what would happen if. . . ?" They
are open to new experiences within and outside themselves. They
like to play with ideas and words. One first grader substituted
"gumdrop" for "Christmas" in the song, "I Wish You a Merry
Christmas." And what a merry time the other children had sub-
stituting all sorts of incongruous words of their own choosing!

Adults can encourage creativity in the child by sharing his interest in making novel combinations of words, ideas, or events.
To prevent the child from concluding that an original production
must be bizarre or absurd, the adult should help him to develop
standards for appraising quality in examples of creative work.

As Margaret Mead has said, all children, whether or not they
are especially bright or talented, can have a creative life.[19] Growth
itself is creative. The first step that the child takes, the singing
sound of a new word that he pronounces for the first time, anything new that he learns all by himself—all these are creative
experiences.

Music and dancing are the earliest and most natural forms of
creative expression. The speech of young children, as you hear
them at play, has a musical quality like that of the street venders
of Old London. Today children can hear the best of music over
radio and television. Sometimes they see the persons and the instruments producing the music. Most of them have a chance to
be music makers, in one way or another, themselves. A few love
music so much that they want to take music lessons. Some of these
will become the great musicians and the popular singers of the
future.

Today it is possible to have reproductions of art works in every
home for the children to enjoy and wonder about. For the older
child, catalogues from art museums serve to open up the world of
art. But looking is no substitute for struggling to express one's
own thoughts and feelings in a painting or a piece of clay. How
else can the child learn what it feels like to be an artist?

For older children, art products may be a means of gaining
recognition, of building status with others. A child who is having

difficulty in reading may find it reassuring to reflect, "Anyway, when it comes to art, I'm pretty good." An assignment to draw illustrations for the story he is reading stimulates him to read better. In a social studies class, the children may make murals to illustrate what they learn about other people, their products, their houses, their ways of life. In science, they may draw a series of pictures or diagrams that express the concepts they have found important.

Words may be more difficult to manage; they cannot be manipulated in quite the same way as art materials. From their earliest years children should hear poetry and stories read aloud; they should memorize them, and repeat them just for the pleasure of the sound. All these experiences contribute to their creativity in language. The experience of looking and listening may lead directly to the experience of writing or "talking poetry."

From playing "peekaboo" and other games invented ages ago, children progress to inventing their own "Let's pretend" games. During the elementary school years they make up their own plays; some want to give them before an audience as the March children did in *Little Women*. In high school, the dramatic club may present Thornton Wilder's "Our Town." All of these creative experiences are valuable to children at different stages of development.

Parents and teachers have many opportunities to encourage the child in creative ways of meeting daily situations. Instead of telling him the answer, they may ask him questions that will lead him to discover the answer for himself. Far too many teachers make it a habit to ask children set questions and insist that they give set answers. In many instances there is no one right answer. The role of the parent or teacher is to provide the learning opportunities and leave the child free to make the discoveries, furnishing just enough explanation to insure his success. Children should be encouraged to look for the answers to many of their questions. When they are bothered by conflicting points of view, the adult can help them to learn that there are some things no man knows—that they cannot always expect to find a sure answer.

Instead of classifying and categorizing perceptions for the child, adults may help him learn to notice differences and similarities, and then make his own categories, provided he has the essential facts with which to think. He can learn to recognize the common elements in the concept of *flowers, animals, charity, courage*. If the child's classification is inaccurate, the adult should help him discover and correct his errors.

When the older child is presented with a new experience, such as an experiment in science, he should be encouraged (a) to recall related patterns of knowledge that he has gained from previous experience, (b) to form hypotheses, and (c) to fit his new knowledge into his established patterns. Thus he continuously rebuilds the thought structures that help him to sort, classify, and draw generalizations from the manifold sensations that are constantly demanding his attention.

Guidance in creative activities is subtle. It is not step-by-step instruction. The initial idea is the child's. The adult provides the necessary time and materials, and sometimes suggests sources of help that the child may consult in developing his ideas.

When the child shows his drawing or painting the adult does not ask, "What is it?" He asks the child to tell him about his work. What looks like a washtub to the adult may be a kitty to the child. By accepting the child's conception, the adult lays the groundwork for helping him improve the quality of his art work. When criticism is necessary, the adult offers it kindly and constructively, keeping in mind the child's point of view. Criticism may block creativity, especially if, instead of pointing out something good in the child's product, the adult makes a blanket criticism—"You could have done better." Or, if the adult steps in and changes the production according to his way of thinking, the child has no chance to learn to make creative revision of his work.

Parents and teachers may either foster or suppress creative tendencies in children. Indifference is a deterrent. If no one cares about his wonderful new ideas, the child may no longer bother to express them. On the other hand, if others show genuine surprise and pleasure at his discovery, and in his poetic way of describing his experience or his original drawing or painting, he is encouraged to create.

In our culture children seem to reach peaks and slumps in creativity at certain fairly predictable ages.[20] A wave that begins at the age of three reaches a peak at about four and one-half years. A slumps occurs at about five when there are increased demands for social adjustment and acceptance of authority outside the home. The curve of creative thinking then rises during the primary grades, only to drop rather sharply when children enter the fourth grade; this is the point at which peer opinion begins to exert a strong influence. The third slump occurs at early adolescence, the period of increased personal anxieties and concern about adjustment to the opposite sex.

Parents have noted these periods. Some have suggested other reasons for the apparent declines in original thinking. Overemphasis on conformity may account for a slump in creativity, as one parent noted:

"Each year since the first grade, the teachers have raved about my son's creative ability, but moaned over his reading development. This year (his fourth in school) has been the first that he hasn't been in the bottom group, but also, since he's learned to conform, his creativity is not as outstanding as formerly. He tries *not* to be different, he says." [21]

It is obvious that creativity is a complex quality. Though intelligence is essential, it is not the only prerequisite. "Productive," as distinct from "reproductive" imagination is an important factor. This factor in itself is highly complex. It includes (a) fluency— an unusual flow of associated ideas and new notions, (b) variety of ideas, (c) ability to see new problems, or to see familiar problems in a novel light, (d) insight, intuitive synthesis, sagacity— ability to single out what is most relevant or essential. There is no merit in mere fluency of ideas, if they are irrational or bizarre.

These aspects of creativity appear at a fairly early age; home and school conditions, as already suggested, may strengthen, weaken, or entirely destroy them.

THE GIFTED CHILD [22]

Among the gifted we should include scholastically gifted children —those who succeed in academic subjects—and a wide variety of talented individuals. By "gifted" we mean "any pupil whose performance, in a potentially valuable line of human activity, is consistently or repeatedly remarkable." [23] Studies of children with IQs of 130 or higher have refuted the popular notion that these children are social misfits with narrow interests. Quite the opposite!

Genuinely gifted children are, in general, superior to the average in physical attractiveness, health, and social competence; distinctly superior in moral attitudes; and two or more years advanced in educational attainments, including reading interests and reading ability.[24]

The following letter by a mother illustrates some of the characteristics and problems of precocious children:

Tommy was talking like an adult at seventeen months and doing puzzles at one year. He began reading at four with no instruction except for the sounds of letters. I have spent a great deal of time with Tommy and his brother who is two years older.

After he was in first grade for two months, his teacher told me Tommy was an exceptional child and was doing second and third grade work. Since school work in the first grade had become so boring to him, he was sent on errands or to the library where he had been given special privileges to read anything he chose.

I pleaded with his teacher and principal to put him in the second grade, but skipping was against school policy. As the months wore on, Tommy became sullen, boastful, happy, sad, lovable, and unbearable, in that order. Although Tommy is a very big boy for seven years, the principal still refused to put him in the second grade, but agreed to follow the recommendations of the psychologist. After a two-hour test and interview, the psychologist agreed that Tommy was a gifted child and said that he scored on the fifth grade level on every achievement test. The psychologist criticized the school for not advancing him to a higher grade this year. She suggested that they promote him from the first to the third grade.

Tommy seems to be much happier now that he knows he's going into the third grade. He has even taken a strong interest in baseball and plays every day. My neighbor said, "Tommy has changed overnight."

This mother's description of her child indicates quite clearly that preschool children with average or above average mental ability can be stimulated to achieve much more than we at present expect of them. The mother gave Tommy a great deal of attention. She probably read to him, talked with him as one adult to another, answered his questions, gave him puzzles to solve, and gave some instruction in reading. As a result, he was far abler than most first graders. The question is whether such special attention and early instruction are beneficial to the child in the long run, especially if other aspects of his development are neglected.

To be sure, some of his problems were caused by the school's failure to make provision for exceptional children. Since Tommy was physically mature as well as academically advanced, he could probably have been placed in a higher grade at an earlier date. But if he skipped two grades he would miss systematic instruction in arithmetic and the language arts that are necessary as a foundation for future academic success. The teacher, burdened by her responsibility for forty other children, made the only special provision that occurred to her—sending him on errands and permitting him to spend a good deal of time in the library. Even under these conditions, Tommy might have been helped to find some interest and value in the group instruction that was given to the class. It would be interesting to have a report on Tommy ten years from now, when he is in high school. Has he maintained his lead in academic achievement? How well has he adjusted socially to classmates older than he?

Gifted children may be provided for in any of the following ways on every grade level. Parents who are familiar with various plans and procedures may be influential in helping teachers and administrators develop programs that are appropriate for other gifted children in the local school system.

In some cases, *acceleration* may be desirable. It may be good policy to let a child complete three years' work in two. However, this depends upon the child's social and physical maturity, his intellectual capacity, and upon the attitudes of the teachers and their skill in making special provision for the gifted in their classes. Any decision to accelerate should be based on a study of the child and the situation.

Grouping should be based on the pupil's competencies in various subjects, rather than on intelligence test scores alone. By this plan a pupil might be grouped with able learners in science or mathematics or English, and with average pupils for the rest of the day. Thus he would have the stimulation of more advanced instruction, more difficult materials, and more informed discussion, without losing contact with less able youngsters.

Gifted pupils should have tailor-made programs. They may be

encouraged to take advanced work in the required subjects, or
left free to take any elective that will enrich their lives—art, music,
typing, a second foreign language, home economics, industrial
arts.

Special after-school clubs offer able students opportunities to
make social contacts, as well as to explore a given field beyond
the limits that usually are reached in regular classes.

In some large cities, New York, for example, there are *special
schools* such as the High School of Science, the High School of
Performing Arts, and others that offer advanced work in certain
fields.

Summer institutes, on the college level, for academically interested and talented high school students are becoming a part of our
educational system. Students are admitted on the basis of
aptitude test scores, academic achievement, recommendations of
secondary school principals, and a personal interview with the
director of the institute. Students who have attended these institutes, highly motivated to begin with, feel that the experience is
worthwhile, not only in knowledge gained, but also because it
fosters growth in independence and responsibility, insight into
one's interests and abilities, and respect for learning.

Under an *Individual Sponsor Program* a student is teamed with
a carefully selected adult who has similar interests. The contacts
between sponsor and student may take the form of conversations,
correspondence, shared excursions, the exchange of books or recordings, etc. If an adult sponsor is not available, a gifted older
student may perform the same function.

Correspondence courses have been used effectively in rural communities where the number of gifted students is too small to war-

Independent study is another way in which gifted children may
explore their special interests. For example, a gifted student might
have two periods a week for special projects, exploratory reading,
independent field trips, and the like.

Counseling helps the gifted student to work out his own educational and vocational plans. The counselor shares his ideas and
sources of information with the student, and listens to the student's
ideas about the kind of program that seems most likely to develop
his potentialities.

We should help gifted children to become aware of their social responsibilities. Good heredity and favorable early childhood experiences carry a proportionate responsibility for service to others.

THE CHILD WHO IS SLOW IN LEARNING

Teachers tend to take a fatalistic attitude toward slow-learning children, instead of helping them to progress as far and as fast as *they* can. Slow learners are learners; they should be given educational opportunities to develop *their* intellectual capacities.

A traveler asked an old native of the village the way to Riverton. "If I were going to Riverton," the old fellow replied, "I wouldn't start from here." This is the way we are likely to feel about the mentally retarded child: we should like to begin instruction at a higher level. However, if we are to make satisfactory progress, we have to start where the child is and build on his present capabilities.

Most parents of mentally retarded children need help in facing the fact of retardation. They need reassurance that both they and the child can achieve some degree of happiness, despite the mental defect.[25]

Education at home can supplement education in school. Parents can easily furnish the child with opportunities for motor-sensory training by giving him things to fit together and games that require eye-hand coordination. They can also provide him with simple card games that give additional practice in vocabulary, or in other reading or number skills that he is learning in school. Like normal children, the mentally retarded enjoy certain hobbies; they can also develop an appreciation of art, music, and drama that are within their mental scope.

"Gifted children and retarded children are first of all *children*. They have many needs in common. They need work that they can do successfully, play and other social experience, approval more than criticism, respect for them as persons, and faith in the resources each has within himself, whether he has one talent or ten talents." [26]

QUESTIONS AND ANSWERS

1. *Are intelligence and talent the same?*

Highly intelligent children are likely to be talented in one or more fields. Among talented children and young people, below-average intelligence is rare. When we find research that fails to find a positive relationship between intelligence and creativity, we must remember that tests of intelligence and especially tests of creativity are inadequate; they measure only a small part of a child's intellectual capacity or creative potentiality.

2. *Should the schools tell parents their children's IQs?*

Different opinions have been expressed on this question. Those who say "yes" believe that parents should know the child's IQ in order to avoid expecting too much if his IQ is low, or too little if his IQ is high. In the first case, the child may be subjected to too much pressure; in the second case, he may languish in idleness and fail to use his talents. In either case, knowing the IQ might enable the parent to make better provision for the experiences the child needs.

Those who say "no" recognize the limitations of intelligence tests that we have mentioned in this chapter, and the dangerous misconceptions that prevail about IQ scores. They are also aware of the possible danger of arousing feelings of inferiority on the part of the child who scores low, and producing a certain arrogance on the part of the child who scores high. In either instance, knowledge of the child's IQ might prevent the parent from trying to help him grow by giving him opportunity to use his powers successfully, regardless of his IQ.

There is a great difference, however, between just telling a parent his child's IQ and interpreting the results of intelligence tests to him.

3. *How much information about test results should I expect the the school to give me?*

The best general answer is: "The parent should be given as much information as he will use for the good of the child." And this information must be given to individual parents in a form that they can understand and use. Certainly, the counselor, psychologist, principal, or teacher should explain frankly the values and limitations of tests, and should state and explain the school policy relative to the use of test results.

Counselors will often interpret test scores to parents in this way:

"Your son (or daughter) scores like . . .

". . . students who find getting into a liberal arts college and getting a B.A. degree something they can attain only with extra hard work. On the other hand, they find a year or two of technical school interesting and they probably do well in the jobs to which that leads."

". . . students who are disappointed later if they don't begin a language in the ninth grade and plan to take more math and science. It's easier to head toward business later if you still want to than to go from the commercial course into a good college."

". . . students who don't often—only about one out of four—manage to earn a C average their freshman year."

". . . students who have more than average difficulty passing in arithmetic—they may need some extra help on this in the next few years."

Many more samples will come readily to mind. The most important thing to note is that a satisfactory report combines two kinds of information: (a) the test results of the individual person, and (b) something known about the test or battery and its relationship to the subsequent performance of others who have taken it.[27]

4. *Will preliminary practice on College Entrance Examination Board Tests help the student make a higher score?*

It is an advantage for a student to know the nature of college admission tests before taking them for the first time. A booklet called *A Description of the College Board Scholastic Aptitude Test* may be obtained from the College Entrance Examination Board, Educational Testing Service, Box 592, Princeton, New Jersey, or Box 27896, Los Angeles 27, California.

It is very helpful for the student to take the Preliminary Scholastic Aptitude Test in his junior year. His scores on this preliminary test are likely to predict quite well his scores on the longer Scholastic Aptitude Test that is usually taken later. A little booklet, also published by the College Entrance Examination Board, gives an excellent concrete explanation of the scores on this test.

5. *Does coaching on intelligence-type tests improve an individual's score?*

Dr. Philip E. Vernon of the University of London found that the effects of mechanical practice at, or coaching on, specific types of intelligence test items are strictly limited, but that stimulating curricula and previous experience with similar tests does make a difference.[28]

6. *How are intelligence test results used?*

Intelligence test scores have been used to group children into separate classes or to form sub-groups within a class. The purpose of such grouping is to enable teachers to provide appropriate methods and materials of instruction for different kinds of learners. However, at present, intelligence tests alone are seldom used for this purpose; they are used in combination with achievement tests (especially reading tests), teachers' marks, and teachers' recommendations. Moreover, ability-grouping is no longer considered the best solution; more and more teachers are trying to provide for a wide variety of individual differences within a regular class.

Intelligence tests are also used for guiding pupils who have learning difficulties. The test results may indicate that a child is doing the best he can, or they may show clearly that his lack of achievement is not due to lack of mental ability.

Another common use of intelligence tests is in educational and vocational guidance.

Unfortunately, intelligence tests are misused as well as used wisely. They have sometimes been used without consideration of the individual's background, and without reference to other information about him and about the testing situation. Important decisions have too often been made on the basis of a single test result.

FIVE

Educational Potentialities

MANY children and adolescents today have unfulfilled intellectual potentialities. These are the underachievers. They *can,* but they *don't,* achieve up to expectation.

In high school we find a high proportion of underachievement among the gifted. For example, in New York City, of the 5,000 ninth-year high school students who scored at the 90th percentile [1] or higher on the Iowa Test of Educational Development, and were rated as 130 IQ or above, less than half were achieving grades of 85 per cent or better in all of their major subjects.[2] When these figures were made known to the students and their parents, improvements began to occur. Merely knowing that they were capable of superior achievement stimulated many of these students to do better. Families who had not even considered the possibility of higher education for these potentially able young people began planning to send them to college. Counselors and teachers began to use different approaches to motivate and instruct them.

Military sources also give us evidence of underachievement. From the end of the Korean War until January 1962, more than one million young men flunked the Armed Forces Qualification Test, yet this is not a difficult test.[3] It consists of one hundred multiple choice questions in four fields—reading, arithmetic, the relations of forms and shapes, and mechanical ability. Some intelligent men gave incorrect answers to as many as twenty-two out of the hundred questions because they had not learned the English language. Others, though they had gone to school, had failed to learn to read, write, or do arithmetic.

Underachievement is prevalent on all levels of intelligence and of socio-economic status. Both mentally handicapped children and gifted children often fail to make achievements that would be appropriate to *their* levels of mental development and *their* rates of mental growth.

What is the solution? More effective teaching of basic reading and thinking skills? More effective methods of stimulating students' desire to learn? Or does the problem stem from a fundamental lack of worthwhile goals and values in our culture?

HOW CHILDREN LEARN TO THINK

Habits of thought begin to be formed in the very earliest years. The mental processes established in infancy exert a continuing—perhaps a life-long—effect upon the person's educational achievement.

In infancy the child learns by endlessly exploring all the things in his immediate environment. A little later on, the child makes boats and wagons from cardboard boxes and blocks of wood, animals from paper and clay, dolls from clothespins and hollyhocks —all, as Wordsworth wrote, "shaped by himself with newly learned art." In the process of making things, he acquires finger dexterity, eye-hand coordination, and a first-hand understanding of the properties of many kinds of materials. From his self-initiated projects and creative activities he learns to think—to perceive, to reason, to relate, to remember. He learns to keep trying until he has solved a problem. The role of the adult with respect to children engaged in creative activities is to give just enough help so that they can achieve their goals.[4]

Language facilitates thinking. Ability to tell his thoughts helps the child to clarify them. As an older girl said, "I talk so I'll know what I think, don't you?" This kind of communication is especially important to the little child.

The element of discovery makes thinking rewarding. Children learn to think by finding for themselves the answers to their questions. A scientist is born when a child shifts his questions from *who* to *why*—when instead of asking who makes the storm, the flowers, or the blue sky, he becomes interested in natural causes— in why things happen. When he asks questions about life and death and other "things that no man knoweth," we should be careful not to close the door on his spirit of inquiry by giving a superficial explanation.

Children's thinking is also affected by their needs. The children of American Indians in the early days had a need to listen and observe very carefully; only by close attention could they avoid danger. Today there are innumerable social needs that stimulate children to think clearly and reason accurately. Television commercials, for example, demand critical thinking. One child began this kind of thinking early when he said, "Mommy, they all say *their* cereal is the *best*."

Children show an early susceptibility to the influence of their parents' ways of thinking. If a father is curious, observant, and eager to learn about the things he sees and hears, his son is likely to acquire a similar habit of inquiry. If a parent is precise in his thinking, the child is likely to follow in his father's footsteps. In psychological words, children tend to copy their parents' cognitive patterns. Their imitation of adult models seems to be most effective when the adult talks about what he is doing and why he is doing it. There is some evidence that a child is likely to make a better approach to problem solving if he has a close and harmonious association with his father during the early preschool years.[5]

Little children, in general, are extraordinarily receptive to casual or unpremeditated learning. They are unconsciously influenced by works of art that are placed within easy visual range. They become acquainted with birds and flowers on their daily walks. They store among their mental treasures songs, stories, and poems that are repeated to them.

But children also need guidance in learning. They need to be shown how to look at things carefully, how to file new observations or ideas in their minds, how to organize, classify, and rearrange the evidence they already have. When they have a new problem to solve, they can be encouraged to ask, first of all, "What ideas and skills do I already have to bring to bear on this problem?"

There seem to be critical periods for learning.[6] The famous experiment with the twins, Johnny and Jimmy, showed that these critical periods vary with the thing to be learned.[7] Learning to walk was not affected by previous practice. Roller skating and some other activities benefitted by early practice. In other activities, early practice slowed down learning. In general, the critical period for many kinds of learning seems to be the time when the individual first reaches his maximum capacity to look, to do things, to want to learn. Any attempt to teach a child motor and intellectual skills too early may result in his learning bad habits or in his "learning not to learn." Either of these results may handicap him in later life.[8]

Poor habits of thinking limit or interfere with the child's subsequent learning. His continued development depends on his previous learning. Once a system or pattern of thinking and feeling is organized, it becomes increasingly difficult to modify. In other words, we tend to "get set in our ways." Habits of thought and feeling are modified only as the individual is actively engaged in forming new patterns of perceiving, reasoning, and acting.

Learning is subject to many influences. A mild or pleasant emotion is favorable to learning. A slight degree of tension is essential to optimum learning. A student can be too relaxed. However, intense anxiety often disrupts the learning process; it may be a cause as well as a symptom of poor achievement. Different degrees of anxiety affect individuals in different ways. High anxiety may increase the achievement of competent students, but prevent less able students from doing their best work. Low anxiety may cause some able students to work below capacity, but free others to do the best they can. The individual's response to anxiety varies with his personality pattern and his self-concept.

Some adolescents feel a need to defy their parents; some fear growing up; some have a feeling of incompetence; some have a desire to be different or unique. Any of these emotional states may influence the individual's thinking.

That a satisfying experience has a favorable effect on subsequent learning has long been recognized. Praise, if genuine, usually promotes learning. Rewards, too, must be deserved, and not given too lavishly; what becomes too common decreases in value. When the child acquires an interest in learning for learning's sake, he becomes less dependent upon adult approval.

Praise and encouragement affect different children in different ways. Praise facilitates the progress of children who are already receptive to learning. To children who are closed or resistant to learning, praise may be threatening. A self-confident child who has a strong desire to learn may interpret criticism from a respected parent or teacher as genuine concern for his best development. Such criticism may stimulate him to improve. However, the same kind of criticism may crush a sensitive, self-depreciating child. One child may be grateful to an adult for overlooking a minor error, whereas another child may consider it a sign of weakness. Even the same child may respond differently at various times to what appears to be the same situation.

Children vary both in their mode of learning and in their approach to a learning task. Some boys, for example, can best discover what is wrong with an engine by tinkering with it; others learn more from a manual; they can visualize the relationship of mechanical parts.

Some children are impulsive—if they do not get the answer or solve the problem at the first try, they tend to give up. Others move in slowly and reflectively. They enjoy complicated, thought-provoking problems.

The way in which knowledge and skill are acquired also affects subsequent learning. A fact will not stand up by itself or be long remembered unless it is supported by the reasoning that led to its discovery. Children who learn facts through the process of discovery are likely to remember and use them.

Teachers should not be content if their pupils merely memorize many separate facts. They should show them how to find basic principles, key ideas, and the structure or plan of a subject. Edgar Dale described a class in Menlo Park School in California where the children, after having mastered fourteen physical science principles, could forecast, with great accuracy, where bananas or wheat or coconuts could be grown.[9]

The clarity with which a subject is presented has a great deal to do with students' learning. The art of saying complex things simply is usually possessed by the persons who have the deepest knowledge of their field. Classroom explanations are often wordy and poorly organized. Even very young pupils can understand quite complicated subjects if their basic concepts are clearly presented. In the case of slow learners, of course, one must take slower and more numerous steps toward drawing a conclusion or mastering a skill.

The "drive to learn" underlies all genuine educational achievement. Its development is based most fundamentally on the presence of consistent goals and values in the home and the community.[10] Some cultures stress competitive achievement to the neglect of kindness and consideration for others. Some cultures build the opposite attitude—their children refuse to succeed at someone else's expense. Still other cultures emphasize collective rather than individual success. In our own adolescent culture, some youngsters will put forth more effort to insure the success of a group project than to attain high marks for themselves.

If a given culture emphasizes the principle that each individual should be helped to develop his potentialities, not only for his own satisfaction, but also for the welfare of society, this goal will be uppermost in the pupil's thinking. He will take the initiative in seeking and undertaking challenging tasks. He will not be deterred by difficulties. He will endure hardships in the pursuit of his purpose.

WHAT MAKES THEM TICK?

When a small boy was told, "You can do anything you want to, if you try hard enough," he asked, "How do you get to want to?" In other words, how are children motivated? Ability or talent combined with drive can surmount enormous handicaps. Without the drive to achieve, ability or talent tend to go to waste.

In the anonymous, unstructured compositions written by a group of gifted ninth-grade students on the subject "What Makes Me Tick" we find a wide range of motivations. A few quotations from these compositions will give us insights about adolescent motivations.

Everyday happenings that give satisfaction

"There are many things that keep me going from day to day. I like to listen to the radio every day, to keep up with the new records. I don't like school work very much, but I want to pass all my subjects."

"From being alone for so long I learned to derive pleasure from small things that no one else really enjoys."

"In some instances, it is the extra-class activities that make school tolerable."

"I really don't get pleasure out of school itself. It's the messing around and being with friends that pleases me."

External compulsion

"I go to school because I have to. So while I'm going to school I might as well learn something. A lot of the things we do in school I don't like, but I have to do them or fail."

Sense of duty, especially to parents

"The reason I want to do well in school is that I feel it is a duty. If I don't do well in school, I think I'm letting my parents down. This is the main reason I try my hardest."

To make a good impression on people

"In sports I try to be the best so as not to be laughed at. People don't like to be known as poor players at whatever they endeavor."

Some goal in life

"My attitude on life is to make something of myself before I die. I don't wish to be a nobody all of my life."

"The thing that makes me tick in my school life is the desire and need for a college education. In order to get a half-way decent job, one must go to college. I will therefore try to obtain good grades in all my majors and secure all the education I need for entering any college. . . . I know what it is to work for what I want."

". . . I have set my goal ahead of time so that in my later life I can have the satisfaction of knowing I did the best I could to achieve these goals. When a person always keeps his mind on what he wants to be in later life and the ways in which he can achieve this—I think that is what makes me tick."

Satisfaction in doing a worthwhile job

"The satisfaction of doing a job worthwhile to the best of my ability is probably what makes not only me but others tick. A person should take pride in everything he is doing that is worthwhile. . . ."

Enjoyment of work itself and one's own competency

"One thing that makes me tick is my schoolwork. I basically enjoy the main subjects. I like to learn all I can about a subject. . . . I like to do well in school for my own satisfaction. I care what other people think, but also what I think. I get satisfaction from knowing that I can do it without anyone else helping me—that I can get along on my own."

Multiple reasons: vocation, parental approval, satisfactions

"If I do well in school, I'll feel that I have accomplished something, my parents will be proud of me, and I will be better suited for my future job. I really like school because I enjoy learning, but in a way I fear it and I guess I always will. I think I find some type of satisfaction in everything I do."

Our idea of motivation has changed over the years. We used to think of motivations as being specific incentives—a gold star, a mark of A, a prize, or some other extrinsic reward. Actually, motivation is far more complex than that. It really comprises a combination of forces—forces within the individual interacting with forces in the environment. It is part of a system that regulates all the individual's behavior. It is goal-directed from within, in accord with his needs, desires, and self-concept. It is goal-directed from without by the people in his immediate environment, the social pressures to which he is subject, and the appeal of the particular thing that is to be done or not done.

The simplest drives to action are most easily recognized in the young. The baby seeks his mother's breast when he is hungry, drinks when he is thirsty, shivers when he is cold, throws off his blanket when he is hot, sleeps when he is tired, moves various parts of his body when he feels the need for activity. Under certain conditions, these basic physiological needs—hunger, thirst, and fatigue—may dominate behavior. Some authorities put sex in the same category, while others believe that this physiological drive is stimulated only by external conditions. The more complex motivations probably stem in part from these basic drives.

To some extent we all continue to respond to these basic biological needs, though we introduce many modifications. Though we are hungry, we delay eating if our hostess is slow in serving dinner. We may not rest when we are tired because a stronger drive toward achievement keeps us up late at night. As the child grows older, his biological drives or needs tend to influence his behavior less than his values, purposes, and goals.

Psychological motivations take many forms—curiosity, interest, difficulty, success, satisfaction, anxiety, and habit. All of these may affect a child's achievement.

Curiosity—the desire to know the "how" and the "why" of things

—is a natural spur to children's achievement. Parents can foster the spirit of inquiry in their children from the earliest years. Teachers can make children's learning an experience of discovery. Any student may ask a searching question that sets other students to work finding the answer.

One aspect of motivation over which teachers and parents have considerable control is the interest and challenge of the immediate situation. The child's environment contains attractions and repulsions that stimulate him to move toward or away from opportunities to learn. For example, the child may be attracted to a reading task by the interest or suspense of the story itself, or by an immediate need to read certain lines well enough so that he can take part in a dramatization. An older boy may desire to read better because he needs to get a job, to read his girl friend's letters when he is away at camp or to avoid the disdain or ridicule of his classmates.

Children's interests are important spurs to their achievement in school. The skillful teacher relates the child's interests to the subject at hand. For example, a child's interest in the flight of the first man in orbit may stimulate him to collect and label pictures of the event, read and compare accounts from different sources, and explore related topics. Similarly, a child's interest in music may lead him to read about his favorite composers and the times and places in which they lived. Certain television programs may give students, especially boys, an initial interest in science that enriches the regular science curriculum. As a result of a trip to some place of historical interest, children may be stimulated to learn why the historical event took place and what influence it has on our life today.

Difficulties or barriers may be challenging, if they do not seem insuperable. Any activity may be unattractive if it appears too difficult—or too easy. Most children like to have graduated goals leading to a successful end result.

The way in which success or failure affects a child's achievement varies with the individual. For some persons, avoiding failure may be a stronger incentive than achieving success. They regard difficulty as a challenge; it arouses their fighting spirit—"I'll show you!" With others, difficulty and deprivation only serve to lower their self-esteem and increase their sense of hopelessness.

With most students, failure depresses the level of aspiration, whereas success raises it.

Some individuals accept failure as part of their personality pattern. They have failed so often that they are afraid to try again. Their level of aspiration sinks lower and lower. This attitude toward failure is the most difficult to overcome. In trying to help such a child, we should direct his attention to his previous successes, however few and small they may have been. If we can find the level at which he can succeed, and begin instruction and practice there, the experience of initial success will motivate him to put forth the effort he needs to gain the knowledge or skill that he lacks.

Sometimes teachers or parents can create situations in which this kind of child can and will succeed; thus they break his vicious circle of self-depreciation, underachievement, and further self-depreciation. They convey to him in subtle ways that they feel he is adequate to the situation and that they have confidence in him. Their confidence helps him to change his self-defeating attitude.

While helping the child to capitalize on his assets, we should also help him correct his faults. Children can learn from mistakes. The child's natural tendency is to do the things in which he can succeed and to avoid activities in which he is likely to fail. Consequently, he gets less and less practice in the very skills in which he needs the most practice.

The response that a person has just made to one situation often determines what he does next. If the response produced satisfaction, he is now motivated by hope, and tends to make the same kind of response again. If the response aroused anxiety, he is now motivated by fear, and tends to avoid doing the same thing again. Thus, previous learning acts as a motivation. The more children see and hear and do, the more they *can* see and hear and do. Achievement leads to further achievement.

Good old-fashioned habit plays a part in motivating a child to behave in certain ways. One psychologist has defined motive as "an incomplete reaction." Once we have started to do something, habit, or the sense of closure, impels us to continue or finish it.

The individual's achievement is also affected by various social motives—to be accepted by people whom he regards as important, to have prestige or power, and to accumulate material things.

By rewarding certain behavior, we may make it attractive; that is, the child will perceive it as attractive. This is what Anatole France may have had in mind when he wrote, "I would make lovable those things which the child ought to love." [11] However, the effect of approval or disapproval depends partly upon who gives it. If the child likes the person, he may interpret even criticism as favorable. If he dislikes the person, he may disparage anything the person says. With this in mind, adults will be cautious in their use of praise and blame. Although the adult may intend his criticism to motivate the child to do better work, its actual effect may be either to make him dislike the adult or to give him a hopeless view of himself. Moreover, a child may become too dependent upon personal approval; his main concern should be with work well done.

For many adolescents, adult approval in the form of commendations or marks may have less influence than peer approval for success in sports, dates, and social activities. Underachievement in adolescents is often due to the adverse social pressure of the group. Adolescents motivate one another. They will frequently put forth much more effort to achieve a group goal than to reach such individual goals as high marks and teacher approval.

Desire for prestige motivates some extremely competitive students. To them, it is all-important to be on the Honor List, to get the highest mark on an examination, to win first prize. To be less than "tops" gives them a sense of failure. A student with a strong desire to excel may choose to work with a capable student whom he hardly knows rather than with a less capable friend.

Motivation to high achievement may have cultural as well as personal elements. The traditional American values have in the past been a pervasive spur to achievement. American achievers have had certain attitudes derived from the Puritan ethic. The Puritans believed that problems could be solved, no matter how complicated they were. They believed in a Power beyond and above themselves that could help them solve problems. In the words of Agnes Repplier, the Puritan was one who "understood that life is neither a pleasure nor a calamity. It is a grave affair with which we are charged, and which we must conduct and terminate with honor." [12]

This traditional attitude is rapidly changing. Many young people place personal gain and material success ahead of social responsibility. For others the Freudian concept has replaced the Puritan ethic; these persons seek to reduce tension by lowering their standards rather than by striving to achieve higher standards. Television, radio, motion pictures, modern novels, and the records young people play interminably are permeated with the "take it easy" and "why worry" philosophy of life. These modern media of communication are subtly conditioning children and young people to values that reduce their need and motivation for achievement. Such outside-of-school influences are often more potent and persuasive than those exerted by teachers who try to raise the achievement level of their classes.

When a culture emphasizes personal development for a social purpose, the individual is motivated to develop his capacities in order to fulfill his obligations. Although he encounters hardships and difficulties, he is challenged and sustained by the ideals set and the rewards provided by his culture.

Values often override adult rules and practical knowledge. A group of junior high school boys were told not to buy from a pushcart vendor who stationed himself outside the school. In health education class they learned that his glasses were rinsed in a pail of dirty water, and his so-called lemonade consisted of some tablets dissolved in water with a few pieces of lemon rind floating on top "for local color." Nevertheless, the boys continued to buy from him. When asked why, they said, "Well, he bought an ad for our school newspaper, and we couldn't let him down."

What a person values, he usually puts forth effort to obtain. When a family or a community values scholarship highly and consistently, its able children tend to be outstanding in their academic achievement. They do not seem to resent adult strictness or pressure, or other conditions that some psychologists consider unfavorable to learning.

Underlying the various motivations already mentioned is the basic desire to make oneself as "good" or complete as possible. The direction of this drive is determined by the individual's concept of himself—what he thinks he is, and what he would like to become (see Chapter One). The individual's self-concept is pervasive and persistent. It strongly influences what he thinks and what he does.

It seems quite clear that focusing a child's attention on his faults, or labeling him as a slow learner, as mentally retarded, or as emotionally disturbed is in most cases detrimental. To encourage a negative self-concept is to invite premature school leaving, delinquency, or mental illness.

In general, a student will be motivated to achieve academically if he knows that his work will be evaluated, if he expects to be successful, if he has previously been successful in similar tasks, and if he thinks that the results of his effort will be worthwhile. However, other strong motives or long-term goals may cause a pupil to achieve even in the absence of these common motivations, and in spite of considerable anxiety and previous failure.

SCHOOL ACHIEVEMENT AND CONDITIONS AFFECTING IT

Parents expect their children's achievement in school subjects to be commensurate with their mental ability. In general, the level of achievement among high school students does parallel the level of ability.[13] A recent survey shows that the ablest 5 per cent ranked in the upper third in achievement. However, some of the brighter pupils ranked in the lowest third. At least one-fourth of the very able learners earned marks that were below their level of ability.

The percentage of underachievers among gifted students varies from school to school. In one school it was 12 per cent; in another, 16 per cent; in another, 42 per cent. This variation may be due to any of a number of factors, including high or low academic standards, good or poor instruction, strict or lenient marking.

On the other hand, high achievers may be found among pupils who score relatively low on intelligence tests. In the survey mentioned above, 10 per cent of the pupils in the lowest fourth on intelligence tests ranked in the upper third of their classes; 34 per cent were in the middle third. Why did they do so well?

There are a number of possible reasons. These pupils may have been brighter than the intelligence tests indicated. They may have studied very hard. They may have had exceptionally good reading instruction in elementary school. They may have had help and encouragement at home. These and many other conditions may affect pupils' school achievement.

We also find a difference between girls and boys with respect to school achievement. Even in a group of boys and girls who are about equal in mental ability, more boys than girls usually rank low. Girls are usually more conscientious than boys about their school work, and less rebellious about taking subjects that they do not think are of much value to them. Sometimes teachers give boys lower marks than they really deserve because they behave badly or show a poor attitude in class. Since girls mature about two years earlier than boys, they have a headstart in language development. This female superiority is often discouraging to boys. The self-concepts of fourth and sixth grade boys were found to be significantly less confident than those of girls in the same grades. In general, the boys who were the most self-confident were the higher achievers.

Many able learners find it challenging to be placed in advanced sections with other able pupils. Sometimes, however, it is better "to let well enough alone." There are instances where this push ahead comes before the child is ready for the advanced work, and ultimately causes a setback. James, for example, had been an honor student until his freshman year in high school, when he was placed in advanced sections in biology and English. He failed miserably, and even began to doubt whether he should continue with the college prep program. Some youngsters do not adjust readily to the intensified competition and extra work that are characteristic of advanced courses. They get discouraged and lose confidence in themselves. When this happens, the best way to restore their confidence is to return them to the regular class and help them achieve success there.

In urging a child to do better in his school work, we sometimes ignore physical factors. He may have a generally low energy level. He may have some sub-acute infection that is sapping his energy, or some unrecognized physical defect that is making achievement impossible, or at least uncomfortable for him. One teacher considered an underachiever "lazy," and scolded her for not getting her work done. Another teacher was sympathetic and advised more rest. Still another thought the student was dull and accepted her low level of performance as the best she could do. A thorough medical examination later showed the girl had an infection that was sapping her energy.

Individual interest and effort are also affected by the achievements that the community, the school, and the family choose to reward. Pressey pointed out that one community was distinguished by very high achievement in music.[14] He attributed this peak of accomplishment to these conditions: children began to study music at an early age; they were given excellent instruction; their performance was applauded; high achievement was rewarded. Similarly, exceptional achievement in tennis occurred in a community where unusual facilities for instruction and practice were available and proficiency in this sport was highly commended. In our contemporary culture where business attainments reap greater rewards than intellectual or artistic talents, the young person's educational concern is often utilitarian. His criteria for judging a given subject or for earning high grades, are summed up in a frequently heard question, "Where will this get me?"

Pupil achievement is affected by the recognition that the school accords to certain kinds of activity and ability. In a high school in the midwest, Dr. James S. Coleman found that the students did not become increasingly interested in their work during the four-year period.[15] Although in the middle of the senior year many students became concerned about getting "good grades for college," they still did not seem to be interested in learning *per se*. The leaders of the school population were the socially dominant girls who controlled important extracurricular activities, and the boys who were athletic heroes. "The young people most attracted to scholastic brilliance were quiet, conforming, unsophisticated boys and girls who remained unnoticed and often unhappy."[16] This condition was more prevalent in well-to-do suburbs than in working class or farm areas.

Parents usually regard teaching skill as the most important factor in their child's achievement. The teacher should know his subject, and should also know how children learn. Lack of variety in methods and materials is detrimental to motivation. The same old routine, day after day, soon makes a class dull. To bright children especially, unpredictability has charm.

Sensitivity to the needs and feelings of individual pupils is also essential; different individuals respond in different ways to the same classroom situation. David has a high achievement motivation and wants to learn; he may accept sharp criticism from a respected teacher, because he sees it as evidence of the teacher's concern for his success. Mary may burst into tears if she is similarly criticized. Bert may become belligerent and hostile. The skillful teacher adapts his approach, his methods, and his materials of instruction to the pupils whom he is teaching.

Family relations and family attitudes have even stronger effects on the child's achievement. The attitudes of the high achiever frequently resemble those of his family. Children from low socioeconomic levels are often relatively low in school achievement. One of the reasons for this may be that their homes are characterized by an autocratic atmosphere and strong emphasis on punishment. Studies have shown positive relationships between democratic family control and a favorable attitude toward achievement on the part of the child.[17]

To the ambitious family, education offers a ladder for advancing socially and economically. When this motivation for achievement is too strong, the student may conform to the school requirements and the values of his peers rather than developing gifts that have less cultural approval but more potential importance.

The following case shows how family attitudes and conditions made it extremely difficult for an able rural boy to achieve his educational potentialities:

"I have one major problem that has been bothering me for some time. My father has lived and worked on the farm all his life. There are six children in our family, and we have all had to stay out of school and work on the farm whenever necessary. Now all my brothers have left to pursue their chosen fields. That leaves only me to help with farm work. It has become a tremendous problem to me. I have to stay out and I miss my school work because of this. The farm seems to come first with my father. . . . School and farming just don't go together. I definitely don't want to be a farmer. Several years ago it didn't make too much difference if one stayed away from school a few days, but now with the intensified school program and terrific competition, it makes an important difference. I feel that I don't have a fair chance with this situation existing." [18]

Marian's high achievement in college had its origins in quite different home conditions. Her mother, although not highly educated, greatly valued scholarly attainment. As a child, Marian was very close to her parents and rather inept in social relations with children of her own age. During college, too, she failed to achieve popularity with the majority of the students. Her feelings of social frustration seemed to find a compensation in her high academic achievement.

Even within the same family, home conditions affect children in markedly different ways. In one lower-class family there were seven children: one was in a state penitentiary, another was in an institution for mental defectives, three left school as soon as the law allowed. However, one became a prominent lawyer. This boy had an unusually great need for achievement. The youngest of the family, he had been given more independence and freedom of initiative than the others. A scoutmaster who recognized the boy's ability encouraged him to do his best in school. The boy also had an innate desire to know, a curiosity about life. Although the neighborhood in which he lived discouraged intellectual achievement, the scout group and the school groups to which he belonged emphasized values conducive to putting forth effort and working independently for a purpose. Lacking the intellectual stimulation and emotional security that are best provided by parents, this boy obtained these outside his home.

"OVERACHIEVERS"

"Overachievers" are students who are getting higher marks in school than we would expect from their intelligence test results. Some of these pupils did not demonstrate their true mental ability on the test. Others may be achieving their high marks by a kind of desperate diligence, perhaps to the detriment of their mental health.

It may be better to set the goal of "optimum achievement" rather than "achievement to the limit of one's capacity." If the latter goal involves constant strain, it may result in a nervous breakdown. We have seen this happen to children who were coached on the specific tests that gained them admission to a high school with very high academic standards. Once admitted, they had to compete with classmates of superior mental ability. It was a constant struggle—sometimes eventually a losing battle. We have evidence that excessive pressure to achieve harms the health of some children.

Intense striving for achievement may also cause neglect of certain socially desirable characteristics. It is significant that certain six-year-old children who were rated high in aggressiveness, self-initiative, and competitiveness tended, as time went on, to score relatively high on standardized tests.

Although "the importance of being earnest" is clearly recognized, it is possible to go too far in this direction. The senior year programs of some seventeen-year-olds seem formidable—at least to older observers. Students in advanced science and mathematics courses work hard. They get up before 7:00 a.m. and often do not go to bed until 11:00 p.m. They study weekday nights and on Sunday. Yet even while following such a program, the truly gifted student finds some time for sports, dates, and club activities. He likes the pace and feels challenged by it.

During examination periods, when conscientious overachievers doubt their competence and become tense and anxious, parents can do several things to ease the strain. Dorothy Barclay has given these sound and sensible suggestions: [19]

Accept the child's worries as real and serious to him. Offering the worrier unfounded assurance may only make him fret the more. Telling him that he should have done his work regularly all year does not help him at all in an examination crisis.

Do whatever seems to ease tension and aid concentration. Some children want to be let alone. Others appreciate practical help—someone to talk to about the paper they have to write, someone to ask them the questions at the end of the chapter, someone to whom they can recite the poem or irregular verbs they are expected to know.

Create the kind of study atmosphere in which your child learns best. Some children actually study best when there are people around or when the radio is playing music. Others say these distractions "drive them crazy."

Help the child to analyze his test-taking approach. This may make him aware of faulty procedures such as not reading the questions carefully enough, or not allowing enough time for the more difficult questions.

Encourage the youngster to learn from his mistakes and help him to find ways to avoid similar difficulties in the future.[20] Several recent books—among them, "How to Study Better and

Get Higher Marks" (Crowell) and "Score: The Strategy of Taking Tests" (Appleton-Century-Crofts)—give practical advice that might make it easier to take tests.

UNDERACHIEVERS

"When I bring home my report card," said one youngster, "my parents always say, 'You could have done better.'" How often parents make this remark! Without knowing what a child's ability really is, they have the feeling that he is underachieving.

Who are the underachievers? Much has been written about them. Ten boys who were enrolled in a science project and twenty who were participating in a program for underachievers were given several ingenious tests.[21] According to the results, the underachievers seemed more impulsive, less oriented to the future, less able to delay gratification, and more concerned with immediate rewards than the high achievers. These are characteristics that might well affect students' success in school. The good student often has to give up immediate pleasures, such as dating on weekday nights, for long-range goals. Another study showed that feelings of hostility and negative attitudes toward school seemed to be more characteristic of bright underachievers than of bright achieving students.

Why are these students failing to achieve their educational potentialities? We might be surprised if we knew how much underachievement stems from resistance to parental pressure. More and more children of average and above average intellectual potential seem to be rebelling against too much regimentation, too little opportunity to take initiative and explore their own interests. By consciously, or more often unconsciously, staging a sit-down strike, they get relief from the pressure. However, there are others who feel they need more routine and firmness than their parents give them.

Many underachievers attribute their lack of academic progress to poor teaching. The following criticism by a high school girl is fairly typical. In this instance the tone is good-humored rather than bitter:

"The main thing that makes me frustrated is the geometry teacher. He forgets what he is talking about and goes off onto another subject.

He tells us stories to get his point across, but nobody in the class can see how the story is even vaguely related to the point in geometry he was trying to illustrate.

"This man is just not a good teacher. He tries to explain the theorems but still no one understands. The only way I can understand geometry is to have another student explain it to me."

An intellectually creative child may fail in a subject for several reasons. He may reject the absurdities that he hears and reads in class. When his original ideas are rejected, he may come to think of himself as stupid. Unenlightened criticism by teachers and fellow pupils is destructive of a child's creative impulses. Parents of such a child can encourage his divergent thinking at home, and help him to be tolerant toward, without being dominated by, the unreasonable demands and distractions of the school. Dr. Leta S. Hollingworth, one of the first psychologists to study gifted children, recognized that very brilliant, creative children had to learn to accept less able people without making them feel inferior. To put it more positively, we might say that the highly creative child, in a school adjusted to mediocrity, should look for "plus values" in class situations and for admirable qualities in the other pupils.

In one class, the teacher was intolerant of highly creative children and the seemingly strange ways in which they prefer to learn. There were many underachievers in this class. Dr. E. Paul Torrance has described some of them.[22]

Dick is an underachiever because he has an unusually large amount of information he is never permitted to utilize. His grade average does not permit him to participate in the school clubs. At school he is listless and withdrawn. At home he works at scientific experiments with endless enthusiasm, has energy enough for ten boys, and reads many books from the library.

Charles enjoys color, sound, light, and texture and loves to create with them. His mother, generally an understanding woman, feels it is effeminate for a boy to be so interested in this kind of thing. So artistic activities are taboo for Charles. At a summer camp devoted to arts and science, Charles has scored outstanding triumphs with his paintings.

Andy likes to take time to think about things. His teachers say he is slow; they keep interrupting his thoughts to instruct him, to hurry him, and to motivate him. In a kindergarten creative thinking test, the class was shown how a triangle could be used as a bird house; then the children were urged to think of different forms which could also be used for the same purpose. Andy sat for over four minutes without visibly doing anything. The teacher was embarrassed and wanted to urge him to get busy, but the school psychologist who was observing asked her not to do this. Finally Andy became furiously busy. He had been thinking all this time how a bird house would look on the *inside*. The teacher's tendency was to place too much value on the *visibly* industrious child.

Jane's problem is daydreams, which are now forbidden to her. In the early grades Jane's teachers valued her ingenuity, enthusiasm, and drive. Now she is getting C's in all her subjects except art. Her parents and teachers are trying to break her of daydreaming, but it is hard for Jane to remember not to daydream!

Ed's underachievement is probably tied up with unexpressed ideas. His judgments or opinions are unsought. Whenever he makes a comment, he is ridiculed by boys his own age because they do not know what he is talking about. He is becoming more and more withdrawn. He has a very high IQ, but his low grades may prevent his admission to a good college.

Less easy to understand than the preceding cases of unused talent are those in which emotional blocks prevent learning. It is difficult to deal with the "feeling storms" that contribute to underachievement. We have all met children who "froze" on a test or were fearful of speaking before the class. We have seen the slow breakdown of confidence in children whose inability in reading prevented achievement in their academic subjects. We have known other children who are so preoccupied with what is going on inside them that they cannot pay attention to school tasks.

What is going on inside children? How can a teacher or parent understand enough to help? One way for an adult to sense how a child feels is for him to relive some previous normal experience with his own emotions. Everyone has at some time been so "floored" that he could not think of a thing to say. A storm of feeling rose up and swept away the ability to think and speak. If a teacher has experienced great anxiety when asked to give a speech, take an examination, or appear before a new class on the first day, then he can appreciate the panic some children feel mounting in them when they are asked to read aloud or recite. The emotionally unstable child, anticipating failure, tenses to the point where thinking is impossible. Dr. Sarason of Yale University, in a study of children who showed "examination anxiety," found that most of them really knew their lessons when informally questioned in an anxiety-free situation.[23]

It does not seem wise to put underachievers in separate classes; they are likely to reinforce one another's negative attitudes. It is more effective (a) to help them establish a personal relation with a teacher who consistently accepts them as persons with potentialities, and (b) to give them effective instruction in reading, arithmetic, and other learning skills that they have failed to acquire.

CHILDREN RETARDED IN READING [24]

Johnny may be having a hard time keeping up with his class because he cannot read books on his grade level. Yet he should not be labeled a retarded reader, because he is reading up to his capacity. Jimmy, on the other hand, *is* a retarded reader even though he has no difficulty with books on his grade level; he has the capacity to read better. Johnny needs praise for doing as well as he does; Jimmy needs to be challenged to read above his grade level.

How can a child's reading potential be determined? Parents can observe how quickly their child catches on and how eagerly he attacks new intellectual tasks. Teachers have a still better opportunity to note how he responds to the best instruction that they can give him. Psychologists may obtain more information about his reading potential from individual intelligence tests and listening comprehension tests. Although an intelligence test score will not precisely predict a child's reading capacity or potential, it will suggest something about the sources of his difficulties in reading. The group intelligence test is also a fairly good measure of reading achievement.[25]

What makes a child backward in reading? Sometimes there is a physical condition. The school nurse and physician should check on vision, hearing, and other physical conditions that may contribute to difficulty in learning to read. Neurological factors in reading disability are often difficult to diagnose, even in the hands of highly trained medical people. Other conditions such as malnutrition, infections, or endocrine disturbances are suggested if the child shows listlessness, fatigue, irritability, hyperactivity, or inability to concentrate on reading.

Backwardness in language development may lead to backwardness in reading. The mother who talks to her baby as she cares for him thus acquaints him with the sounds of his native language. The baby associates the sounds produced by a loving mother with a feeling of comfort and reassurance. Through imitation and interminable repetition and practice, the child learns to produce the sounds, words, and sentence patterns of his native language. This speaking ability is the prerequisite to writing and reading.

Retarded readers are likely to be children of parents who are indifferent to reading. If reading has status in the home, then reading tends to have status with the child. The Friday night dinner table review of the week's news stimulates all the members of the family to read newspapers and magazines with discrimination, and to listen selectively to radio and TV.

Getting off to a poor start in the first grade is a common cause of later retardation in reading. Some children are not ready to begin reading instruction. Others miss basic reading instruction because of frequent absence during the primary grades. Sometimes a child has an unhappy relationship with a teacher that interferes with his learning. In the upper grades, the teachers are often too busy to help a pupil overcome his reading deficiencies. Reading materials that are too difficult, or that have no interest, meaning, or use for the child intensify his sense of failure and inadequacy, and his dislike of reading.

Increasing attention is being given to dynamic personality factors which may play an important role in a child's reading achievement. There is often a significant improvement when the child establishes a good relationship with his special reading teacher, or when there is a change in the classroom atmosphere. A poor reader may improve when he changes from a woman teacher who hurries and harries him to a man teacher who is casual and unhurried in his approach.

Parents who become over-anxious about the child's reading, or more concerned about the reading than about the child as a person, may also contribute to his retardation, as in the following case.

Mrs. Y. had become over-anxious about ten-year-old Sandra's reading. She had some cause for concern because Sandra was getting D's in her fifth-grade reading. Mrs. Y. was putting a great deal of pressure on the child. Even though she realized it was wrong, she couldn't seem to help making acid comments: "You're intelligent, so why can't you read?" "Why don't you ever read; are you stupid?"

Sandra and her sister took music lessons, but the parents had stopped Sandra's lessons temporarily until her school work improved. Sandra enjoyed music, swimming, and ice skating. She said she had many friends. She liked her teachers with the exception of the reading teacher, who was somewhat autocratic and accepted only one answer to a question.

A friend who was a reading teacher agreed to help Sandra on the condition that her mother would stop nagging the child about her reading and would have her eyes checked by an eye specialist. The mother agreed. She said she would be more relaxed once she knew that Sandra was getting help.

The reading teacher's first step was to learn all she could about Sandra's reading problem. In this endeavor, Sandra was of little help. She shrugged her shoulders and said she didn't know why she was having trouble. All she knew was that she had difficulty answering questions about the readings assigned in class.

Tests gave more information. On the Durrel Analysis of Reading test, she read orally with expression and fairly good phrasing. But she made several errors, mainly additions and substitutions of words. Some of these seemed to be due to carelessness. On the more difficult words she figured out the first part of the word and guessed the rest. More important, she did not seem to care whether the substituted word made sense in the sentence. On the Silent Reading paragraphs, too, Sandra showed equal lack of concern for meaning. Her score on the Listening Comprehension test was even lower than her scores on the silent and oral reading tests. Like some other retarded readers, Sandra did better on tests of specific reading skills than she did in the reading of paragraphs which test the application of these skills.

The reading teacher also noticed that Sandra's scores were affected by her interest or lack of interest in the materials: she did well on a story about clothes, and poorly on one dealing with deep-sea fishing. These observations suggested a lack of interest and motivation; a possible emotional conflict; and a lack of the kind of reasoning ability that is required in reading for meaning. There was also some evidence that her anxiety to be as brilliant as her mother and father wanted her to be might be interfering with her ability to concentrate on the material she was reading.

To develop her ability to recognize syllables at sight, Sandra played the Dolch word games, *Syllables* and *Take,* with the reading teacher—and sometimes beating her.[26] From the beginning, Sandra was good at learning syllables. Her pronunciation of words in the Dolch games was excellent. To improve her ability to apply word analysis skills to her oral reading, the reading teacher constantly encouraged her to use these skills and to check her accuracy by testing whether the word she pronounced made sense in the sentence.

To focus her attention on reading for meaning, the reading teacher brought to each session a humorous article and a list of questions that directed Sandra's attention to its content. At first she gave Sandra one question at a time that could be answered by reading a paragraph or two. This method proved successful until the teacher inadvertently said, "See, when I force you to read for an answer by asking you the question first, you get it right." "Force" was the wrong word to use. Sandra instantly bridled and said, "You didn't force me to do it. I did it because I wanted to." Here was a clue suggesting that pressure was still being put on Sandra at home, and that she was resisting it. This impression was strengthened by Sandra's replies to some incomplete sentences; for example:

I'd read more if *I wanted to and not when anyone tells me to.*

Sandra still reads passively. The reading teacher's main job was to get Sandra actively involved in her reading, and to make sure that she read with a purpose and an awareness of what the author was trying to say.

To give her practice in paragraph reading, the reading teacher chose well constructed paragraphs and typed out the individual sentences. Sandra combined the sentences to form a paragraph and then compared her organization with the original version.

As a further aid to reading for meaning, the teacher asked Sandra appropriate questions on many interesting articles. Some articles called for a simple factual answer; others required her to find the main ideas. Many called for a statement of the author's pattern of thought.

Helping Sandra develop her potential reading ability was difficult for several reasons. Her mother seemed to be haunted by a fear that she was not doing the right thing. Her intense concern with both her children might be relieved if she had some interests outside the home.

However, this case has a number of positive aspects. Sandra acquired the basic word recognition skills, although she did not yet apply them to reading for meaning. She showed interest and persistence in word analysis. She enjoyed the word games and demonstrated an ability to read to answer specific questions. The mother may come to demand less than perfection from her daughter, or Sandra may gain immunity to her pressure. With continued instruction, reading may become an important source of satisfaction to the child.

We have seen many reading cases in which the individual's resistance, indifference, or apathy could be attributed to his self-concept. For example, one fourteen-year-old non-reader said in a confidential conversation, "I'm the black sheep of the family; I suppose every family has to have one black sheep." His lack of effort and motivation to read better seemed to stem from this hopeless attitude toward himself. Emotional and personality disturbances may be both a cause and an effect of a severe reading problem or disability.

The multiple causes of backwardness in reading have been clearly stated by Dr. M. D. Vernon.[27] Different patterns of factors appear in different cases. The only common factor seems to be the child's confusion in seeing the relationship between the printed words, their sounds and their meanings. The backwardness of a child of illiterate parents who has had no experience in reading at home, or instruction in school is different from that of a slow-learning child who has had no opportunity to learn to read. Even at the beginning, difficulty with reading is not simple and it becomes increasingly complex as the child's confusion and anxiety about his failure increases.

Some children learn to read in spite of detrimental home environments, inferior teaching, poor vision or hearing, and emotional or other problems. Even a handicapped child will learn to read if he has other abilities that compensate for his deficiencies and if he has a favorable reaction to difficulty.

There are some reading cases with whom everything has been tried and with whom nothing has worked. Why they cannot learn to read and write, why they fail to respond to instruction is a mystery. Perhaps something could have been done earlier. Perhaps something will still be done.

Danny was such a case. Early identified as a reading problem, he had been given remedial instruction during several school years and also during one summer session. In spite of all this attention, he was unable, at fourteen years of age, to read first grade books independently.

Danny was a thin, undernourished boy from a poor socioeconomic background. He was third in a family of six children, and the only boy. One of his sisters also had trouble with reading, but the two older sisters completed the tenth grade before they left high school. At the time of the thorough diagnostic study, his mother was in the hospital due to a leg injury. The aunt who brought him to the clinic said, "Danny used to be healthy, but now his father drinks, and everybody in the house is a bundle of nerves."

Like many retarded readers, Danny said he "did not begin to worry until he was in the fifth grade." He blamed his poor reading on the "nervousness" that overcame him when he tried to read aloud. "When I'm in front of a class," he said, "my voice gets low and I can't read some of the words." He had a very low estimate of himself.

Several tests gave this picture of Danny's reading: he had no fluency in oral reading. With many repetitions, hesitations, and misreadings of small words, he could stumble through reading material up to third grade level. However, his recall of what he had read was close to perfect. He could comprehend second and third grade material when he read silently.

Why didn't Danny read better? His mental ability was above average; he should have been reading seventh grade books. Possibly the illness that he had in infancy caused some slight brain damage. If so, this might have been aggravated by emotional disturbance arising from the home situation—the mixed religious background and the father's drinking. As the only male child Danny had only his father to identify with—a man who had come to accept himself as a failure. It is also possible that Danny had accepted and adjusted to his reading disability, and was enjoying the attention it brought him as "a remedial reading case."

If Danny were your child, what would you do about his reading difficulty? One thing the parents could do would be to help Danny's all-round development: encourage his interests in swimming and other sports, his scout troop, camping, and pets. Success along any line might give him the increased confidence he needs in order to improve his reading. Obtain, if possible, individual or small group reading instruction for him in a calm, quiet atmosphere, free from time pressure. This instruction should give him a series of successes in reading appropriate material. Fortunately, there is now an abundance of material on second and third grade levels that Danny could read silently with enjoyment.[28] He might want to reread some of these books. Youngsters like to do the things that they can do well. In his reading lessons, the teacher could help him select simple rhymes and stories and learn to read them fluently so that he could read them aloud to his four-year-old sister. This would give him the practice he needs without the embarrassment attached to reading "baby stuff."

Danny was beginning to be concerned about getting a job. All jobs require some reading. Here was a mature motivation: he needed to read well enough to fill out an application blank, understand signs and directions, and do any other reading that might be required in the jobs that were open to him.

Three basic conditions underlie specific techniques of teaching reading:

1. Provide the best possible learning experiences for each child and observe how he responds—how well he can learn to read under the most favorable conditions, regardless of his measured IQ.

2. Realize that learning takes place in a relationship of affection, firmness, and consistency.

3. Reward successful performance immediately; do not wait until the end result has been achieved.

"BILINGUAL" CHILDREN

Many people think of bilingualism as a handicap. Actually, it should be an asset. The child who is proficient in two languages from his early years has a headstart in the linguistic aspects of his education.

Many children from a foreign culture, however, are not truly bilingual; they are not proficient in either their native or their second language. They do not have the oral English on which teachers build reading instruction. Often they do not understand what they are expected to do in school. Some are so emotionally attached to their native tongue that they resent the new language as an interloper or competitor.

Little children learn to speak a second language by playing with children who speak that language. They enjoy singing games, music, stories, toys, and art work that lead from their old culture to the new. Their parents should share these new experiences with them.

Every culture has its admirable customs and behavior patterns. Every people has certain admirable characteristics. For example, Puerto Rican children usually possess emotional warmth, sensitivity, and trustfulness. They are often quick to enjoy humor. They respond to music, rhythm, color, and nature. They respect their parents. The Navajo Indians have many of the same qualities, though Indians are generally more reticent. They do not have the typical American drive or competitiveness. Their philosophy of life is to live in the present, to respond to the sun, to fire, and to the voices of many waters. We should recognize the admirable characteristics of children from other cultures and use them in helping the children to develop their potentialities. Their experiences should be used to enrich the understanding of the other children. Their communication skills should be developed.

A foreign language background is often associated with problems of economics and family life. Mrs. R., far from her native land, in a large city, was handicapped by lack of training and limited education. She kept her home clean and sent her children to school with much-mended clean clothes. The father was not interested in the welfare of his family; he deserted them early in the school year. Three of the children did not graduate from high school. Maria had to live at a friend's house and pay for room and board by washing dishes in a small restaurant.

Under these conditions, Maria could not concentrate on her studies. She was slipping behind in her work. Her inability to keep up with the class was undermining her interest in school. She said that life seemed to be all mixed up. She felt like a complete failure. At this point she dropped out of school. Four months later she said she would like to come back, and wanted to know what she could do to graduate with her class.

In this case the mother did what she could. She was overwhelmed with responsibilities. Poverty, family disorganization, lack of vocational training, all intensified her problems of adjusting to a new language and a new culture. Maria had to work out her own salvation with the school counselor's help. By returning to school, she maintained the one positive relationship in her turbulent life. She is interested in nursing education and has the ability to succeed in this field which will open to her the door of a useful and satisfying career.

A clash of cultures sometimes causes antagonism between parents and children. Josie complained that her mother was harsh to her. Her mother complained that her older children wanted to adopt the "Anglo attitude" of doing what they pleased. This kind of behavior she was determined to prevent at any cost. The cost was high. Her harshness alienated the children. Their resentment was intensified by her marriage to a man whom they did not like.

It was not easy for the mother either. She said that trying to keep the children from going wild had been very hard. She felt that she had become a very strict, harsh parent. There were many things she regretted—making the oldest girl leave school, nagging her son so incessantly, and being too easy with Josie who could be "very good one minute and ugly the next."

In this case, the problem was not one of language; it was a matter of the social and economic conditions involved in a clash of cultures—two different sets of values and standards of behavior held by two different generations.

The experience of Miss Sylvia Ashton-Warner in teaching the

Maori children in New Zealand has relevance for our work with children from non-English-speaking homes. She has discarded the formal school procedure, and begins by asking each child for his own words. As they come out—words of love, fear, desire, *intensely personal*—she prints them on cards and gives them to the child: *Mummy, truck, ghost, kiss, jet, beer, police, frightened* (not always pleasant words and stories). "First words," she thinks, must be already "part of the dynamic life of the child. If reading is begun in this way, a love of reading, a realization of what reading can mean is born, and this is carried over with confidence to the books of the new culture, to all literature. Thus a bridge is formed from the inner world outward, and the wholeness of personality can be preserved. . . . Destructiveness—often the product of hoarded fears—fades out, the creative takes over, and real learning occurs." [29]

A young child is constantly trying to deal with his own experience. This is also true of school children. They soon progress from single words to phrases and sentences or paragraphs about something that is vital to them. They can dictate these into a microphone, so that their stories can later be typed as reading materials.

POTENTIAL DROPOUTS

If one of your children or a neighbor's child is thinking of leaving high school before graduating, try to find out why he wants to drop out. Usually the underlying reason is dissatisfaction with school; he is not succeeding. The trouble may stem from inability to read. Because he cannot read well, he cannot do his reading assignments. Because he fails to do his homework, the teacher scolds him. Because he feels discouraged and embarrassed, he dislikes school. Because he dislikes school, he plays truant, which makes failure inevitable.

Dissatisfaction with school may have a social as well as an academic basis: the other kids don't like him; he has no friends; he feels left out of the social groups in the school.

Outside activities often have a stronger attraction than school. The part-time or summer job with its paycheck fosters a feeling of independence. The money the youngster earns makes it possible for him to afford commercial recreation. It tempts him to drop out of school and set up a home of his own. This temptation is very strong when a young person's homelife is barren or blighting.

When interviewed by Dr. Ruth Penty several years after they had dropped out of the Battle Creek, Michigan, schools, young people of average intelligence gave the following reasons for leaving school:

"I didn't think that I was getting any place in school. I was working part time and wanted to work full time. I had trouble reading and understanding assignments. I couldn't remember what I read and didn't like to recite as I wasn't sure of myself."

"I didn't like school too well. I wanted to get married. I couldn't remember what I read. I didn't like to go to classes and be around other kids who seemed to learn easier than I did."

"I had difficulty with school work. I quit school and went to work. I couldn't get interested in English or history. I had trouble in reading. I felt inferior. I got the most from class discussions."

"I wasn't interested in school because I had no friends. No one cared whether I came to school or not. I got a job at a drive-in when I left school. I felt all right out of school. I felt sick a lot of the time when I was going to school. I guess part of it was that I didn't like school."

Some poor readers of average ability did graduate from the same high school. These were some of the reasons they gave for continuing in school, even though they had difficulty:

"My Dad and my counselor encouraged me."

"I liked classes, especially the discussions. I also liked band and physical education."

"I had a deep desire to graduate. I am the only one in the family who did."

"My mother, father, and brother graduated. It was understood that I would. I like activities and the kids. It was my own desire to graduate, too."

"I realized that you couldn't get much of a job if you did not graduate."

Dr. Penty summed up their reasons for remaining in school as follows: "Personal desire to graduate, encouragement of family, family expectation, interest in specific subjects, interest in sports and other extracurricular activities, desire for a better job, help of counselors and teachers, special instruction in reading, and liking to be with other young people." [30]

The best approach with potential dropouts is to try to get to the roots of the problem. If poor reading and study habits are causing discouragement and failure, begin there. These youngsters need expert instruction and practice, not admonitions or advice. They need to see evidences of progress in reading.

In many cases, these youngsters need more rather than fewer recreational activities. It is no solution to deprive them of privileges—"no more playing after school; you come home and study until your marks go up." Everyone must have some corner of his life in which he feels successful and happy. The feeling of self-confidence and worth that a child gets from being good in baseball or dramatics or mechanics is likely to spread to other areas of his life; it may cause him to put forth more effort in his school subjects.

The potential dropout also needs to get perspective on his life; he needs to see more clearly and realistically the kind of person he can become. He also needs an accurate picture of the job situation (see Chapter Six).

With students whose aptitude for school work is low, the prospect of eventually getting a high school diploma is insufficient motivation for enduring several more years of frustration and near failure. What they want is an opportunity to get a job and earn money; these are the satisfactions and rewards they want. If they are to stay in school, their experience there must offer an equally satisfactory reward. As one counselor said, "We should reevaluate the success structure for all our terminal students."

GUIDANCE TOWARD HIGHER ACHIEVEMENT

There is no one best way to deal with underachievement. A bright, creative boy may sit idly in his classroom because the school work is too easy for him. Neither the boy, his parents, nor the teacher have found projects that would enlist his wholehearted interest. Consequently, he may fool around with his classmates, irritate the teacher, or withdraw into a dream world that is more satisfying to him than the real world.

An equally bright boy may give up trying to reach the impossible standards his high-powered parents set for him. He cannot stand their intense and persistent pressure.

Even though not exposed to overt parental pressure, a sensitive, conscientious child may become very tense and worried about his school work. More reassurance does not help him. A high school teacher-counselor helped Jane, a worried adolescent, to find a way out of failure. The following are excerpts from their short interviews:

Counselor: Come in, Jane, and have a chair. Miss Smith tells me that you've been having difficulty with math, and I thought maybe I could help you get things straightened out. What seems to be the trouble?

Jane (in a low voice): I just can't understand it, Miss M. All the others in the class get it all right and I try. But I just can't understand math. I can't.

C. Well, that's not unusual. If you've done your best, there's no disgrace in failing.

J. But my father—(weeps silently).

C. What about your father, Jane? Does he scold you because you don't do better in math?

J. (Indignantly: There's evidently love and understanding between these two.) Oh, no, no! But he's in the Army, and he uses math a lot, and he keeps telling me how important it is, and—and I don't want to let him down. . . . My father wants to send me to college. There wasn't money enough to send Eleanor (an older sister), but he wants me to go. And I keep thinking, "If I should fail!" All the girls I go with are in the accelerated group, and they're smart. I've never failed anything in high school. And I keep thinking, "If I should fail!" All night long I think about it—suppose I can't get into college.

C. Have you thought of any way out?

J. No, my thoughts go around and around in circles and never lead anywhere.

C. What do you think of this idea, Jane? Suppose we shift you into another math group? In a class that does not move so rapidly as the accelerated group, there would be more chance for you to ask questions.

J. (Eagerly) Oh, could you, Miss M.? Could you?

C. I'm sure we can arrange it. We'll try to, anyway. Stop in to see me before you leave today, and I'll let you know what luck I have had in shifting you to the other class. . . .

Two weeks later Jane stopped by the counselor's office.

C. Jane, I was thinking about you this morning and wondering how you are making out in your new class. How are things going?

J. Fine! Just fine! They go more slowly in that class, and I'm beginning to understand it now. I think I'm doing all right.

Jane's new math teacher later told the counselor that Jane was "one of the best in the class." [31]

In other cases, youngsters have become overconfident as a result of easy success in elementary school. Having got by with a minimum of study, they have never acquired the efficient reading and study methods, and the habit of wholehearted effort, that they need in high school and college. Many youngsters wake up to this need, and either learn to study by themselves, or take a special study course; such courses are sometimes offered in the summer, or during the school year in addition to the regular subjects. They find that this is a good investment.

Some children have been "spoiled"—overprotected from difficulty. They have never learned how to work; they have never had to do anything that they found distasteful. School achievement requires effort. Effort that stems from interest in the task itself is superior to forced labor. Helping these students to make a shift in their values is the best way to release their energy for active learning.

In New York City's Talent Preservation Project, a number of methods were used to improve the academic achievement of potentially able high school students.[32] Some of the students were tutored in their subjects, received intensive individual and group counseling, and participated in discussions of study methods. Groups were formed primarily for the purposes of motivating the students, for therapy, or for instruction and practice in reading. Other students, and their parents, were interviewed by social workers and psychiatrists. The most frequently recommended method—tutoring in a given subject—seemed to be less effective than the other approaches.

The most important factor in a student's achievement seems to be his desire or drive to achieve.

Many parents have been provoked by a child's lack of drive or motivation, especially with reference to his school work. This was true of the Browns, who were at their wits' end. They knew that George had ability. They knew he should go to college. But in his junior year he was doing everything but getting the grades that are necessary for college admission. He was on the baseball team, had the lead part in the school play, and spent untold hours just fooling around with the other kids. On rare occasions, usually just before examinations, he would get down to work and learn enough to make a barely passing grade. When his parents reproached, reprimanded and berated him, or pleaded and remonstrated with him, he appeared contrite, but did not change his ways.

Finally a teacher whom he liked and admired took a hand in the situation. He studied George's cumulative school record and the results of a scholastic aptitude or intelligence test that he had recently taken. He asked George to keep an accurate record for several days of the way he spent his time, item by item, from the time he got up until the time he went to bed. He also asked the boy to be thinking about what he would like to be doing ten years from now.

In the interview with George, the teacher put all the cards on the table. Together they examined the records. George began to see himself as a boy who had potential ability that was being wasted. He saw how he let periods of time slip away. He began to realize that he needed to get from where he was to where he wanted to be ten years from now. He recalled times when he had concentrated on his school work with a feeling of satisfaction and times when the rat race of extracurricular activities had given him a sense of futility.

Then, using his daily schedule as a starting point, he decided to make a few changes. Now that the school play was over, he would not get involved in another dramatic activity. He found in the daily schedule several blocks of time when he could study certain subjects. The teacher suggested that he could also save time by cultivating more efficient listening, reading, and study habits—which he knew but did not practice. These habits would also be valuable equipment to take to college.

It was a very good plan. But would George carry it out? He had made good resolutions many times before. But now he saw himself in a different light—as a boy with unrealized potentiality that should be developed for his personal happiness and social usefulness. Now was the moment of decision. He had acquired a certain feeling of urgency, which was reinforced by continued contacts with his teacher and by an inspiring essay that the teacher had given him.[33]

Ten-year-old Jim's lack of motivation was more deep-seated than George's. Jim was so completely discouraged that he had given up trying. He seemed resigned to chronic failure. This attitude had spread to his social relations as well as to his academic work. More and more, daydreaming gave him the satisfaction that he should have obtained from accomplishment.

The teacher attacked Jim's discouragement by giving him experiences of success with puppets. Though Jim had withdrawn from other children, he was able to give his puppet shows first to the teacher and gradually to larger audiences. Success in this kind of communication led him into more active social participation. Soon he was learning magic tricks to perform for the class. Later his teacher gave him step-by-step instruction and practice in reading. His teacher's confidence that she could teach him to read gave *him* confidence in his ability to learn. His small successes gave him courage to move to slightly higher levels of difficulty.

John Henry was a high achiever. In his family background, there were a number of factors that seemed to have contributed to his high achievement. From early childhood—even from infancy—his parents expected him to do things without help. As a baby he helped pull on his socks and put his hand through the sleeve of his jacket. As a toddler he figured out ways of fitting his blocks together, getting hold of an object that was out of reach, or solving the innumerable problems that confront a young explorer in a new world. As a preschool child, he solved many of his problems of social relationship with just a few suggestions from the more experienced adult. When he came home with school problems, his parents encouraged him to use the skills he had learned. For example, instead of always telling him the unfamiliar words in his reading, they helped him to apply the phonetics and other word recognition skills that he had learned.

John Henry's parents expected him to do things the best he could. However, they were careful not to demand a perfection that was incommensurate with his age. And when he did something well, their approval was evident to him. They maintained standards without being authoritarian, and seemed to have fewer difficulties than the average parents in bringing up their children.

Somehow John Henry caught his parents' attitude toward achievement. Both he and his parents took a college education for granted. John Henry's father, whom he admired and respected, was a teacher. Ever since the fantasy stage of vocational choices, John Henry had been looking forward to a career in education. His mother, too, had high educational aspirations for her only son.

Like many other high achievers, John Henry engaged in a number of nonrequired, academically related activities. He was on the staff of the school paper and president of a drama club in which the members read parts rather than putting on finished plays. He was also active in the youth group of his church.

The picture of the equally intelligent girl is somewhat different. Girls do not seem to have as much unconscious need for achievement as boys. Although the high-achieving girl is more likely than the low-achieving girl to plan to attend college, her interest may be diverted by thoughts of love and marriage. Some regard college as an opportunity to find a mate.

Many differences have been noted between high-achieving and low-achieving boys and girls. In one study, the low-achieving boys tended to be aggressive; the low-achieving girls, withdrawn. The boys seemed to perform better under democratic rule, while some of the girls responded better to authoritarian control. More of the low-achieving boys had mothers who interfered with or controlled their sons' activities, and thus fostered a dependency that was unfavorable to achievement.

High-achieving boys have a higher need for achievement than low-achieving boys. They usually give evidence of better adjustment; they score higher on leadership skills. High school boys and girls who are motivated to go to college usually have families, friends, and teachers who set college as a standard of achievement for them. According to a study, college-bound students appeared to be more mature, responsible, and capable than the other pupils in the top 25 per cent of the class who were not planning to go to college.

The child who is highly competent in some aspect of school experience and also highly interested in it finds it easy to achieve self-esteem. It is usually the child with low competence who feels inferior. It is often possible to teach children the special skills they need. A coach may spend a little extra time showing Teddy how to hold the bat, follow the ball with his eyes, and learn other ways to acquire greater skill. A parent may teach a child little courtesies that make him more socially acceptable.

Development of educational potentialities begins at birth or before. The child who comes to school with a built-in readiness to learn usually gets off to a good start. Effective instruction at every stage of development is in general far more profitable than remedial work, tutoring, or coaching. Day-by-day learning receives too little attention in proportion to its basic importance in building the foundation for further learning.

Questions and Answers

1. *Should parents teach their preschool children to read?*

Some bright children teach themselves to read. Marie Curie learned to read by sitting beside her older sister who was struggling through the first grade primer. Even within the same home, children may vary widely in their interests and abilities.

The role of the parent is to respond to the child's initiative, curiosity, and desire to learn. There are many ways in which parents can build a child's readiness for reading: reading aloud to him; setting him an example in the enjoyment of reading; supplying him with picture books; giving him experiences to talk about; listening to him and answering his questions about words and other things; carrying on conversations with him at mealtime and while working around the house; using correct speech; and talking about the things he is doing. Any preschool child who has these experiences is getting the prerequisites for success in reading.

Parents have always been concerned about their children's reading. They can do more to develop the child's reading potential in the informal ways suggested above than by giving him reading lessons to which he responds with restlessness, resentment, or anxiety.

2. *What are some of the ways in which parents can help an older child to improve his reading at home?*

Establish a regular time each day for reading "just for fun." Fifteen minutes is usually enough. In consultation with the child, choose the time of day that is best for him, and for the family routine. It may be early evening, first thing in the morning, before dinner when Dad has some time and Mom is getting dinner. This fifteen-minute period may develop into a reading time for the whole family.

If the child is interested in an article or book that is beyond his ability, the parent or older brother or sister can read most of it, letting the child supply the words he knows.

Give the child printed directions to read silently and carry out, beginning with something short and easy and gradually increasing the length and difficulty.

If the child likes to use the typewriter, encourage him to write stories, messages, and notes. This is a good way for him to practice spelling, if he has a dictionary handy and uses it. Some of his stories he may first dictate into a tape recorder and then type.

Make suitable books readily available to him. Buy books with high interest that he can read independently. Go to the library with him, at first, to help him choose books he can read and enjoy. Show interest in the class newspaper and other samples of his work that he brings home.

When discussing the child, recall all the good things about him, and recount them.

3. *What can I do for my child to stimulate his mind?*

Children need the example set by parents who are themselves intellectually curious, who read, look at educational TV, go to the library, and are interested in good schools and youth group programs.

Games often unlock mental potential. Old games like "Twenty Questions," "I Pack My Trunk," and the several varieties of charades, all stimulate thinking as well as remembering. Another good game is seeing how many ideas one can think of quickly on a given topic, e.g., how many uses one can think of for a newspaper.

Children are also stimulated by thought-provoking questions involving "Who is it?" "What is it?" and "Why is it?" with respect to important people, places, and things.

Parents can encourage thinking, especially with adolescents, by giving them opportunities to explore the consequences of certain acts or events in their own lives.

Other sources of stimulation include books and magazines that are always on hand to be picked up in leisure moments, trips to many places of interest, friends, hobbies, and selected TV and radio programs. Children need time and place for all these things as well as for study.[34]

4. *Why are some bright children underachievers?*
There are many possible reasons:

(1) The underachiever is the child whose desire to think and to know has not been stimulated. He sees no meaning or purpose in the subjects he is studying. He finds the textbooks and the instruction dull and boring. Perhaps he lacked proper parental or environmental stimulation during the years when he was especially eager to learn and be industrious.

(2) He may be so keenly interested in one particular field that he neglects the required subjects.

(3) He sometimes overestimates his knowledge and does not study.

(4) He has not learned or been taught efficient reading and study methods.

(5) He does not want to be "different," and is afraid of being called a "brain" or an "egghead." He is greatly influenced by the attitudes of the peer group.

(6) Emotional conflicts may prevent him from concentrating and putting forth effort; he may be worried about personal matters.

(7) He may resent the imposition of too much pressure by parents or teachers.

(8) An unhappy relationship with the teacher may cause him to resist learning.

(9) Scholarship is not truly respected in the school; his teachers and parents do not seem to value it. Sometimes the teachers expect so little of able learners that they become indifferent or lazy.

(10) The curriculum does not offer the kind of experiences he needs or the subjects in which he wants to achieve.

(11) The most pervasive motivations include a fundamental drive toward self-realization, interest in the activity itself, a social purpose, and desire for prestige.

5. *Do scholarships, honor societies, science fairs, Mathematics Olympics, etc., offer valid motivation?*

These devices motivate many students. For example, it was found that a large proportion of the articles in science journals had been written by scholars who had once been on Mathematics Olympics teams.

Special science projects give youngsters opportunities to release creative energy and face frontiers on their own. They offer opportunities for independent study. However, participation in these programs should be voluntary.

These devices may discourage some youngsters because of the competitive elements involved.

6. *How are children affected by being pushed to achievements beyond their years in order to satisfy parental pride?*

When children are deprived of the natural experiences of childhood, important developmental needs may be neglected. Too much parental pressure may cause resistance to learning, with consequent underachievement. Thus the pressure defeats the very purpose for which it is applied. Some children respond by undertaking passive resistance; others adopt a more open form of rebellion—they may become delinquent or defiant. Still others turn their frustration or hostility inward against themselves, and actually become ill.

At the same time, we cannot deny that a certain amount of pressure for achievement works well with some children. They acquire skills that make them socially competent; they reach a higher level of accomplishment than would have been achieved by a laissez-faire method.

However, it is not "either-or." Most children need firm parental pressure at certain times. But in the long run, the pull of a goal is more effective than any amount of pushing by an adult. The best results will be obtained under conditions in which the child's initiative is reinforced by adult guidance.

For questions about college entrance, see the end of the next chapter.

SIX
Vocational Potentialities

IF YOUR child has developed, year by year, his physical, intellectual, educational, social, and emotional potentialities, he will have the foundation—the broad base—for a number of possible careers. However, if he has not learned to organize and remember ideas, think clearly, speak with clarity and precision, read effectively, and get along with other people, he will not be ready for specialized vocational training. These educational skills are essential to success in one's chosen field of work as well as in school.

The development of vocational potentialities involves the whole person. From early years, the evolving self-concept influences vocational choice.[1] Self-appraisals such as "I am bright enough to go to college," or "I am happiest when I'm tinkering with machines," serve as one basis for planning an educational program or choosing a career.

Some children have a better chance of success in life than others. Jim is one of the lucky ones. He is a senior in high school. His father is a practicing physician. Jim looks forward to a career in medicine, preferably in research or as a teacher in a medical school. He has clear-cut plans to attend a university that has an excellent medical school. He has sent for the bulletins of several outstanding universities. He is taking summer school courses in history and reading. He has also worked several summers in a medical laboratory, to help pay his way through medical school, although he knows that his family is willing and able to finance his education. He is an able youngster—secure and poised. He has a pleasant personality, and evidently has a fine constructive relationship with his family.

Marian, fourteen, a Negro and a junior in high school, is a living illustration of the importance of factors other than race in choosing a career. She is a most unusual girl. Her mother is a school counselor, her father is an X-ray technician, and her aunt is a librarian. Marian plans to become a pediatrician. She is well informed about the various medical fields and their requirements, and about several schools that she would like to attend. Since she is a Negro, she feels that she might have a better chance at an institution such as Howard University. However, she has not yet decided; she would really like to go to an integrated college that has a good medical school. Her parents are very cooperative and ambitious for her. She has received A's in algebra, geometry, and chemistry, as well as in other high school subjects. During the summer session she is taking advanced mathematics; she is planning to take physics in her senior year. Though she is well fortified to handle any prejudices against minority groups that she may meet in the educational and professional fields, she would profit right now by more opportunities to participate in high school student activities; this would help her to feel more comfortable particularly in mixed groups.

If a child belongs to an upper social class, he has a relatively good chance for more education, high occupational achievement, a substantial income, and the fulfillment of his potentialities. However, inequalities among the various social classes are decreasing; some persons born in the lower classes achieve a better life than some born in the higher classes. "Do we not too often attribute the pattern of people's lives exclusively to something too loosely called 'social class,' thereby losing both in our scientific understanding and in our consequent power to control and alter the pattern?" [2] For example, in a mid-west city one-fifth of the high school graduates who came from the lowest income group went to college. Nevertheless, it is still true that "values, aspiration, knowledge or ignorance, child-rearing patterns, and personality syndromes affect the life-chances of the different social classes." [3] Some children are brought up with the idea of "getting by" instead of "getting ahead"; this is a specific example of the way family or peer attitudes may limit a child's educational progress and vocational success.

The complex process of developing one's vocational potentialities requires (a) self-appraisal and self-understanding; (b) acquaintance with educational, vocational, and avocational opportunities; and (c) ability to make and carry out wise decisions. The individual should first consider his abilities, interests, and values, and ask himself what kind of person he wants to be. Second, he needs to know all he can learn about the colleges, courses, training programs, and other educational opportunities that are available to him. His first major educational decision concerns which high school course to take. His next questions are: Shall I go to college, and if so, which college? How can I finance a college education? If I do not go to college, what other opportunities for further education are open to me? What kinds of education are needed for different kinds of work? Third, he should be aware of the over-all range of occupational possibilities and have some acquaintance with the major vocational fields, as a background for studying the specific requirements and opportunities in the jobs that seem to be most suitable for him. In this area he will be concerned with such questions as these: On what basis should I choose my vocation? Where can I obtain up-to-date information about vocations? And, finally, how can I get a job and find satisfaction in it—in other words, "make a life as well as a living?"

SELF-APPRAISAL

Self-appraisal begins early. In the first grade, Johnny knows he isn't as good in reading as Susie, even though Teacher has not yet divided the class into different groups. Bobby, in the sixth grade, knows he likes to work with numbers; arithmetic is his best subject. Teen-age Tom has always liked to tinker with cars; he can fix anything mechanical. Bill is an outdoor boy. The summer that he enjoyed most was the one he spent working on his grandfather's farm; the most distasteful job he ever had was the one in which he was cooped up in an office. Ann loves books; they are her best friends.

Parents notice these differences in the interests and abilities of their children. As the children grow older, the parents should help them study and understand their abilities, aptitudes, changing interests, and needs. This kind of study forms a basis on which the young person can make his own choices and take responsibility for the results of his decisions. The adult should respect the child's right to have different views. Many adolescents are surprisingly mature in their insights and judgments.

The tests given in school are a further help toward discovering one's vocational aptitudes and interests. However, tests are not a substitute for individual self-appraisal that is based on school work, part-time work, and other experiences. Test scores can be misinterpreted, especially the results of vocational interest tests. Parents have actually said to counselors: "My son wants to go into business. But the tests show he should be an engineer. How can I help him change his mind?" Or they ask, "Will the tests you've given my daughter tell us why she isn't doing better work in school?" Students often complain about tests and misinterpret their results. They say, "I've taken a bunch of tests, but I don't know what they're for." "I guess I'm OK for college—my tests show I'm pretty smart." Or the student simply asks, "What did the tests I took tell about me?"

The answers to such questions are not simple. Tests alone cannot supply adequate answers, though they may contribute valuable information about an individual's aptitudes and abilities. Interpreting test results is a technical matter, on which most teachers, pupils, and parents need expert help.

There is a bewildering variety of standardized tests and inventories from which to choose—tests of intelligence or scholastic aptitude, tests of achievement in many fields, aptitude tests, interest and personality inventories or questionnaires. The counselor or school psychologist helps to select tests that will supply evidence that is meaningful in light of the educational objectives of the particular school. He sees that the tests are administered and scored correctly. However, if the money expended on testing is not to be wasted, the tests must be properly interpreted and used.

When high school pupils have taken a test or a battery of tests, they want to know the results. In some schools the counselor or psychologist meets with the teachers and goes through the process of test interpretation with them. The teachers, in turn, explain the significance of the test results to the students. They emphasize positive, objective self-appraisal. The counselor stresses caution in the interpretation and use of test results. A test, he says, measures the individual's performance at a particular time on particular tasks. Scores on comparable forms of the same test may vary from one testing to another. The results of tests should be used in connection with all the other available information about the individual. No important decision should be based on a single-test result.

Occupational interest inventories do not, as some students think, indicate what occupation one should enter. They do not give assurance that a person can succeed in a given occupation; they merely tell whether the student's interests are similar to those of older persons who have been successful in that occupation.

Paper-and-pencil personality tests or inventories have little value in guiding individuals; the student's responses are affected by the degree of his psychological sophistication, by the manner in which he interprets each item, and by his unconscious desire to present himself in as favorable a light as possible. Moreover, certain personality or mental hygiene inventories may be disturbing to some children and young people.

These and other cautions in the use of tests should be made clear to all concerned with their use.

The counselor should bring together, interpret, and synthesize all the available information about the individual—test results, school marks, attendance record, health information, comments by teachers, and other data. As he surveys this accumulated information, he perceives certain trends and relationships that help him to understand the student more accurately and fully. He can then use this understanding in helping the young person to understand himself, and in trying to provide conditions that are more favorable to his best development.

In some schools the pupils make their own profiles and discuss them with the school counselor. The test profile of a tenth grade girl is given on the following page.

It will be noted that Karen has high scores on the tests of reasoning, numbers, and reading. In fact, she is above average in everything except arithmetic fundamentals and the kind of memory that this test measures. Although we should not put too much reliance on sub-test scores, we do get the impression, as her parents have already guessed, that Karen is a girl of many abilities.

Her interests, as shown by the test, are most similar to those of people in social service; to a somewhat less extent, they resemble those of people in artistic and musical occupations. Many people make the mistake of interpreting the scores on the Kuder Preference Record and other tests of vocational interest as evidences of ability. Actually, a person may have a high interest score in art, for example, but lack the ability to succeed in that field.

Karen's tentative choice of nursing as a profession seems to be

PROFILE CHART SELF-APPRAISAL PROGRAM OF GUIDANCE IN THE __WEST__ JUNIOR HIGH SCHO(

PUPIL'S NAME __KAREN HARVEY__ DATE OF FIRST ENTRY __SEPT 1945__

RESIDENCE __514 FAIRVIEW RD__ ADVISER __MISS LARGE__

CAREER PLANS: 1- __NURSE__   2- __TEACHER__

TENTH GRADE SELECTIONS: SCHOOL __STAR HIGH__ CURRICULUM __ACADEMIC__

| | APTITUDES | | | | | | | | | | | | INTERESTS | | | | | | | |
| | CHICAGO TESTS | | | | | CITY WIDE TESTS | | | | | | KUDER PREFERENCE RECORD | | | | | | | |
	NUMBER	VERBAL	SPATIAL	WORD FLUENCY	REASONING	MEMORY	7B PROB. IN ARITH.	7B READING	8A ARITH FUND.	8B ENG. USAGE	9A PHILA. VERBAL	MINN. PAPER FORM BOARD	MECHANICAL	COMPUTA-TIONAL	SCIENTIFIC	PERSUA-SIVE	ARTISTIC	LITERARY	MUSICAL	SOCIAL SERVICE
TEST SCORES	134	74	75	70	76	10	3	4+	3	4-	28	42	40	36	42	50	60	36	25	114	6

School District of Philadelphia (Feb. 19

PROFILE CHART FOR SELF-APPRAISAL PROGRAM OF GUIDANCE
IN THE WEST JUNIOR HIGH SCHOOL, PHILADELPHIA

in accord with her abilities and interests. The question is whether she should not also consider other careers such as social service or teaching. She does not have to make a definite vocational decision as early as the tenth grade. However, if she takes a college preparatory course that includes science, she will be prepared for whatever specialized training she later desires.

A useful guide for adolescents in their efforts at self-appraisal, *You: Today and Tomorrow*, helps the individual to understand and appraise his abilities, values, and interests with reference to educational and vocational opportunities.[4] The last chapter shows how five pupils made educational and vocational choices, step by step, while in high school.

The career of Anthony J. Celebrezze, Secretary of Health, Education, and Welfare, illustrates the importance of planning and working for an education.[5] His father was a railroad track walker who came here from Italy. One of thirteen children, Anthony started selling newspapers when he was six. In high school he earned money at odd jobs and as a laborer on a railroad-section gang. He helped pay his way through college and law school by working on the freight docks of Cleveland. He has said that his present position as a member of the President's Cabinet was "made possible through the sheer magic of education." [6]

Although creativeness, persuasiveness, a cooperative spirit, or other personal qualities may be important qualifications for certain kinds of jobs, the fact remains that "the fastest growing, the highest paying, and the most secure jobs will be those requiring the greatest amount of education." [7] Lack of appropriate education not only shuts the door to good beginning jobs; it may also block subsequent retraining.

A study of the men in top positions of leadership in the United States government showed that most of them came from well-to-do or economically secure homes; 97 per cent attended college, 91 per cent graduated.[8] However, their grandfathers, in many cases, had been farmers, industrial workers, or clerks. In three generations, these families had moved rapidly up the social-vocational ladder. Moreover, several of these national leaders themselves came from poverty-stricken immigrant families. A few were children of tenant farmers, unskilled laborers, or storekeepers; they worked their way through college.

All of them seem to have certain abilities and characteristics in common. They are eminently able "to make friends and influence people." They are fluent in speech and have pleasant personalities. As young men they were ambitious and hard-working. Their ambition was encouraged and furthered by their parents, and later by their wives.

The future may require a special type of leader—one who is flexible, but has a sense of commitment, one who has insight into the desperate needs of our times, the ability to convey his vision to others, the wisdom to find sound solutions, and the courage to confront and confound the small but very vocal minority whose aim is to degrade and demoralize the unthinking part of our country's population.

Two-thirds of the parents interviewed in a nationwide survey expected their children to continue their education beyond high school. Yet some youngsters definitely should not plan to go to college. Nearly a third of those who do enter drop out during their first year. They learn "only the bitterness of failure." [9] Some who do graduate may not find a college-type job that is congenial to them; they may drift from one job to another.

College is not the only road to vocational success. Slightly more than two-fifths of the nation's business leaders are not college graduates. Although it is true that the average income of college graduates is much higher than that of high school graduates, the difference may be due not to the college education per se, but to the qualities of intelligence, drive, initiative, and application that success in college requires. Some youngsters who are influenced by parental pressure or by a desire to go to college with their friends, buckle under the strain of meeting the increasingly difficult requirements of the academic high school curriculum and of

Enrollment in a four-year college is not the only way to continue learning after high school. Other avenues include the junior—or community—college, vocational schools, hospitals that offer training programs for nurses and medical technicians, apprenticeships in industry, on-the-job training programs, and the Armed Forces Institute. Most firms that are worth working for provide their young workers with a chance to learn the job, partly by training in the firm and partly by attending classes that are scheduled as part of the day's work. The young person who takes advantage of these learning opportunities is the most likely to get promotions.

Why, then, do we have such a large army of aimless unemployed youth? Why are they not enrolled in these after-high-school training programs? There are three possible reasons for this: (a) these educational opportunities are not actually available to all young people; (b) the young person to whom they are available may not have acquired the reading skills and other techniques and knowledge that he needs to take advantage of them; and (c) the young person may have acquired habits of indolence and irresponsibility.

Many young teen-agers are not aware of the extent to which their high school record affects their chances for vocational training and success. Such lackadaisical youngsters might profit by reading the following composition written by a senior high school pupil on the topic, "The Person Who Has Helped Me Most."

In my life the person who has helped me most has been my father. . . . He said in junior high that I should start early to prepare myself for college, but I dilly-dallied around and goofed off and ended up getting bad grades. . . . My father said that with my ability I could do good work if I would just put my potential to use. But, like most kids my age, I was more interested in playing around than in planning for college.

After seeing me make bad grades for a while, my father made me settle down and start doing homework and studying for tests. Strange to say, studying has become more or less a habit. I can't seem to rest until I have done an assignment due the following day. It seems to me now very sad to think how much harder it will be for me in college because of the playing around that I did in my early years at junior high. More students should wake up to the fact that their fathers aren't trying to be mean when they insist on good grades. They are just trying to show the path of life that is best for you to follow.

THE WORLD OF WORK

Out of the more than 23,000 kinds of jobs, the large majority of high school students focus on a few—doctor, lawyer, engineer, teacher, nurse, secretary. They ignore many other kinds of work that our society needs.

We should help children develop the attitude that any job that is suited to the individual and useful to society is worthy of respect and approval. In the wide world of work, the individual has the obligation to serve as well as to achieve. He should ask, "What can I do for others?" as well as "What satisfactions will my work bring me?" Many of the present generation *are* concerned with both service and job satisfaction.

Since our work occupies such a large part of our life, job satisfaction is very important. Our satisfaction is increased as we recognize the inherent value of the work. For example, during World War II, workers in airplane factories were shown how a small monotonous job, such as tightening a bolt on a plane, contributed to the war effort. Some idealistic young workers became disillusioned when they find that they are expected to exploit, rather than serve, the public. For example, an advertising man may have to think up ways to persuade people to buy a product that they do not need, or should not have.

Job satisfaction is enhanced by the feeling that we have some part in planning and decision-making, and that our work is appreciated.

Association with fellow workers is another element in job satisfaction. Many young women prefer to work in offices or factories rather than as domestics in private homes because the former jobs offer greater opportunities for social relations.

Automation may reduce job satisfaction in several important respects. Tending automatic machines is a job that may have little meaning and satisfaction for the worker. It also offers him little chance of bettering his position by increasing his knowledge and skill. Moreover, automation decreases social satisfactions by making jobs more impersonal and lonely.

Occupations have been classified in various ways. The main categories are usually listed as follows:

1. Professional and Managerial Occupations
2. Clerical and Sales Occupations
3. Service Occupations
4. Agricultural, Fishery, Forestry Occupations
5. Skilled Occupations
6. Semiskilled Occupations
7. Unskilled Occupations

The largest numbers of young people have been employed in clerical work, semiskilled occupations, and service occupations. However, the occupational field is shifting so rapidly that one must constantly keep up with the latest sources of information.

Automation is affecting different occupations in different ways. Jobs of the unskilled, mechanical type are becoming more scarce as machines replace manpower. Opportunities for certain white collar jobs are also being decreased by automation. For example, the Bell Telephone Company, over the past ten years, has been able to handle twice as much business with only a 10 per cent increase in persons employed. In 1960 the Census Bureau required only fifty statisticians to do the work that had required four thousand employees in 1950. Nevertheless, it is predicted that white collar jobs will multiply more than twice as fast as blue collar jobs. While technology is taking away more and more jobs that used to be available to the young inexperienced worker, it is creating more jobs for highly trained technicians. The number of service occupations is also increasing.

Since the close of World War II there has been a shortage of candidates for one of the most vital professions: teaching. The need for teachers and specialists in education may continue during the next decade, especially in junior colleges and in fields such as reading and special education.

In addition to the main categories of work already listed, we must mention two that actually involve the largest number of young people: homemaking and military service.

It is strange that we do not think of homemaking as a career, when homemakers are the largest occupational group in our society. Even though your daughter may be planning to work outside her home, as eight out of ten women in the country do, she should take at least one of the home economics courses offered in most high schools. The content of these courses is broad. It includes home management and buying; family health; understanding of family relations, child care, and child development; selecting, planning, and serving nutritious family meals; making clothing; caring for the sick and the aged; furnishing a home attractively; and providing wholesome recreation. Home economics courses have two main values: (a) to help the student improve herself both in her present status and as a future homemaker, and (b) to prepare her for any of the paid positions that are open to persons with education in this field.

From recruiting posters we get a favorable view of the opportunities for young men in the Armed Forces—a chance to see the world, take any of a wide variety of high school and college courses, learn a trade, become more mature. On the other hand, many service men only eighteen or nineteen years old, just out of high school or college, and removed from the security of their own homes, have serious problems of adjustment. Some of them just cannot "take it." They cannot adjust to crowded quarters and lack of privacy, to long hours of work and the constant demands that are made upon them, to receiving no appreciation for a job well done, to receiving a severe punishment for not doing a job exactly right. They have no one to listen to their troubles. They are cut off from normal social relationships and especially from "the girl they left behind them." If their high school record has been poor, they feel anxious or hopeless about the possibility of going on to college when their term of service is over.

As long as service in the Armed Forces is required, it is evident that we must prepare young men who are just out of high school, or who are in their college years, to fulfill their obligations. The home, school, church, and government all share this responsibility. In the home, children should learn to tolerate a reasonable amount of frustration, which is inevitable in any life situation. In school, each pupil should develop his intellectual and educational potentialities so that appropriate opportunities for further study or vocational experience will be open to him. The church has special, but by no means exclusive, responsibility for developing values and a sense of commitment to what is right. And it might be well if the Armed Forces reviewed their methods of training in the light of evidence on the optimum personal development of future citizens, and the personal qualities essential to achieving World Peace. The policy of having service personnel serve the people in the countries in which they are stationed by helping them attain a better way of life is an important step in the right direction.

OCCUPATIONAL INFORMATION NEEDED

To make wise vocational choices, one needs information about the amount and nature of the education required for different types of work. The following figures represent the percentages of persons, who had had some college education, engaged in different types of work in 1959: 75 per cent engaged in professional and technical occupations; 29 per cent—proprietors and managers; 22 per cent—clerical and sales workers; 8 per cent—skilled workers; 6 per cent—service workers; 3 per cent—unskilled workers; and 5 per cent—farmers and farm workers. Of the service workers, unskilled workers, farmers, and farm workers, more than two-thirds had stopped short of high school graduation.

The young person also needs to know the specific courses required in engineering, nursing, secretarial work, or any other vocation in which he is interested. The following are some of the most accurate and up-to-date sources of information about occupations:

United States Government publications, especially the Occupational Outlook Service, Bureau of Labor Statistics. You can obtain their list of publications and subscribe to the *Occupational Outlook Quarterly* by writing the Superintendent of Documents, U.S. Government Printing Office, Washington, D.C. 20402.

Science Research Associates, 259 East Erie Street, Chicago 11, Illinois.

Selected pamphlets from the many issued by professional, occupational, and civic organizations such as the National League for Nursing, A.F.L. and C.I.O., American Medical Association, General Electric Company, and many others.

Chronicle Guidance Publications, Moravia, New York.

Dreese, Mitchell. *How to Get a Job*. Science Research Associates, 1960.

Forrester, Gertrude. *Occupational Literature*, An Annotated Bibliography. New York: H. W. Wilson, 1958.

Zapoleon, Marguerite. *Occupational Planning for Women*. New York: Harper, 1961.

After seeking out the best available sources of information, young people and their parents need to (a) evaluate the information they get; (b) anticipate potential obstacles to be overcome; (c) realize that their decisions must be subjected to revision as new evidence presents itself, and make such revisions without fear of being thought "wishy-washy"; and (d) make practical, realistic plans. This rather technical process demands the participation of teachers, counselor, librarians, state employment officers, and the young people themselves.

In considering vocational possibilities, people often neglect several important factors: the social contribution made by a given vocation, the personal satisfaction to be derived from it, its effect on mental health, and the recreational opportunities that it may afford.

As the young person approaches the time when he must seek a job, he needs to know what jobs are actually available and whether he is prepared for them.[10] The biggest growth is predicted in these fields: construction; finance; insurance and retail real estate; retail and wholesale trade; federal, state, and local government; and service industries which include hotels, restaurants, beauty parlors, and other establishments offering personal service. To be ready for the best opportunities, the able young person will prepare for professional or technological work, especially in science or engineering; or for work in the clerical, sales, and managerial fields.

The May 1963 Bulletin No. 3, *Young Workers: Their Special Training Needs*, U.S. Department of Labor, Washington, D.C., U.S. Government Printing Office, is an excellent example of up-to-date, factual, clearly presented information about vocational opportunities for non-college youth, who comprise about three-fourths of the 26,000,000 new young workers. This bulletin gives special attention to unemployment problems intensified by poverty, racial discrimination, delinquency, and physical and mental handicaps, and discusses the lack of employment opportunities in rural areas.

VALUES AND OPPORTUNITIES FOR WORK EXPERIENCE

The high rate of unemployment among youth under twenty-five is alarming. In 1964, there were more than 300,000 young people who were not in school, not in work and not looking for work. It is estimated that during the 1960s, 40 per cent more young people will enter the labor market than in the previous decade. If present trends continue, 70–80 per cent of the young people in this age group will be unemployed. This is a situation that should concern all parents, even though "the bell tolls" for somebody else's child.

Why are so many young people unemployed? Many lack the skills, work habits, and attitudes that they need for available jobs.

Some of them have difficulty in getting the necessary training. Others have secured their first jobs, but left them because they found little satisfaction in the work. The Manpower Development and Training Act of 1962, amended in 1963, was designed to help youngsters bridge the gap between school and work. More recent programs with the same aim are the Job Corps and work-training programs in which the Federal government will subsidize some state, municipal and nonprofit work for those in school.

If a young person develops his educational potentialities, the chances are that there will be job opportunities for him. In the words of an old proverb, "Get the distaff ready and God will send the flax."

A young person's vocation plays an important role in his personal development: a congenial job helps him find himself. The case of Mrs. B's family will illustrate concretely the role that vocations may play in personal development.

Mrs. B's oldest son, Stanley, successfully completed engineering school and immediately got a job that many older, more experienced workers would envy. Her younger boy, Bert, was still in high school. He had never done as well as Stanley in school, although he studied many more hours. Mrs. B knew that Bert tried hard, but he could not seem to grasp the abstract academic subjects. The school counselor explained to Mrs. B and Bert that his aptitude tests showed he had mechanical ability and a preference for mechanical things. His scores and marks in academic subjects were all in the lowest quarter. Success in college seemed very doubtful.

Mrs. B's husband had died some years ago, and she had taken over the responsibility of supporting the family. Since Stanley was now married and had his own family to support, it was important that Bert choose and prepare for a vocation.

The counselor first helped them to face the employment situation. At that time, in 1962, nearly a million people twenty-five years of age and younger were unemployed and out of school.

Bert was fortunate in having a fine trade school within commuting distance of his home. This was the Los Angeles Trade and Technical College, a two-year accredited junior college that teaches sixty trades ranging from industrial electronics to dry cleaning.

The first decision they made was that Bert should graduate from high school with the best record possible. Higher educational institutions of all types seemed to be raising their admission standards.

Bert applied for admission to Trade-Tech and was accepted. He spent most of the school day with an instructor who was himself highly skilled in the trade and could teach theory as it related to practice.

After completing the course, Bert obtained a job which he felt fully competent to hold. His first pay check raised his self-esteem immensely. Now he felt independent—a young man who could take his place in the world of work. Mrs. B was proud of both her boys; each of them had developed his potentialities.

Ability to hold a job is one evidence of coming of age. In our country, work has traditionally been considered commendable, virtuous, and satisfying. Has this attitude toward work changed during the last generation?

In general, adolescents who are still in school and intending to graduate want part-time work. Almost half of the youth between the ages of fourteen and seventeen have some paid employment during the school year; three-fourths work for pay during the summer.

Through work experience, they may acquire habits of responsibility that they did not establish as children. On the job, they may associate with a socially responsible person, develop efficient work habits, and come to appreciate the value of dependability. They also learn to accept authority and adjust to their co-workers. Significant work experience that demands a high standard of performance is an important factor in self-development and independence. Doing worthwhile work for pay gives the adolescent a feeling that he is learning and growing; it is tangible evidence of his worth as a person.

In the book, *Slums and Suburbs,* Dr. James Conant has pointed out that the presence of large numbers of unemployed, alienated youth is an unfortunate circumstance, both for the young people themselves and for society as a whole.[11] Havighurst and Stiles suggested ways to "provide a pathway to adulthood" for young people who do not profit by staying in the schools as they are now constituted, and who cannot find regular jobs.[12] They need work experience that has growth value, even though it may not be a regular job. The following are some of the current programs and proposals:

In-school, non-remunerative general education work-experience programs.

Remunerative after-class work in the school, such as typing, filing, etc.

Out-of-school, non-remunerative educational work-experience programs in libraries, parks, social agencies, elementary schools, offices, hospitals, etc.

Remunerative educational work-experience programs in junior and senior high schools, in which scholastic credit is given for work experience that is coordinated with school subjects.

Remunerative vocational work experience in senior high school.

To be most useful, a work-experience program should begin at age thirteen or fourteen and continue to age eighteen. It should progress through three stages:

1. Working in groups under school supervision—in parks, on school grounds, at the beaches, etc.
2. Part-time work on an individual basis with an employer.
3. Full-time employment in a stable job.

This kind of program would teach good habits of work as well as specific skills. As part of the public school curriculum, it should be adapted to the abilities and interests of the students.

Many features of this proposed "national policy" have already been tried out at certain times and places. Work-experience programs have been expertly handled in some high schools, for example, in the Oakland public schools during the war years. Resistance on the part of labor and industry is partly responsible for their not becoming more widespread.

Another type of service already in existence provides "job-exchanges" for summer employment. Sponsored by newspapers, PTA, service clubs, and other agencies, they list young people seeking work and try to create or find jobs for them.

Early leadership in the development of volunteer work programs was taken by the American Friends Service Committee. Various youth-serving groups and church groups whose goals in-

clude character building or the improvement of international relations now sponsor different kinds of volunteer service groups.
Other young people perform volunteer service in schools, settle-
ment houses, on summer playgrounds, and in similar projects. The
Job Corps and the Peace Corps are outstanding examples of this
service pattern.[13]

In Berkeley, California, young people may enroll in a program
of paid summer work in the city parks, combined with recreation.
This is a promising pattern for youngsters who need both responsible work and social group experience.[14]

THE ROLE OF GUIDANCE IN DEVELOPING YOUR CHILD'S VOCATIONAL POTENTIALITIES

Parental guidance comes first. Parents are in a unique position. No
one else knows so much about the child; no one else is so inti-
mately concerned with his welfare and so sincerely wants what is
best for him. As one gifted young adolescent said, "The kids I
truly feel sorry for are those who can't confide in their parents."
Children who can confide in their parents usually mention them
first as a source of guidance, as in the following quotations:

"When I have school troubles or just the problems of growing up, I
usually go to my mother because I feel that I'm closer to my mother
than to anyone else. She understands my problems and explains them
clearly."

"The type of guidance I think is best at this age," one adolescent
wrote, "is the frank and adult type. Sometimes teachers tend to talk
down to students. My parents are always truthful to me and try to explain my problems in easy but grown-up terms. If teachers and parents
continue to talk down to children in order to spare their feelings, I don't
see how the student can grow up very much mentally."

Some youngsters recognize the need for both parents and counselors:

"When I am bothered by something, I usually go to my parents for
help because they are the closest to me and I feel that they understand
my problems and I really think that I can confide in them. But sometimes I don't exactly know what to do; so if it concerns school or voca-

tions and my parents don't understand these problems, I go to my guidance counselor who is supposed to have more information."

Since vocational success depends so largely on educational preparation, every young person should receive guidance in making plans for further education. Why do such a large percentage of high school students who rank in the top quarter in intelligence fail to go on to college? The most important reasons seem to be lack of purpose, a low level of aspiration, inefficient reading and study skills, dissatisfaction with the schooling they have had, and inability to finance a college education. If potentially able young people have no long-distance goals or purposes that are commensurate with their ability, they see no need for further study. If they are poor readers, they are handicapped in passing college entrance examinations and in meeting college reading requirements. If they know their parents cannot afford to send them to college, they may not even consider the possibility of further education.

Here are a few examples of the ways in which counselors have helped students to make and successfully carry out sound, realistic educational and vocational plans.

Let us first take a look at an eighth grade boy who is in the highest tenth of his class on intelligence and achievement tests. He has superior mental ability, but is doing only average work in all his classes. He appears to be bored and wastes his time.

From the first grade on, his scores on standardized tests have been high—in the upper 10 per cent of students of his age. But his marks have been only average; in the eighth grade they dropped still lower. His teachers' comments about him have been sometimes favorable, sometimes unfavorable. From the early years, his record has shown unsatisfactory social relations on the playground, poor work habits, and lack of interest in school.

In the seventh grade, when the teacher told his mother that he was the only underachiever among the very bright students in five classes, she said, "I think he lacks initiative and drive. I wish you would talk to him. You always boost his morale."

The psychologist who gave this boy an individual intelligence test came to a similar conclusion. He said, "His analytical ability is high, but he is not motivated toward excellence. He shies away from hard problems; he does not exert himself to give the right answer."

Although the teachers have been aware of these fault lines (to use a geological term) and have tried to correct them, their efforts have not been consistent or coordinated. Since they are responsible for thirty other pupils in each class, they have not had time to get perspective on the problem, view it from many angles, and help the boy to change his attitude toward himself and toward school.

Here is where the counselor comes in. The counselor has time to review previous records, interpret standardized test scores, interview the student and, if it seems desirable, his parents. The following is an excerpt from the counselor's first interview:

"Gosh, I'm just an ordinary boy. I don't know what I should be, but my folks keep after me all the time. They look at me and say, 'You're big enough to be deciding what you want to do—do you want to be a doctor or an engineer or what?'" With this he straightened up his big frame, looked a bit sheepish, and said, "I guess I am big enough, but I still don't know."

As the counselor smiled sympathetically he said,

"I wish I did know, for it sure would be easier. You see, in this school they teach for the bright students, and I'm only average or less, I guess."

During this and other interviews, the boy talked about his summer jobs and his satisfaction or lack of satisfaction in each one. The counselor interpreted the boy's test results to him, and stressed his better-than-average ability. Gradually the boy modified his idea of himself. Instead of thinking of himself as "only an average boy" he began to view himself as "a boy who could succeed in college" and could make a contribution in the field of his special interest. Over a period of time the boy formulated three goals: (a) to become a person who understands his abilities and knows what he wants; (b) to get good marks in his present high school subjects; and (c) to enter a carefully selected college after graduating from high school.

Another boy of sixteen who, according to all test records, belonged in the high ability group, was taking a course of study that would not lead to college or to a suitable vocation. He was getting high marks in all his subjects, and his parents seemed well pleased. Two weeks after school began, the counselor called the boy in for a conference. Together they reviewed his record of high test scores and high grades throughout his junior and senior high school years. The boy said he needed to study less than two hours a week and that he spent much of the rest of his time watching television. When asked about his vocational goal, he said he hadn't thought about it but that he probably would serve his term in the army and then go into business with his father. When asked about going to college, he said he had never considered the possibility and that no one had suggested it to him.

The counselor then held a joint conference with the student and his parents. He pointed out that the boy was "college material" and had considerable ability that was being wasted. Since both the boy and his parents were interested in his having a business career, the counselor mentioned the demand for college-trained men in business, and gave them bulletins regarding colleges, scholarships, and business courses on the college level.

At the parents' request, the counselor had another conference with the boy soon afterward. As a result, he changed to five college preparatory courses, two of which were on the honors level. At the end of the first six weeks, he was doing above-average work, and by the end of the second six weeks he was getting superior grades in all his subjects.

A high school girl has described how a counselor helped her in deciding to go to college and in making suitable vocational plans:

When I was a sophomore, I was determined that I did not want to go to college. After I talked with our counselor, I saw the importance of a college education. I have thought about it a great deal and talked with a lot of people about it. At last I have decided: I'm going to college. Mathematics is my favorite subject, and most of my tests have shown me to be highest in math. I may become a math teacher. I don't know how I will finance a college education, but I'm quite sure I will find some way. I think I owe my decision to the guidance department of our school.

The counselor's interviews will be much more effective if they are reinforced by concerted action on the part of teachers, the reading consultant, and other members of the school staff. Conferences on individual cases are extremely valuable: everyone present gains an understanding of the pupil and learns what kind of stimulation, encouragement, instruction, and counsel he especially needs.

Deciding *not* to go to college is a problem that some students have to face. Such a decision is painful both for the ambitious student and for his parents. However, the counselor must say what he thinks about the probability of the student's success in college in the light of standardized test results, previous school record, and all the other complex factors that may be involved. Most important, he should be prepared to suggest other avenues to further education in which the student's chances of success are high.

The freshman year of high school is not too early for students to begin making tentative long-term plans. Eighth or ninth grade students and their parents need to have detailed information about the subjects and the curricula offered in senior high school. Counselors are responsible for getting this information, putting it in readable form, and discussing it with individuals and groups who are at the moment of decision. In beginning to think about college, students should consider such questions as these:

Should I plan to go to college?
If so, what college?
How can I get help in financing a college education?
Does my high school record count?
What do college freshmen wish they had learned in high school?

The counselor can discuss these and other questions with groups of students. He also makes available in his office or, preferably, in the library, a shelf of general books about colleges, current sources on available scholarships, and pamphlets on how to finance a college education. In addition, he has a file containing folders on all the colleges likely to be chosen by the pupils in his school. In each folder are to be found the latest catalogue of the college in question, supplementary booklets that the college has prepared, articles about the college from magazines and newspapers, reports from parents who have visited the college, and letters from high school graduates who have attended it. This information the coun-

selor describes, explains and discusses with any student who is—
or should be—interested in entering the particular school of nursing, college, or professional or technical school.

The counselor also calls students' attention to the many other
means by which they can continue their education: the public
library; evening school courses; educational television; and educational opportunities offered by the YMCA, YWCA, and other
youth-serving organizations.

In similar fashion, groups of pupils can explore the broad field
of occupations in order to acquire the information they need for
thinking about the education that is essential to their future
careers.

QUESTIONS AND ANSWERS

1. *How can parents finance a college education for their able
children who should go to college?*

The cost of going to college ranges from almost nothing (for
students in the Labor Program of Berea College) to $12,000 for
four years in a prestige college. A youngster living at home and
commuting to a state or land grant university in his own southern
or western state might finance a four-year college education for as
little as $1,000. But most medium-priced state universities now
charge $6,000–$7,000 for out-of-state students. Tuition fees are
constantly increasing.

Parents and students meet college costs in various ways:

About half of the parents put aside money to pay for their children's college education. At an early date they start a "college
fund" for each child.

Some mothers go to work to help finance college educations for
their children.

Many children work during summer vacations to pay part of
their college expenses.

Fewer students now than in past years work their way through
college; this is because the academic requirements are becoming
more demanding and the opportunities for part-time work are less
plentiful.

Although the number of scholarships is increasing, most of them meet only one-fifth of the cost. There are many sources of scholarships. Some are given by industries, such as the General Motors scholarships. Others are given by departments of colleges and universities, such as the music scholarships distributed by the Peabody Conservatory of Music, the scholarships in pharmacy offered by the Alumni Association of the School of Pharmacy at the University of Maryland, or the scholarships offered by Goucher and many other colleges. Scholarships are offered to veterans and to the orphans of veterans. Most numerous are the scholarships offered by foundations and by the government. However, scholarships are not plentiful. Most colleges and universities are able to award scholarships to only three out of five, or in some cases one out of twelve, applicants. Only about half of the most able high school graduates—those in the top quarter of their class —attend college. If more scholarships were available, about one-fourth more would probably attend.

The present trend is toward borrowing. The National Defense Act loans have become the main resource. These loans are available to freshmen at a true interest rate of 3 per cent, which does not begin accruing until a year after graduation. College and state-sponsored loans are less likely to be available to freshmen. Most state long-term loans carry a higher rate of interest; finance companies may charge a true interest of 8 to 10 per cent or more.

A good plan for a middle-income family with several children is to start a savings plan early; $1,100 should be available to finance the first term and part of the second, so that the student need not do part-time work while he is getting adjusted to college.

2. *Where can a high-school-age child who is keenly interested in science get special instruction?*

The National Science Foundation, Washington 25, D.C., has offered summer science programs of various types for secondary school students of high ability. Most of the programs delve deeply into some subject such as biology, mathematics, or physics. Others offer students opportunity to engage in scientific research under the direct supervision of a scientist. Many combine both these kinds of experience. Application blanks should be secured from the directors of colleges and universities in your own state.

3. Who chooses a child's college?

The choice should be the youngster's, not the parents'. The role of the parents, and of the school consultant or counselor, is to supply information, encourage careful thinking on the basis of all the available information about the college and the youngster, and veto any choice that is clearly foolish from the standpoint of his goals and capacities.

James Bryant Conant in his study of suburban high schools says that one of the most serious guidance problems is the emotionally charged pressure that parents bring to bear on children to gain admission to prestige colleges.

4. Will intensive last-minute tutoring help students improve their college admission test scores?

Investigations to date have shown that last-minute tutoring has but little influence on the College Board scores. There does not seem to be much danger that the test scores of tutored students will mislead college admission officers.

The important factor in college application is the student's readiness for college education, which is a slow growth that has been acquired over a period of years. Effective study methods, the habit of critical thinking, and the ability to organize are the result of a long process of education; they cannot be mastered in a few weeks. If these essential elements of education have been neglected, parents cannot compensate for them by sending the boy or girl to a tutoring school.

5. What can I do if the college we have chosen rejects my child's application?

Don't over-react. Perhaps your first choice was the wrong college for your child. By being rejected he may have been saved from flunking out.

Probably his high school record and college admissions tests were not up to the college's standards.

Perhaps his application blank was not carefully or thoughtfully filled out.

Consult the counselor or teacher-counselor who does the college guidance in the high school. He will go over the records with you and suggest other colleges that are still accepting students to fill out their freshman classes.

If you are not satisfied with the school counseling service or want additional help, write to college admission centers such as College Admissions Center, 610 Church Street, Evanston, Illinois; College Admissions Assistance Center, 41 East 65th Street, New York 21, New York; Catholic College Admissions Center, 500 Salisbury Street, Worcester 9, Massachusetts. For a fee of $10 to $15, they will go over your child's application and records and make them available to colleges that still have room for students.

Consider junior colleges, too. Some of these have better teachers and give better education in the freshman and sophomore years than some of the larger universities. At the end of the second year, your child might even transfer to the college that rejected him.

6. *When they get married, should girls plan to work outside the home?*

There are vocational opportunities for women in many fields. The distinctions between "men's jobs" and "women's jobs" are growing less and less sharp. Women will find increasing opportunities in new fields—space exploration, atomic energy, research in medicine and biology, and automatic data processing. Women are needed, as always, in the fields of health, community and social service, and education. New professions in home management are developing. As more married women seek employment outside the home, the need for housekeepers and child care specialists increases. However, homemaking is still women's No. 1 job. Their role as wives and mothers is of prime importance. In speaking to a group of deans and counselors, Mrs. Esther Peterson, Assistant Secretary of Labor and Director of the Women's Bureau of the Department of Labor, said, "Your role is to awaken girls' interest in their probable life pattern and to guide them in selecting training and goals appropriate to their individual capabilities." [15]

SEVEN

Emotional Potentialities

EMOTIONAL health is difficult to describe. It does not consist in maintaining a perfect adjustment under all circumstances. It is not being always happy and free from anxiety and tension. It is not conformity. It is rather the ability to respond to life situations appropriately. This is the quality that Jacqueline Kennedy showed to such a remarkable degree during the three days following her husband's assassination. She used her social skills to deal effectively with a crisis; she showed ability to cope with extreme environmental stresses. Such self-control could only have been learned as a result of innumerable previous situations of minor stress; by responding appropriately to each of these, she had become increasingly competent to handle the awful tragedy with so much dignity and courage and resolution.

The development of one's emotional potentialities involves accepting oneself, maintaining constructive relationships with other persons, facing reality and dealing appropriately with it, and making active efforts to master one's environment.[1] Another essential characteristic of emotional health is flexibility as contrasted with rigidity. A four-year-old, naturally indifferent to table manners and cleanliness, might nevertheless wash his hands before dinner if he felt that this was important to his parents and he wanted to please them. We should realize that this would be a major concession and a major effort on his part. Similarly, we should always appraise a child's behavior in accordance with *his* frame of reference and *his* degree of maturity.

The development of children's emotional potentialities can be discussed under three main headings. The first and most important concerns the development of their potentialities for a creative life. The second is the avoidance of hazards to mental health, and the third is the treatment of mental illness.

CONDITIONS RELATED TO EMOTIONAL HEALTH

"David gets upset easily, just like his mother," Grandmother said of her son's little boy. "Betty is emotionally unstable, just like her father," Betty's mother complained. There is some truth in statements like this. Predisposition to emotional instability is in some measure controlled by hereditary factors. Studies of twins have shown that heredity may be a contributing factor in certain psychoses, notably some of the schizophrenias.[2]

The chemistry of the body may also play a part. Recent scientific advances have called attention to the possible role of biochemistry in the promotion of mental health and in the treatment of mental illness. Psychiatrists have found that certain cases did not need psychological treatment, once certain vitamin and mineral deficiencies had been detected and corrected under expert medical supervision. Numerous experiments have enabled Dr. Selye to describe the effect of prolonged stress and strain on the chemistry of the body. For a time, the glands of internal secretion enable the individual to live with the stress. Eventually, however, as the adaptive mechanism wears out there is a breakdown of body cells which leads to serious illness and the impairment or deterioration of learning.[3]

Social and cultural influences also contribute to mental illness. For example, in a community where there had been considerable disintegration in social relationships, the percentage of psychiatric disorders was twice as large as in a neighborhood in which there was little or no social disorganization.

Some mothers wonder whether working outside the home has a detrimental effect on their children's development. At some time in their lives eight out of ten women in this country do work outside the home. Of all the married women in the country, about one-third were employed in 1962. The effect of the mother's employment depends on a number of factors:

1. *The age and personality of the child.* The younger the child, the greater his need for someone to mother him. The more sensitive the child, the more deeply he is affected by the withdrawal of the mother's attention. The more dependent he is, the harder it is for him to let his mother leave each day to go to work.

2. *What the outside employment means to the mother.* If the mother must work in order to supply essential food, shelter, and clothing, she should have no feeling of guilt about leaving the child. If she wants the job primarily to satisfy her own needs or ambitions, the situation is more complicated. If she stopped working, she might consciously or unconsciously blame the child for depriving her of this opportunity for self-realization. Since she would be sacrificing her own interests for his, she might expect more from the child than he could give.

3. *The kind of mother-substitute that is provided.* Some substitutes have a beneficial effect on the child; others have a detrimental influence.

4. *The mother-child relationship.* Some working mothers give their children their exclusive attention for at least part of the time that they do have at home. This is a happy experience for both mother and child. Other mothers are too tired, too worried about their work, or too burdened with home duties to enjoy their children.

5. *The father's attitude toward the mother's working outside the home.* In some cases the husband resents having his wife employed; it makes him feel inferior. Other husbands actually urge their wives to contribute to the support of the family by getting a job. "A working mother need not be a deserting mother."

Children whose mothers work outside the home may have special problems. Some children manage to cope with these difficulties. Self-reliant Marie gets breakfast for her younger sisters, dresses them for nursery school, and takes them there before she goes to her own classroom. She is only eight years old! Of course, some mornings she is late. When a little sister is sick, she has to stay home and take care of her. This responsibility deprives her of school instruction that she needs.

Some children of working mothers depend heavily on the teacher for mothering. They cling to her in their hunger for affection and reassurance. Others bring to school the resentment they feel at being pushed about and hurried at home. The child who is emotionally neglected may become aggressive and demanding, or apathetic and withdrawn.

If a mother wants a job primarily or solely because she is bored by taking care of children all day long and craves adult companionship, she may meet this need through friends, mothers' clubs, or a moderate amount of service activities. If she is young and full of energy, she may find volunteer work or a part-time job to use up her surplus time and strength. If she wants extra money for expensive things her husband cannot afford, she should consider whether such possessions are more important than meeting her children's present emotional needs. If she craves the sense of accomplishment and gratification that comes from a regular job, she should reconsider the possible satisfactions of motherhood as a career. Women who choose careers in teaching, psychology, psychiatry, social work, and pediatrics find it fascinating to watch children and help them grow. Too many mothers see only the dull side of this job. Perhaps the best solution for the modern mother is to appreciate motherhood as a career, and to do only part-time outside work during the preschool years when the child has such a vital need for constant and reliable mothering.[4]

Emotional behavior, like other behavior, is influenced by our environment—or rather by the way we perceive our environment. A certain degree of order and stability helps to create an atmosphere of relative tranquility. If a child learns to enjoy an attractive, uncluttered home, and to make his own appropriate contribution to its order and beauty, who knows what beneficial long-term effects this may have on his mind and spirit? "A thing of beauty is a joy forever."

Most important of all are the interpersonal relations in the home.[5] Even a child who is constitutionally unstable may make a good adjustment under favorable conditions. From the earliest years, children can begin to develop in the home and at school the emotional strength they need for mental health.

Of the various persons in the home, each may have a unique influence on the children's emotional development. Grandparents sometimes play a major role. They have time to listen to the child's chatter and to answer his questions. They have ideas about amusing things to do and interesting places to visit. They can give a child perspective on the past "when Mommy and Daddy were your age." They have time to read to him and tell him stories that will enrich his sympathy and understanding.[6]

While grandmother may make a real contribution to the child's development, she should also be a person in her own right, with her own friends and interests. She should have leisure and privacy. She is not to be taken for granted as a "built-in-baby-sitter," even though she takes pleasure in being able to free the parents of unrelieved responsibility for the care of their children.

Too often, however, a third adult in the family causes conflict. Grandma is overindulgent; grandpa insists upon good old-fashioned discipline; Uncle Jim criticizes the parents' ways of handling conflicts. The little imps are quick to take advantage of dissension among their elders; they play parents off against grandparents in order to get what they want.

Jealousy, too, may enter in. If grandmother enjoys her grandchildren and has much more time to give them than their busy mother does, the children may show more affection for Grandma than for Mother. This is hard on Mother. However, if she is uncommonly mature and truly wants what is best for her child, she will appreciate the plus values the child is getting from another loving adult.

The housekeeper, cook, or maid, the janitor in the building, or a neighbor's child of the same age—any one of these may meet the child's particular emotional need at some psychological moment. For example, in one wealthy home the butler and his wife served as parent-substitutes for an alcoholic mother and a father who was away from home much of the time. The two preadolescent boys were becoming behavior problems. They refused to do their homework and found excuses for playing truant. The fatherly butler began work on the home study problem by telling the boys that if they got their homework done right after school, they could play all the rest of the afternoon until dinner time. At first, he did a large part of their homework for them. Gradually, they did more and more of it themselves, and thus experienced the satisfaction of achievement. They enjoyed the leisure that followed the completion of a task. He was kind but consistent in his treatment of them. He never let them "get away with anything." Underneath his firmness was an affection such as they had never received from their parents.

These represent only a few of the many patterns of personal relationships that are important influences on children's emotional development. Relationships change as the child grows older. Many parents fail to recognize this fact. Just as some children do not want to grow up, so some mothers do not want to relinquish the pleasure of having a child dependent upon them.

Children catch their values, their fears, and their anxieties from the adults who are important in their lives. Children are affected not only by what adults say, but by what they feel and think to themselves. Uncertainty in adults breeds uncertainty in children. When adults show feelings of hopelessness, children and adolescents take the attitude, "What's the use?" Children respond to each other as they see adults responding to children. All of this has been pointed out by Dr. Buchmueller, Executive Director of the Child Study Association of America, in his introduction to Sibylle Escalona's significant study, *Children and the Threat of Nuclear War*.[7]

There are several reasons why it is so difficult for adults to answer children's questions about nuclear war. When they ask, "Will there be a war?" we do not know. When they ask, "What will happen to the world and its people?" we cannot fully imagine the devastation and suffering. When they ask, "Where will we go?" we have no reassuring answer. We cannot answer children's questions because we do not know the answers ourselves. Children often know more about these matters than we think they do. Instead of playing house and school as they used to do, little children often dramatize bombings. Preadolescents play "Russians bombing us," instead of Cowboys and Indians. Adolescents talk about fallout, Sputnik, H-bombs, and radiation.

Can parents provide an area of security and trust in the midst of this persistent threat of war? Escalona seeks the answer to this question by inquiring how children at different stages of development protect themselves from fear. "When parents can fit their answers about nuclear dangers to the ways of thinking most natural to the child, they are likely to be most successful in helping their youngsters to deal effectively with frightening ideas."[8]

With preschool children from four to six years old, understanding and reassurance work best. The preschool child does not need a scientific explanation. His erroneous ideas can be flatly contradicted, and he will be satisfied with only a brief plausible explanation. He only needs to feel that his parents will take care of him. At the same time, he should be protected from TV programs that show violence and destruction and the noise of war.

Children six to twelve years of age often begin to feel a sense of their own inadequacy in a larger and less sheltered world. They realize that the forces at large in the world can now affect them. They do not have the security of knowing how to meet the threat of nuclear war because older and wiser people do not know what will happen or what to do to insure their own safety.

However, there are still ways in which parents can help. They can focus the child's attention on the positive factors in the situation—on the space heroes, and on the efforts of scientists to intercept bombs and other missiles, and to combat other dangers. To talk calmly about these things helps children to clear up misunderstandings. But as with preschool children, information should be limited "to those aspects of the situation of which the children are already aware." [9] Going beyond the child's present concerns may suggest new dangers to him. He may also be reassured by the knowledge that millions of friendly people in the world want peace.

Adolescents are particularly disturbed by the nuclear threat. Their moods are more intense than those of younger children; the future is of the greatest concern to them. They fear that "nuclear weapons might destroy much of the future they are counting on." [10] Adolescents respond to this threat in many ways. Some give up trying to succeed; they use world conditions as "a ready-made excuse for behaving as they do." [11] Others put the blame on adults, often with some justification. Still others retreat from reality; they refuse to accept danger as a part of life. But there are some who take a much more mature approach. They want to understand and take part in adult efforts to save the world from destruction or, more positively, to build a better world.

Parents can help by sharing their points of view with their adolescents on a man-to-man basis. Young people want to know what adults think. They are disappointed when adults' values turn out to be wishy-washy or selfish. They appreciate integrity on the part of their parents, teachers, counselors, pastors, and the scientists and political leaders whom they see and hear on television and radio. Our own survival and the future of our children depend upon the ways we think and feel about our destiny and our present responsibility for it.

Fear is restrictive; it discourages responsiveness to new situations. It causes a child to view a new experience as something to be avoided. Our perception of a situation is affected by our beliefs, values, needs, attitudes, and self-concepts. For example, if we believe a child is doing his best, we will act kindly toward him. If a child believes he can learn to read better, the chances are that he will put forth effort to improve.

EMOTIONAL DEVELOPMENT AND PROBLEMS

Children's emotional potential gradually develops as they encounter experiences that are appropriate to their years. As they learn to cope with minor conflicts and frustrations, they become increasingly able to tolerate greater degrees of stress. For example, a certain amount of sibling rivalry that is skillfully handled in the home may help the child to manage subsequent competitive relationships at school and at work. The home in which the parental guidance is both reasonable and affectionate offers the child opportunities to learn how to cope constructively with numerous reasonably difficult situations.[12]

During Infancy and Preschool Years

The feeding of an infant involves much more than satisfying his hunger for food. During the feeding process, the mother and the child achieve an emotional closeness. The mother learns her baby's bodily rhythms. By falling in line with them, she protects him from undue tension. She introduces order and control into his life. Starting with the feeding schedule that seems best suited to the child's own timetable, the mother can gradually adjust the intervals so that the feeding times are more convenient for her.

In the first month, the baby may need the comfort of being held and cuddled. Parents need not fear spoiling him at this stage. Indeed, some infants who have been deprived of the normal amount of mothering have failed to develop a sense of trust, an outgoingness, a desire to reach out to new experiences, an ability to relate themselves warmly to others.

Later on, when the baby cries, it may be good to let him fuss a bit in peace. He will often drop off to sleep without being picked up or hovered over.

Weaning marks an important stage in the emotional separation of the child from the parent. Sometimes babies are ready for weaning before their mothers are ready to relinquish this close relationship. Walking is another milestone toward the child's emotional independence.

At first, the child fears to venture very far from his mother. Between the ages of nine and fifteen months, he often resists letting his mother out of his sight. At this stage no one is acceptable as a substitute for her. When later, separation is necessary, as when the mother must go to the hospital, she can explain her absence and reassure the child about her return in ways that the child can understand. Role-playing is often an effective way of helping a child to understand this kind of situation. If the mother goes away for brief periods, the child learns to expect her return. During his second year, the child can tolerate brief absences.[13] While early separation may have a serious effect on the child's emotional development, even abandoned children can pull through if they have someone to turn to. Every child must eventually learn to share his mother with other members of the family, and to recognize her other responsibilities.

Building on the sense of trust he has established in infancy, the child develops independence during his preschool years. Gradually he learns to play by himself or with other children.

He also learns from experience to cope with his impulses. Although parents cannot—and should not—protect the child from all frustrations and unpleasant realities, they can furnish the support that enables him to handle the inevitable frustrations that arise from his inexperience, his lack of verbal and motor skills, and the aggressiveness of his playmates.

Children show their feelings in different ways. Some cry when they are angry; others go off by themselves; still others have temper tantrums. Bobby is brave when the dentist hurts him, but cries if mother brushes him aside or does not understand.

Preschool children often lack the words to express their feelings. Their only outlet is crying. Though it disturbs us, it may be a relief to them. It also gets results; someone comes to the rescue of the injured arm or bruised feelings. Children who cannot cry are more likely to show physical symptoms such as loss of appetite or listlessness. Sometimes children are inconsolable. All efforts to comfort them fail. But it helps just to have mother near. It helps to have her say later, "I'm glad you feel better now," and suggest something that is fun to do.[14] While some children are comforted by an adult's quiet verbal reassurance, others seem impervious to words and want only to have loving arms around them. With these children, comfort comes first; words may help later. The things that satisfy one child may not appeal to another.

Parents can help the child learn to cope with emotional stress. They may suggest that he dispel sadness by playing a favorite record, or that he try various ways of letting off steam when he is angry. Some children pound nails or saw wood to relieve their feelings. Some splash around with finger paints. Others find release in running or in other kinds of physical activity. There are individual differences in the efficacy of any safety valve. No one of them works for all children. If parents can help the child understand why he feels guilty or afraid or anxious, he may feel less emotional disturbance.

During the child's early preschool years, parents tend to see more problems than potentials. It is easy for them to forget that thumb-sucking, bed-wetting, jealousy, fears, temper tantrums, and destructiveness may represent ways in which the preschool child is solving his problems of growing up. The way the parents handle any one of these problems can be more important for the child's development than any other effect of the problem. In fact, our overconcern about the first signs of problem behavior may make the child feel inferior and overanxious.

If instead of paying attention to children only when they do something wrong, what would happen if we paid attention to them when they were doing things that we approve? An interesting experiment with five preschool children suggests an answer to this question. In the experiment there was one child who withdrew from the other children and played by himself most of the time. The more attention the nursery school teacher paid to his solitary play, the more he withdrew from the other children. However, when she paid attention to him on the occasions when he did play with other children, he became more sociable.

Another child preferred to crawl around, though he was quite capable of standing and walking. He stopped his crawling when the teacher ignored it, and gave him her attention only when he stood up or walked.

A third child cried frequently. When the teacher stopped paying attention to his crying, and gave him her attention only in his happier moments, his excessive crying stopped.

These and other recorded instances show how we can have a favorable effect on children's social and emotional development by focusing attention on their desirable actions rather than on their undesirable behavior.

When thumb-sucking, bed-wetting, jealousy, unfounded fears, temper tantrums, and destructiveness persist without apparent provocation and unaccompanied by observable gains in independence and self-direction, we should look below the surface for the possible causes. There is usually no single cause; the whole network of family life and relationships may be involved. Nor is there any quick and easy way to correct these undesirable trends. While "don'ts" and restrictions may deter the child from continuing the problem behavior, they may also decrease his spontaneity. Nagging or withdrawal of affection may simply cause the child to seek satisfaction in other undersirable ways.

Jealousy can disrupt otherwise happy relationships. It is a painful emotion that can warp a child's personality. When there is a new baby, the older child usually finds it hard to share his parents' love and attention. He does not realize that they have enough love for both children. It is hard for him not to feel neglected and jealous when everyone in the family is preoccupied with the new baby, and visitors exclaim over her and bring her presents. Parents can often minimize, though not completely eliminate, this kind of jealousy. They may let the child share in making preparations for the new baby. They may help him to understand his mixed feelings of jealousy and love. If the mother can create loving relationships throughout the family group, jealousy becomes unnecessary.

Like the other problems that we have mentioned, certain fears may be natural and normal. Fear that produces caution is essential in this dangerous world. Thunderstorms, large dogs, and spiders can be very frightening to a young child. However, in a secure relationship he can learn how to handle his fears. In some instances, knowing just what to expect and do in a strange situation is the best preventive of fears and worries. Intelligent action often casts out fear. If the child is encouraged to bring his fears to the surface, they are not so likely to become intense and prolonged.

Social fears increase as the child grows older. Many children today fear not being able to live up to their parents' high standards and expectations. They fear failure in the competitive classroom. Girls have a special fear of not being popular.

Around the age of two, temper tantrums and obstinate behavior may be indications of the child's efforts to move away from the dependency of infancy. Adults often fail to recognize the motivation of the child's angry behavior, or the accumulation of frustrations, disappointments, and resentments that precipitated it. It is especially hard on the child to find himself at cross-purposes with someone he loves. It is no solution either to "get tough" with the child or to give him freedom to do anything he pleases. The child needs to learn to control his anger for the sake of his own security and his adjustment to society. As children are helped to discover new and satisfying outlets for their aggressive impulses, they learn to behave in ways that are more acceptable socially.

When a child is ready to talk about his feelings, it is helpful for him to do so. Other avenues of emotional release such as active physical exercise are also helpful. It is still better if the release of tension is accompanied by a feeling of accomplishing something worthwhile. In time the child will observe that a temper tantrum only makes him unhappy and annoys other people.

Destructiveness in young children often evokes a response from adults that is out of proportion to the child's intention in committing the act. This is because the adult does not make a distinction between accidental and deliberate destructiveness. Many destructive acts prove to be due simply to lack of experience, or to curiosity.

Constant criticism tends to make a child feel that his parents are dissatisfied with him and want to change him. He may suspect that they are using him to satisfy their own ambitions and needs. Patricia may feel that she is being sent to dancing school so that Mother may show off her accomplishments to friends or relatives. Junior, who is not naturally athletic, may resent the lessons in horseback riding and swimming that his father insists on his taking. This kind of pressure seems more like exploitation than real concern for the child's welfare.

On the other hand, over-indulgence is no better solution; it usually lessens the child's determination to achieve. The child who has everything tends to value nothing very highly. If he has no wants, he has nothing to strive for. He may have all sorts of material possessions but lack what is most important—his parents' love.

Preschool children sometimes comfort one another. They may have a capacity for sympathy as well as for aggression. Their ways may not be our ways, but they are good ways if they make another child feel accepted and secure.

Although we cannot always accept the child's behavior, we can accept the child. We can encourage him to tell us how he feels. Feelings often need to come out, though actions sometimes have to be held back. Donald may want to hurt his baby brother, but he must not do so. If he does, he may lose the very thing he wants most—his mother's love. The child has to learn that he cannot always *do* what he *feels like doing*.

During Elementary School Years

When the child enters kindergarten or first grade, success in school becomes important to him and to his parents. But his "success" should be measured against his ability to succeed, rather than against school standards and patterns which may or may not be applicable to him.

School children who are continuing to move from dependency to independency often experience frustration, conflict, and feelings of failure in an autocratic classroom atmosphere that demands subordination and submission. Their "normal" reactions to frustrating conditions are too often treated as "problems," rather than as signs of conflict between their needs and the school's demands and expectations. Fear, anger, envy, loneliness, bitterness, dejection, or despair may preoccupy a child's mind, drain his energy, and leave him incapable of applying himself to his school work. A change in the child's program or a transfer to another classroom sometimes frees him to engage in more independent, satisfying, and successful learning experiences.

Skillful teachers attempt to meet the child's needs in the group setting, which is the area of their special competence. The child should feel that he is part of a group engaged in a worthy enterprise to which he can contribute. Youngsters often recall the projects that they have carried out, individually or in groups, as their most satisfying school experiences. Through group experiences teachers can help children learn to live responsibly and effectively. They cannot be expected to change the way parents feel and act toward a child, nor to do much about his past experiences.

A classroom environment in which children feel that they are learning and growing can bring about desirable changes in their personality and behavior. Success in reading and other school subjects enhances competency; competency contributes to self-esteem and self-confidence. Every time a child resolves a conflict or meets a crisis successfully, he takes a step forward toward self-realization. These early successful experiences with problems in living fortify children to meet the crises that arise or will arise at home, in the community, with their peers, in their later school life, and, finally, in their adult life. Continuous studies of the circumstances that give rise to emotional disturbances in individual children and of the conditions that affect the emotional health of all children are of basic importance.[15] To develop his emotional potentialities, a child needs (a) adults who are sensitive to his emotional needs, and (b) experiences that satisfy those needs.[16]

Every morning an elementary teacher may take a "feeling inventory" by watching each child, observing his appearance and behavior, and listening to the tone of his voice.[17] These observations give her clues for teaching the child during the day. At other times she notes when "feeling storms" are interfering with a child's learning. To some children, she gives a smile of encouragement; to others, a pat on the head; to still others, just enough help so that they can succeed in the appropriate work they are doing. She programs the children's learning so that all can enjoy small successes on the path to a completed product or performance. Her classroom shows a high degree of "positive regard" between teacher and pupils, and among pupils.

Children in the intermediate grades need the security of knowing that grown-ups will set limits for them that are appropriate to their age and development. Eleven- and twelve-year-olds especially depend on these limits to help them "save face" with their peers; they can say, "I can't do that because 'they' won't let me," rather than "I can't do that because I'm afraid to."

Their security is further strengthened by knowing what to expect. They like adults to be consistent. It is confusing to have a certain activity allowed at one time and prohibited at another. They become angry and antagonistic if a punishment seems unfair, or if they are punished for something they did not do. They like strict but understanding parents and teachers who will hold them responsible for the kind of emotional control that they are capable of.

Children learn ways of working with others by watching how teachers do it. They see a teacher trying to understand a pupil who has been caught stealing, before she passes judgment on him. They observe the teacher's interest in finding out why another pupil caused a disturbance in class. If they get the idea of looking below the surface of their own and other people's behavior, they will tend to use this approach in their daily social relationships.[18]

If a school-age child is disturbed by disagreements among members of his family, he can be helped to realize that fundamental agreement does exist, and to accept differences of opinion. It is not so much the conflicting views as the conflicting feelings of his parents that bother the child. Without attempting to conceal his genuine feelings, the parent may avoid violent and angry expressions of emotion in the child's presence.

During Adolescence

Adolescents often tend to be excitable and moody; to be nonconforming when it comes to adult social requirements, but subservient with respect to the standards set by their peers. They are often confused about their identity and their roles—whether they are child or man, dependent or independent, masculine or feminine. Adolescence is the time when youths should achieve a sense of identity and be able to answer the question, "Who am I?" Many cannot rely on parental authority or neighborly surveillance to steer them in the right directions. These are normal problems of growing up. How young people handle them has a strong effect on their progress toward emotional maturity.

Some adolescents seek the solution of their problems in early marriage. Early marriages often spring from a kind of immaturity, an emotional dependency accompanied by a need to claim full adult maturity. Often both the girl and the boy who enter into such a partnership expect to obtain from each other the kind of security that would prolong the parent-child relationship.

Responsibility, which seems to have its roots in early identification with socially responsible adults, should increase with age. During adolescence, this increase seems to be largely due to the demands of work experience. Even children prefer serious, grownup assignments to trivial childish duties. As the eminent psychologist, Dr. E. L. Thorndike, once said, "Children would rather make real pies than mud pies." The main value of a job to young people lies in the opportunity it offers for self-development and independence. Doing useful work helps the individual to prove himself; it gives him a sense of worth. It is also a learning experience. He may even view a reasonable amount of floundering or failing in the first jobs as an exploratory experience, essential to learning.[19] To be sure, the money earned also increases his sense of independence, though the way he spends it may neutralize its psychological value.

EMOTIONALLY INSECURE AND DISTURBED CHILDREN

These labels are too freely given out. It is easier to label a child than to describe and understand his behavior. Once labeled, the child tends to think of himself as that kind of child. The label influences his self-concept. Knowing this, we should avoid making such remarks as "Jane has always been nervous," "Teddy gets upset so easily," "Bill makes me nervous, too," or "David acts just like his uncle" (who has been in a mental hospital).

Occasionally we are all "nervous," emotionally insecure, or disturbed. If we have to give a talk for which we feel unprepared, we are sure to be nervous. An irritating succession of annoyances during the day is likely to culminate in an immature, emotional outburst. We cannot appraise a child's emotional stability without knowing his developmental history, his environment and the conditions with which he has to cope.

The age of the child should also be considered. A two-year-old who throws his dish of spinach on the floor may be responding quite normally; if a twelve-year-old did the same thing, we should be justifiably concerned.

Characteristics

Of the children in public elementary and secondary schools, from 2 to 12 per cent have been diagnosed as maladjusted. These children show undue passivity, anxiety, fear, restlessness, day-dreaming and withdrawal tendencies, or aggressiveness and hostility. Not only do they fail to make a wholesome social adjustment, but many of them also fail to make an appropriate academic achievement. Among the sixteen emotionally disturbed children in one class, all but three had failed or been retained in one or more grades, mostly in the kindergarten or first grade. Nine had

Since the emotionally disturbed child is self-impaired, he is consequently handicapped in his ability to give, to receive, to perceive, to react normally. He is too self-absorbed to sustain interest in matters that do not relate directly to him. Because of inner conflicts that block, distract, or retard him, he is potentially limited in learning.

However, success in reading and other academic work may contribute to a child's social and emotional maturity. Failure, on the other hand, may cause decreased self-confidence, excessive submissiveness, and difficulty in concentration. The child who is already blighted by unfavorable circumstances must be spared a recurrence of these if he is to rebuild his self-esteem, confidence, and security. It is sometimes necessary for a child to regress before he can progress, to catch up on certain preschool experiences that have thus far been denied to him.

Multiple Causes

Many conditions conspire to produce emotional disturbance. Biological, social, and psychological factors all interact and overlap. Physical factors may initiate secondary emotional problems. Physical irritations may contribute to psychological irritability. The discomfort of poor vision, the strain of not being able to hear clearly, a nagging pain, or poor muscular coordination may cause frustrations that lead to emotional disturbance. The film about Helen Keller presented an extreme instance of what it would be like to be incapable of understanding or being understood. A child who is physically attractive is more likely to be accepted than a child who has physical defects. For example, a child born without fingers on one hand may not be accepted by his family or treated as a normal child. This lack of affection and acceptance may cause secondary emotional problems.

Sometimes physical causes are so basic that psychological treatment alone would be ineffective and a waste of effort. Six-year-old Alice had become generally irritable. She had frequent temper tantrums. A thorough medical examination revealed a very low blood count. She needed medical treatment rather than psychotherapy. Sometimes a thorough medical examination, including tests of blood chemistry and vitamin deficiency, make psychiatric treatment unnecessary.

Children with varying degrees of brain damage show various disturbances in behavior. Charlie was overactive in a restless, explosive way. He pulled open drawers and frequently tore his toys apart. His concentration was poor; his attention span was so short that he darted from object to object, from one idea to another. He was in perpetual motion. Any activity such as climbing, which involved danger of falling, made him exceedingly anxious. These signs of mental disorganization were observed in Charlie's free play, and also in his retarded language development. He had special difficulty in seeing, hearing, and feeling things as children do. In other words, his perceptions were distorted. When reading, he tried to pay attention to the page as a whole, rather than to a specific word or group of words. To overcome this, the reading teacher would cover the page with a piece of cardboard that had a slit which let him see only one group of words at a time. He was also below average in spoken language—understanding commands, recognizing and naming objects, and remembering letter-sound associations. Moreover, his eye-hand coordination was poor. His movements were impulsive and badly controlled.

Because of these deficiencies, he was constantly frustrated. Sometimes he reacted with anger, sometimes by withdrawing from the situation. The competitive atmosphere of his school accentuated the frustration he felt in being unable to achieve normal satisfactions.

Parents and teachers can help to reduce the severity of the frustrations suffered by such a child by providing conditions that he can handle more or less successfully at every stage of his development. Patience and continuous cheerful encouragement may help him to gain better motor coordination and to learn to see and hear a little more effectively.

Many emotional difficulties undoubtedly have their roots in

unfavorable neighborhood conditions. Some emotional problems stem from lack of food, shelter, and clothing. Johnny was only ten years old when he was referred by the school to a child guidance clinic for truancy and stealing. He was one of six children whom his widowed mother, herself mentally ill, was trying to support. Johnny had repeated colds, earaches, and other conditions caused largely by neglect and an inadequate diet. His truancies occurred on days when he had no shoes to wear or food to eat. When asked to state his three wishes, he asked for money so there would be enough to eat, shoes to wear, and books for school. When Johnny went to live with his kind and understanding grandmother, who was able to supply his basic needs, his stealing and truancy disappeared, though he was still restless and retarded in his school work.

Parents of children who are favored by fortune should feel some responsibility for children whose home conditions are unfortunate. A wealthy father whose own children had every advantage gained a sympathetic understanding of less fortunate children by serving on the Advisory Board of an Urban Society for the Prevention of Cruelty to Children. He was shocked at the cases of cruelty that were brought to court. Poverty, ignorance, disease, and crime are burdens too heavy for children to bear.

Lack of parental affection and acceptance intensifies bad social conditions. In the following case parental cruelty was combined with racial discrimination. A Negro boy, Tom, only ten years old, stole from his family and fought with his younger brother, whom the father favored. The father himself could "pass" as white if Tom, who was dark-skinned, was not with him. Finding himself generally resented and rejected, Tom became aggressive. His hostility naturally increased the dislike that his father and other people felt for him. This dislike, in turn, further stimulated his aggressiveness. Although the home factors in this case could not be altered, a teacher helped by accepting Tom and praising him for his accomplishments. His school work improved, and he became a leader in his Scout group, though his hostility to his younger brother still persisted.

Emotionally deprived children often present a picture of disorganized or diffuse activity and infantile behavior. They do not love or accept love, or identify themselves with other persons.

They feel rejected by their parents. This apparent rejection is often the result of the parents' own frustrations and the emotional turmoil caused by their heavy burdens and unmet needs. Sometimes they lack knowledge. Sometimes their very anxiety may preclude a more relaxed attitude toward the child. One mother was very anxious and upset because her three-year-old child had not learned to speak. Her husband thought she was to blame. The child himself, frustrated because of his inability to communicate as his parents obviously expected him to, was restless and destructive. After the psychologist had reassured her that the child was of normal intelligence and had discussed the family situation with her, the mother felt less guilty. Two months later the child had begun to talk and was more cooperative and pleasant. In another month he was no longer a problem. Very often a little insight and a few suggestions have an almost miraculous effect on children's emotional difficulties in their initial stages. Child psychiatry has gradually become a kind of family psychiatry which aims to help parents, not to blame them.

Unfavorable school conditions may create or intensify existent problems. Seven-year-old Ellen presented problems of thumbsucking, temper tantrums, nightmares, fears, failure in school, and jealousy of her younger brother. These symptoms had become increasingly severe when she enrolled in an overcrowded school in a low-economic neighborhood. There were fifty children in her first grade class. It was obviously impossible for the teacher to give enough individual instruction to so many children.

The mother tried to help the child with her homework. This attempt was worse than useless, because the mother's impatience with Ellen's slow progress caused more emotional difficulties.

Although Ellen's IQ of 90 was probably not an accurate measure of her true mental ability, it did show how she might be expected to perform mental tasks at present. Ellen's father preferred her older brother, who was a good student; this made Ellen jealous of her brother. Grandmother's gratuitous advice about bringing up children further complicated the home situation.

Ellen was transferred to another school where the classes were much smaller. She was placed in a grade corresponding to her present mental age. In two months, the initial symptoms, which apparently were temporary, had disappeared except for her continued sibling rivalry. Although Ellen's disturbance had been due to a combination of home and school influences, the change in the school situation altered her behavior dramatically.

Ellen was not an emotionally sick child, though she certainly was an emotionally disturbed child. Sometimes a change in a single aspect of the environment will check a trend toward persistent self-defeating and inappropriate behavior. All disturbed children do not, of course, respond so promptly and completely to an environmental change. Much depends on how long they have been disturbed, and how deep-seated and pervasive the disturbance is.

Children may be sensitive about failure in any aspect of school life. Jerry was sensitive about his poor writing. One day when the teacher merely remarked that he could make his paper neater, he tore it up and threw it on the floor. The teacher said nothing at the time. But after class she talked to him kindly, first saying how good he was in reading and arithmetic. Then he confessed that he was very sensitive about his poor handwriting, that his mother was always nagging him about it and making him rewrite his papers, and that his older brother was far more skillful with his hands than he was. The teacher reassured Jerry about his many good qualities and promised to give him extra instruction in writing.

Children respond to failure in many different ways. Some may regard a mistake as a chance to learn not to fail that way again. Failure may affect others in these ways:

They may think of themselves as "no account" or "stupid," and stop trying.

They may try to withdraw from an unhappy situation by retreating into a world of fantasy or by sitting passively in class.

They may develop physical symptoms such as morning headaches or upset stomach that prevent their attending school.

They may become hostile and aggressive, blame the teacher, and hurt other children.

They may become discouraged, irritable, or troubled in their sleep.

These responses are significant for emotional health insofar as they become habitual ways of responding to difficulty and disappointment.

The skillful teacher helps children to view failure as an opportunity to learn. He helps the child to channel the aggression that arises from frustration into an attack on the particular problem. Otherwise the child might use his pent-up hostility to destroy property or hurt people, or he might turn it inward against himself.

Ways of Helping

When a child is emotionally disturbed, there are two general ways of helping him. One is to correct, where possible, the conditions in his physical or social environment that have caused or are aggravating the disturbance. The other is to strengthen the child's ability to handle these situations and react in a healthy way to new situations. In other words, if conditions can be changed, do something about them. In any case, help the child develop the resources within himself that will enable him to handle frustrations and annoyances. Mother Goose said it in this way:

> "For every evil under the sun,
>   There is a remedy, or there is none.
>   If there be one, go and find it.
>   If there be none, never mind it."

Children are remarkably resistant to experiences that might cause psychological damage. Whether a given child becomes emotionally disturbed or not depends a great deal on what adjustments can be made in his environment, and how much understanding he can be helped to gain.

The school attempts to help emotionally disturbed children in a variety of ways.[20] First, the teacher may make the classroom environment easier for these children to handle by:

Finding activities in which they can participate successfully and helpfully.

Helping them individually to develop the skills needed by children of their age.

Placing them in a small congenial group engaged in some activity in which they are interested and competent.

Second, the severely disturbed children may be placed in a special class, if one is available. With a well qualified teacher and appropriate instructional materials, they can learn to handle their emotional difficulties. They should be with their regular social group part of the day. Whenever possible, the program for emotionally disturbed children should be a part of, rather than apart from, the regular school program.

Third, the child may be referred to the school psychologist or the school social worker (visiting teacher), who works with him and with his family. The specialist tries to help the teacher understand the child's emotional difficulties, and the conditions in the home or the school that might be changed for the better. However, schools frequently fail to provide the kind of re-education that emotionally disturbed children require. Too early a return to ordinary classrooms and a regular curriculum may reactivate their problems.

THE CHILD WHO IS MENTALLY ILL

There is a great deal of controversy over the name and nature of mental illness. One authority says it is a myth; another, that it is a sin. A psychologists' symposium asked, "Is there such a thing?" Some experts would substitute such terms as "maladaptive behavior" or "psychological disorder" for "mental illness." However, the name is unimportant except as it affects the treatment.

There are cases which the teacher cannot help in the ordinary classroom situation. These severely disturbed pupils show different patterns of symptoms such as the following which tend to become progressively worse despite the teacher's best efforts:

Extremely Passive

They continually work below their ability.

They lack the abilities and skills that they might have obtained.

They cannot concentrate on school work.

They show an extreme lack of self-confidence.

They complain of headaches or other illnesses for which the doctor can find no physical basis.

They are tired all the time, for no apparent physical reason.

Extremely Tense, Nervous and Inhibited

They are in a state of constant, extreme anxiety; fears and feelings of guilt are prominent.

They often appear bright.

Their reaction to difficulty is intense.

Extremely Withdrawn

They withdraw completely from other children, fantasy, and engage in solitary, aimless activities.

They show a pattern of declining school grades.

Extremely Hostile and Aggressive

They hate school, hate adults, have difficulty in adjusting to school.

They are hyperactive.

Their action is directed toward relieving tension rather than toward reaching a goal.

Their superego, or conscience, is weak.

In an entirely different situation, some of these children might not show these signs of emotional disturbance. If they could be put in a play therapy group that was geared to their present level of ability, they might learn to relate themselves to others.

Many factors have been suggested as contributing to children's mental illness. Being hospitalized as an infant may cause separation anxiety. The broken home is frequently mentioned, though this may not be any more detrimental than an intact home where there is quarreling and lack of love. Alcoholism, family quarrels and fights, crowded living conditions, extreme poverty *or* affluence, and frequent change of residence have also been mentioned as causes. Misfortunes such as the loss of several loved persons, other than one's parents, or the loss of wealth, of home, or of social standing have been thought to precipitate mental illness. The child who is either smothered with love or who feels unwanted and rejected is also susceptible to mental illness.[21]

In general, *feelings* of deprivation seem more important than the *fact* of deprivation. Children who are actually deprived may not see themselves as disadvantaged, whereas children who are actually in fortunate circumstances may consider themselves emotionally deprived. The most important factors in emotional health seem to be the capacity for loving, and the experience of being loved by parents or parent substitutes.

Subtle signs of emotional illness appear early. At six years of age Danny had more in common with a three-and-one-half-year-old than with other children of his age. His muscles had a "doughy" quality. He clung to his mother as though to separate himself from the rest of the world. He showed a diffuse anxiety. He repeated certain questions over and over again: "What's your name?" "Where is Danny?" "Who is Danny?" He often had digestive disturbances and refused to eat certain foods. He learned to read and spell, but tended to use these skills in a mechanical way, rather than as a means of communication. Since he was learning the school subjects and was docile and dependent on the teacher as well as his parents, nothing was done about his emotional difficulties.

However, between the ages of ten and eleven, the picture changed. Though his immaturity had become less obvious, his anxiety suddenly increased, and his behavior symptoms became more pronounced. He became aggressive and hurt other children. He had many fears—of ghosts, of people stealing into his room to kill him, of evil spirits inside him, telling him what he must do. Symptoms of this extreme kind indicate clearly the need for expert clinical treatment, the earlier the better.

In such cases, the child's teacher may be very helpful. If the teacher is baffled by the child's behavior, he may get help from the school counselor or adjustment teacher. If the problem is too serious for the counselor to handle, he may obtain assistance from the psychologist, the visiting teacher, or the psychiatrist employed by the school system. Outside clinics and social agencies are additional sources of help for emotionally disturbed school children.

The psychotherapist uses various methods to help the child obtain a less distorted or confused picture of his world and his relationships. He uses the therapy situation itself as an opportunity to work out ways of behaving in everyday living. For example, if the child expresses hostility toward the therapist, the therapist does not retaliate—within limits, of course. He accepts the child in spite of his unfriendly acts. The child then needs to find another way of responding. A relationship of mutual respect may gradu-

ally develop. Having learned to relate himself more satisfactorily
to one person, he may be able to apply his newly acquired learning to other situations.

Some children can work out their feelings in play therapy.
Others may gain more insight by discussing their problems. The
expert therapist tries to find the approach that seems most appropriate to the individual child. "The therapist accepts the child
where he *is* for what he can *become*. He respects him as a person,
with a right to his own healthy individuality. . . . The task of
therapy is to help the child to expand his own emotional horizons,
to increase his understanding, to enable self-defeating, self-
isolating rebellion to become constructive, socially-directed activity." [22]

It is sometimes hard for parents to accept the child's fondness
for the therapist. They feel they are being displaced in the child's
affection. However, any feeling of jealousy on their part increases
the child's difficulties. The effect of psychotherapy should be to
enhance the relationship between parent and child.

Only by recognizing that time plays a vital role in child and
adolescent development can parents and teachers avoid undue
discouragement. It takes time to effect changes in an individual's
behavior. Miracles do not happen often. Long-standing habits and
deep-seated attitudes do not change overnight. The path to
progress has its ups and downs, its detours and roadblocks. For
example, the boy in the film, "The Quiet One," after months of
psychiatric treatment, lapsed into behavior that was as violent and
destructive as any he had previously exhibited. Not until he had
finally worked through the problem in his own way was he able
in some measure to reorganize his life.[23]

It is often possible to treat mentally ill persons successfully in
their own communities and to find useful work for them to do,
instead of confining them to institutions. To carry out this policy,
the late President Kennedy proposed to Congress in February,
1963, a plan to establish comprehensive community health centers,
which would use existing community resources and provide additional facilities for all aspects of mental health care. Prevention
would be a major objective of this program. The community
health center would have the advantage of enabling those concerned to secure a better understanding of the person's needs, a

closer coordination of services, and a more consistent progression of treatment.

Every child has potentialities for emotional health. Our first concern is to create favorable conditions under which we can help the child build psychological resistance to the common causes of emotional disturbance.[24] The aim is not to avoid life's inevitable frustrations and disappointments, but to become better able to handle them. The young have considerable capacity to recover from unpleasant or even shocking emotional experiences.[25] If signs of serious emotional disturbance appear, we may be able to take corrective steps at an early date.

QUESTIONS AND ANSWERS

1. *What are the effects of city living on the mental health of children?* [26]

A large city may be stimulating to the growth of children. It offers opportunities in science, art, music, and drama that rural communities cannot afford. It has many more health agencies and specialized services.

But how many city children are able to enjoy these opportunities? And in the case of those who are able, do the cultural and educational advantages compensate for the crowding, the pushing, the hurrying, and the complexity of city life—not to mention the fumes and soot?

Moreover, city life is usually devoid of neighborliness. The child is not deterred from undesirable behavior by the example or advice of neighbors who know him and want him to do what is right. On many streets, the child sees examples of depravity, crime, and drunkenness. He may well have some unfortunate experience with a stranger which causes him to develop a not entirely unwarranted fear of people.

A disadvantaged child may join the gangs in his neighborhood, or go to the opposite extreme of isolating himself in his own home.

We must face these and other unfortunate aspects of city life and counteract some of them if possible. The schools are the basic agency for doing this. They reach all the children five days a week, ten months a year, for at least ten consecutive years of their lives. Surely much can be accomplished in this length of time.

The churches are next in importance. Though they have far fewer hours with the children, they have the advantage of working with the whole family. The educational focus of the church should be on the development of moral values and specific goals of conduct.

Community centers, social agencies, and an enlightened police force meet other special needs.

Parents living in cities can try to meet their children's needs in various ways. They can find out what recreational resources are located in their vicinity, accompany a shy or immature child on his trips of discovery, or give an older, self-reliant child a guidebook and map to do the exploring himself with a special friend of his own age. To offset the feeling of haste and hurry, some parents try to provide a relaxed home environment for their children and the children's friends. To counteract the impersonal quality of a city neighborhood, the parent may try to give extra personal attention to the children. In some neighborhoods block organizations have been able to establish a small-town kind of friendliness among the families on the block.

2. *How are the three basic needs of children related to emotional health?*

The three basic needs are the need to love, curiosity or the need to know, and the need to grow. If these needs are not satisfied at critical periods early in life, the child may make little effort to satisfy them later on. From this viewpoint, mental illness and underachievement may be regarded as "deficiency diseases" comparable to vitamin deficiencies, or as neuroses—self-defeating ways of attempting to meet basic needs.

3. *What are the main ways in which children learn to cope with their emotional handicaps?*

Children learn various ways of maintaining their self-respect and sense of worth when they are faced with conditions that prevent satisfaction of their basic needs. Some of these mechanisms of adjustment are socially approved and personally beneficial, such as the following:

To try to excel in spite of the handicap, as Edison and Beethoven did.

To find something good in every situation, as Pollyanna did; to "see opportunity in every calamity."

To seek satisfaction in art, music, religion, work, recreation, or some other activity that is not closed to him by the disability.

To atone for a socially disapproved act by doing something that will be commended.

Other mechanisms of adjustment, while not leading to the original goal or a satisfactory substitute, do help the individual maintain his self-respect. He may identify with some admirable person, blame circumstances beyond his control, get attention in ways that are not socially approved, do the opposite of what he really wants to do, or try to do everything perfectly.

Still other mechanisms only make it more difficult for the individual ever to reach his original goal. He may insist on being "babied," become overdependent on someone, feign illness or physical disability, or become stubborn and rebellious.

Other ways of coping with life's problems and one's own inadequacies are not only self-defeating but socially disapproved. These include imagining oneself a great hero or the victim of tragic circumstances, rebelling against authority, becoming hostile and defiant, developing extreme fears, or exhibiting compulsive behavior. Responses like these make it increasingly difficult for the person to face reality and to achieve his goal. (For more detail on these adjustment mechanisms, see Louis P. Thorpe, *The Psychology of Mental Health,* pp. 126–150. New York: Ronald Press, 1950.)

4. *Why may it be difficult for parents to accept their child as he is?*

It is difficult for parents to accept a child who does not come up to their expectations. Sometimes they even say, in the child's presence, "I never wanted a child like that." It is natural that parents should have a feeling of defeat or humiliation when their child does not fulfill their hopes and dreams. It is difficult for them to accept him as he is and love him as he is—not as they unrealistically hope he will be some day.

5. *What are the possible dangers of giving children aspirin and other commonly used drugs?*

Almost all modern drugs have predictable "side effects." A cartoon in *Punch* depicted a patient saying to the doctor, "Drugs, side effects, more drugs, more side effects—couldn't I go back to the original cold?" Some side effects, as in the tragic case of thalidomide (see Chapter Three), are not immediately detected —sometimes not until the next generation is born.

Moreover, many of the drugs given to calm children down— the so-called "tranquilizers"—give no better results than a placebo—a pill that contains no drug. This has been demonstrated experimentally. Those that do have an effect are likely to be dangerous. Instead of dispensing drugs, doctors may more and more dispense with drugs, except for real emergencies.[27] Parents should do likewise.

6. *Why is it so important to understand a child's feelings?*

Each child has his own unique way of responding to the stresses and the opportunities in his environment. Parents need to understand what is going on in the child's mind in order to give the help, approval, or explanation that he needs. It is most important to sense how a child feels. How does he feel when Grandfather shows his preference for the older brother? How does he feel when Father takes the part of another child in a quarrel? How does he feel when Mother keeps on reading instead of listening to his discoveries? Problems of this kind are not easily solved because they often involve a complex network of family relations. However, understanding the child's feelings and helping him to deal with each enables him to build better ways of handling his feelings of jealousy or rejection.

EIGHT

Social, Moral, and Spiritual Potentialities

PARENTS want the school to contribute to their children's social and moral development as well as to their intellectual and physical development. They want their children, especially their daughters, to be popular, courteous, socially competent.

SOCIAL POTENTIALITIES

Some children have from birth a special physical attractiveness; as babies they are more appealing than others; people respond to them with smiles and approval. Similarly, some preschool children just naturally handle social situations more skillfully than others; they think of ingenious ways of resolving conflicts and solving problems in social situations. The socially gifted child is sensitive to the situation and to the feelings of the other people involved in it. He also has verbal ability, which helps him to handle social situations flexibly.

Every child has the potential ability to get along well with others. Even children who have a physical or emotional handicap or are retarded in mental development may not necessarily be handicapped in their social relationships. We all know of handicapped people whom everyone loves. Children do not have predetermined personalities. Under favorable conditions, they can develop positive attitudes toward themselves and toward others.

Although intelligence and creativity contribute to a child's social development, he acquires social skills largely through his social experiences. He learns manners and proper ways of behaving as well as consideration for others by observing the actions of the people in his home, school, and neighborhood environment. The child's social self develops through his interaction with playmates and friends.

However, it is not necessary to be with people all the time to be a socially adequate person. A feeling of belonging and of concern for others can be developed by people who spend much of their time alone, doing things that benefit others. Social interests may develop in solitude. Too many people dissipate their energies through a multiplicity of social contacts.

Nor is it necessary for a socially adequate person to occupy positions of leadership. He may exert a beneficial influence as a member of the group. Whatever the situation, he is sensitive to the needs of others and does what seems necessary to meet those needs.

In the adolescent culture of today, there is a strong urge to belong to the leading crowd or social set in the school.[1] A youngster is considered socially adjusted if he has a wide range of friends, is chosen and accepted by his peers, and participates in sports, games, or other extra-class activities. If the teen-age crowd places a high value on being pretty, having "a line" with boys, and wearing the right clothes, then the girl who is not successful in these ways is left out. Similarly, the boy who is not athletic or does not have a car has a low status in many adolescent societies. These prevalent false values are harmful to the popular as well as to the unpopular youngster. Being a football star is a poor preparation for professional and family life. And the girl who could qualify as a model or a chorus girl does not necessarily make a good secretary or a mother.

The youngsters who do not conform to group ways soon find themselves isolated. Those who are among the "outs," who are relegated to the fringe of the group because they do not meet its superficial and shoddy requirements for popularity, may react in several ways. They may retreat into the world of their own daydreams. There they can be socially successful—until faced with reality. Sometimes it is so easy for a child or an adolescent to enjoy his inner world of emotions, hopes, and fantasies that he is reluctant to face the real world. Others express their resentment and frustration in violent acts such as vandalism. Emotionally healthier youngsters recognize the superficiality of the group goals, and calmly set more mature goals for themselves. However, there are many gifted youngsters who have not resolved their conflicting desires to develop their unique potentialities, and at the same time to conform to the demands of the group.

SOCIAL DEVELOPMENT

Social growth takes place over the whole span of childhood and adolescence. The infant's egocentric outlook slowly gives way to wider interests—in most cases; some individuals never get off the self-center.

The child's social relationships move in ever-widening circles. His first contact is with his mother or mother-substitute. Soon his social circle includes his father and other members of the family. At three and four years, he prefers to play with one or two younger children. Seven-year-olds will take part in a group, but they still need careful supervision. Nine-year-olds begin to manage group activities themselves. They will express appreciation as well as criticism of other children's accomplishments. By eleven or twelve years of age, the child is capable of real friendship. A friend's well-being becomes as important as his own; he wants what is best for the other child. During adolescence, social growth takes place outside of adult control, sometimes even in opposition to it. Teenagers tend to resent it if their parents expect to have any say about their choice of friends.

There seem to be critical periods in children's social development.[2] Especially critical are the early periods of life in which the first new social relationships are initiated.[3] Young puppies separated from their mother and the other puppies in the litter for twenty hours per day showed a strong emotional attachment to the people who took care of them. Birds, too, became attached to any person or object with whom they were associated during the critical period of socialization. Although social attachment through contact and emotional arousal is more rapid at certain periods than at others, "the capacity for such an attachment is never completely lost." [4] It may take place throughout life.

The critical periods for the development of social behavior patterns depend on the individual's sensory, motor, and learning capacities. In the human infant, the process of socialization begins before mature motor patterns develop. The tendency to be "a little friend of all the world" is held in check by fear of strangers, which increases between the ages of five and twelve months.

During the preschool years social growth may take place through imaginative play. Later on, children may gain social insights through reading. Sympathy aroused for characters in a story may carry over to persons in real life. Social growth is also promoted by sharing keen interests with others. One's best friends are usually chosen on the basis of common interests.

One aspect of child development is particularly basic to social adjustment—namely, achieving the role appropriate to one's sex. Boys should be boys, and girls should be girls. As children, boys tend to be more clearly aware of their sex-appropriate behavior than are girls. Girls seem to be more flexible in this respect. At the junior high school age, both sexes value the possession of masculine traits, though boys find greater satisfaction in masculinity.

However, ultimate achievement of the appropriate sex role is usually more difficult for boys than for girls. At least, this has been so in the past. As infants, both boys and girls tend to identify with the mother because they are with her most of the time, and she meets their needs. Later, boys must shift from this feminine identification to masculine models and behavior. Most of them accomplish this shift despite a shortage of male models. Many fathers, especially in the suburbs, are away from home part of the time. Studies of father-absence suggest that it is especially important for the father of a boy to be often at home during the boy's elementary school years, when most of his teachers are women.

The boy's early identification with his mother is usually weakened by the father's desire to have an "All-American boy" and by people's unfavorable attitude toward effeminate boys or "sissies." Masculine expectations encourage boys to play boys' games and act tough. Peer preferences for boys who are good in sports have a strong influence during pre- and early adolescence. Consequently, most boys learn to assume a cultural stereotype of the masculine role. They do this not so much by imitating their fathers as by setting the masculine role as their objective and finding ways to achieve it.

Girls do not have to alter their early identification with the mother. They keep the mother as a model, and learn specific feminine ways from their close personal relation with her, and by imitating her. The girl is rewarded in subtle ways for learning feminine characteristics. The way fathers, especially southern gentlemen, treat little girls emphasizes their feminine role.

Finding the appropriate sex-role helps the child or adolescent to make a satisfactory adjustment and accomplish his learning tasks. It is usually relatively easy for boys with a high degree of masculinity to gain social acceptance. Social acceptance is associated with a low degree of anxiety. Failure to obtain social acceptance may cause some youngsters to seek substitute satisfaction from good school attendance or substitute academic achievement.

Boys typically think in different ways than girls. They tend to surpass girls in problem-solving and in deriving abstract principles, especially with reference to moral standards.[5]

SOCIAL PROBLEMS

Self-consciousness and Shyness

Some problems of social relations have their origins in personal feelings. Many youngsters are self-conscious about being shy. Instead of seeking experiences that would help them solve this problem, some children avoid situations in which they would be likely to feel shy. For example, one bright seven-year-old told her mother she had learned not to be shy about speaking in class. When asked how she had solved the problem, the child replied, "I don't raise my hand to recite any more." Other youngsters face the fact of their shyness and resolutely change their habits of responding to people.

In the following composition, fourteen-year-old Mary Ann tells how she overcame feelings of embarrassment and shyness:

"My biggest handicap was shyness. I used to be very shy when I was younger. I think I really overcome it mostly by myself. . . .

"It was embarrassing having my mother yelling at me every minute, telling me to shake hands and talk with everyone. It was embarrassing having people trying to help me overcome my shyness. It was embarrasing having people staring at me or talking about me behind my back.

"Finally I decided to do something about it myself, and before long I had overcome my shyness. I guess I owe the overcoming of my shyness to the feeling that you could change your whole life for better or for worse. For me, it was for better."

Sally also described how she overcame her self-consciousness in social situations:

"For a number of years I have lived with a feeling of self-consciousness. Perhaps this started in first grade when I first got glasses, and worried about how funny they looked. I was one of a few classmates who wore glasses. Now I notice them less and less, as more people wear them.

"Another cause of self-consciousness was the fact that my teeth aren't straight and have not yet been corrected. Unlike my feeling about glasses, I seem to notice my teeth more instead of less and less.

"With this handicap it is difficult to speak to a group or even to meet new friends. I have sometimes felt that everyone is watching me and trying to analyze my appearance and actions, picking out all the flaws. And this, of course, leads to a great deal of nervousness.

"No person has been of outstanding help to me (except possibly my sister who is nearly always encouraging and insists that no one notices my glasses or teeth). I'm beginning to realize better that everyone has his own personal defects whether in appearance or personality. It is also beginning to be clear to me that those who have a defect notice it more themselves than others do. This is helping me to overcome self-consciousness."

Problems Arising from Social and Economic Conditions

Other problems of social relations are created by socio-economic and racial differences. Each social group sets a pattern of behavior for its members. Middle-class parents tend to expect their children to go further in school than do most parents in the lower socio-economic groups. In disciplinary matters, middle-class parents tend to rely more on reasoning, and are more inclined to accept the child's impulses.

However, there are individual differences within all groups. Extremely poor parents may be concerned about their children's social education. A child from a slum area may be interested in art and music. We should be cautious about attributing to any individual the characteristics generally ascribed to his social class or ethnic group.

Migrant children have special problems of social adjustment. They do not stay long enough in any one place to have their special abilities discovered and developed. These children are of three main types: the children of service men and other able fathers whose work requires frequent change of residence; the children whose families follow the crops, staying in one place just long enough to harvest the fruit or vegetables there and then moving on; the children of shiftless, restless parents who are not able to hold jobs and keep seeking what they hope will be greener pastures.

The children of families that travel from place to place seeking seasonal agricultural work or temporary industrial jobs are often lonely. They have no permanent neighbors or friends. They may be dressed differently from the local children, and have more difficulty in keeping clean. Since they seldom stay in one school for long, they are likely to become confused by a succession of different methods of teaching and different school books. These conditions lower their achievement, their self-esteem, and their standing with other children.

Teachers can do much to make these children feel that they belong. They have had first-hand experiences that are of interest to other children. The child who has traveled can make a special contribution to the class when it is studying geography. One migrant girl was brought into the group activities by her ability to weave wicker baskets and make a campfire. Teachers sometimes ask migrant children to keep travel scrapbooks which they can show the class when they return the next year. Permanent residents of the community also have a responsibility for helping the migrant child to feel at home.

An individual's social status today depends a great deal on how far he has gone in school. Relatively few underprivileged children continue their education beyond high school—or, indeed, finish high school even when the courses are modified. Among these are many able pupils whose abilities are unlikely to be recognized. To identify these pupils and stimulate them to develop their potentialities, the Demonstration Guidance Project in New York City was initiated.[6] In this special demonstration program, 54 per cent of the 365 pupils were Negro, 26 per cent Puerto Rican, 18 per cent white, and 2 per cent Oriental. Many of these pupils were victims of broken homes, and other serious family problems, as well as poverty and harmful neighborhood influences. They lacked sustained interest in academic achievement. However, a number of the families, though poor, were sufficiently stable to motivate their children to do their school work.

The program for these pupils included the following features:

cultural enrichment, small, fairly homogeneous classes, special tutoring and instruction in reading, group guidance and counseling, and assistance in making the transition from high school to employment or further education. Clinical services were also available. The cost of this program was $250 per pupil per year beyond the usual allocation.

Work with parents was an important part of this project. The counselors and social workers described the objectives and benefits of the program and sought the parents' cooperation. They asked the parents to lighten the children's excessive home chores, provide them with privacy for study, encourage good school work, and give them more chances to participate in the discussion of family problems. In case the parents could not be reached, the counselors tried to work with other relatives. The school gave some pupils the financial assistance they needed.

Of the total number who entered the project, 108 graduated with academic diplomas; 147 with "general" diplomas; and 71 dropped out for a variety of reasons, some of which the school could have done nothing about.

As compared with past records of comparable pupils, the pupils in the demonstration project earned higher averages in their major subjects. Two and one-half times as many received academic diplomas, and a larger number obtained honors and awards for academic excellence, leadership, cooperation, and achievement in the arts. With financial help, 96, or 89 per cent, of the 108 who earned academic diplomas went on to higher education.

A few quotations will indicate how the pupils themselves appraised the program:

"It has been of great benefit to me because it gave me information on careers, improved my school work, and gave me the chance of taking up all my problems with my counselor."

"The guidance project is of priceless value to those going to college. It also helps people who are floundering and don't know what they want to do."

"The education I am getting in the project is giving me an understanding of how to take advantage of the wonderful things the world has to offer." [7]

Parents who live in wealthy suburbs or in privileged sections of cities cannot ignore the consequences that deprivation has for other children. Lacking goals and objectives, lacking opportunities to learn and earn according to their real capacities, these children become the "social dynamite" that Dr. James Conant described in his report *Slums and Surburbs*.[8] Such social dynamite may in time undermine the security of more fortunate children.

Serious Social Problems Caused by the "Sex Revolution"

"There are more than 20,000 young people between the ages of twelve and fifteen in this country who are actually married and more than a million young people who are married by the time they are nineteen. . . ." [9] This statement was made by Dr. Emily Mudd, Professor of Family Study in Psychiatry at the School of Medicine of the University of Pennsylvania in a forum on "Sex without Love and Marriage without Responsibility." Moreover, out-of-wedlock birth rates for unmarried women between the ages of fifteen and forty-four increased by 194 per cent between 1940 and 1957, while the birth rate of legitimate children was increasing by only 80 per cent.

At the same conference Dr. Sternback pointed out that:

More freedom and fewer sexual taboos have *not* been accompanied by better mental health.

The "infantile pleasure principle," which decreases the individual's tolerance of any kind of frustration, is encouraged by advertisers and by some economists as "necessary for the continuation of an affluent society."

"Youth experiment but learn nothing"—they gain no real understanding of sex, and little sense of responsibility toward marriage.

After her stand against drinking and premarital sexual indulgence on the part of students at Vassar College, President Sarah Blanding received many letters from parents who feared the demoralization of their talented daughters during the college years. Unmarried mothers whose careers had been interrupted by pregnancy and young mothers who had precipitously left college for early forced marriages described their frustrations. President Blanding urged parents and educators to prepare young people to live in our culture "built around the monogamous family unit . . . not as something that is repressive and imprisoning, but as a background for creative development and responsible freedom." She urged against accepting "self-indulgence and moral laxity, however well rationalized, as a desirable direction of change." [10]

Juvenile Delinquency

Juvenile delinquents suffer from lack of moral, social, and/or psychological roots. Newspaper and magazine accounts of juvenile delinquents often indicate a history of early failure, frustration, rebellion, and anti-social acts. Their records of delinquency may begin as early as eight years of age. However, delinquent tendencies have their origin still earlier. Social and moral development is the best preventive of delinquency.

Recognizing the special vulnerability of these children, teachers and parents can try to change conditions that contribute to delinquent tendencies.

Since delinquents lack inner strength and convictions, they are unusually susceptible to the pushes and pulls of their environment. They are ready to accept gang standards rather than those approved by society. Once they have taken a step on the road to delinquency, they are likely to persist in the same direction. There is a certain satisfaction in habitual behavior. As with neurotics and victims of mental disorder and drug addiction, the temporary relief of tension leads them to continue their self-defeating behavior.

Delinquency is also associated with absence of mental resources. Juvenile delinquents often lack knowledge that would help them to understand and handle reality. Knowledge may help a person to change conditions as well as to understand them.

Frustration is another basic factor in juvenile delinquency—frustration stemming from lack of affection and understanding in the home, or from failure in school. The delinquent does not understand the goals of the school or does not see how he can attain them.

In addition, he may find little or no satisfaction in his social life. He is not accepted by the students whom he would like to have as friends. Consequently he seeks to be accepted by the out-of-school gang. The gang meets his needs for recognition and acceptance.

If neither home, school, nor neighborhood offers proper outlets for his energies, he turns to delinquent activities. If his first offense meets with disregard or anger instead of sympathetic guidance and intelligent discipline, he may become alienated from his family and from society. He gets the feeling that no one cares; no one expects the best of him. Narcotic addiction is a desperate form of escapism that attracts the members of the gang who are unusually susceptible or who have been subjected to especially severe frustration and deprivation.

Severe Aggressive Tendencies

Other serious social problems stem from a character disorder known as sociopathic personality. Richard, at ten years of age, showed many characteristics of the sociopathic personality. He was repeating the fourth grade. Although he had been privately tutored for eighteen months, he was still not reading well enough to succeed in his grade. His comprehension was poor and he lacked word attack skills. He had begun reading instruction with a very strict teacher. According to his mother, he had built up a "mental block." His performance on the Durrell Analysis of Reading Difficulty was marked by extreme frustration. Whenever he did not know a word, he would become angry; his anger increased with each successive word failure until he would refuse to read at all. He followed this pattern at home and at school. On the Durrell test, he scored at the mid-first-grade level.

On the individual Wechsler Intelligence Scale for Children, he rated as average in intelligence. On the Mental Health Analysis, he seemed to be giving the answers that he thought were right and proper rather than expressing his true feelings. Following are several of his significant responses:

"Some brothers . . . treat me bad."
"I wish my mother would . . . stop screaming."
"Most people don't know that I . . . can't read well."

His responses on a clinical personality test, the Rorschach, showed that he felt a great deal of hostility, and considerable anxiety about his ability to control it. In taking this test, his behavior toward the clinician was hostile, uncooperative, and hyperactive, though he was extremely cooperative and well mannered while taking other tests. On his walk through the campus, he seemed suspicious and threw stones at pigeons.

He had had several serious accidents; according to neurological reports, however, they had apparently caused no brain injury.

Teachers reported that he did not respond to kindness, and that he frequently got angry and hurt the other children. He had no friends. He took no responsibility for his actions and did not profit by experience.

We observe some of these characteristics in many children. It is only in their more intense and pervasive form that they add up to a full-blown sociopathic personality.

It is impossible to know whether the reading difficulty stemmed from the sociopathic tendencies, or whether the child's whole behavior pattern was the consequence of intense frustration in learning to read. His difficulties were perhaps partly due to his failure to meet his own aspirations and the expectations of his parents and teachers.

With these characteristics, despite an unimpaired intelligence, the sociopath may be expected to be an underachiever. Since he resents authority figures such as the teacher, he does not develop the favorable pupil-teacher relation in which learning takes place. Since he does not relate to others, he does not have the learning stimulus that comes from good group interaction. His goals are immediate, whereas the goals of education are long-term. His anxiety is intense; a mild degree of anxiety is most favorable to learning. He is irresponsible; therefore the teacher marks him down for not handing in his assignments on time. He does not learn from experience; therefore he repeats his mistakes.[11] Severe aggressive tendencies must be recognized early if they are to be diverted into socially acceptable behavior that brings satisfaction to the child.

A MODERATE EMPHASIS ON SOCIAL ADJUSTMENT

Some of the problems we have mentioned may arise when parents overemphasize social adjustment and become anxious about it. In their zeal for the child's social success, they may fill his whole day with social activities and leave him no time to be alone with his thoughts. Their over-concern may also increase the child's anxiety about his social relations.

Children should, of course, become interested in each other. Finding a good, true friend is one of the keenest human joys. They should enjoy being with others and sharing experiences. They should learn the give-and-take of social relations and gradually grow in sympathetic understanding of others.

But parents may interfere with this natural, spontaneous growth in social interests and relations by pushing children prematurely into social situations—for example, the social dancing class—for which they are not ready. If this happens, the child may either build defenses against social participation or learn to act in a superficially proper way without any real feeling of warmth or kindness. This superficial compliance may forestall genuine social growth. Social participation is not a sure cure for personality problems; overemphasis on this one goal has possible dangers.[12]

MORAL DEVELOPMENT AND THE ROLE OF VALUES

Moral development involves taking personal responsibility for oneself and for one's fellow man. There is no conflict between the concepts of "every man for himself" and "unselfish service," if we think of man as a social being, naturally concerned with the welfare of others. Unless a person develops his potentialities, he cannot be of maximum service to society. ". . . God and the world cannot be better served than by each specific self pushing forward to its own perfection, sacrificing the superfluous or hindering elements in its structure, regardless of side issues and collateral considerations." [13] Conversely, unless a person has the quality of loving-kindness, his acts of generosity are mere gestures, and "profit him nothing."

The first twelve years of life lay the foundation for an individual's moral development. At first this consists largely of learning specific things to do and to avoid doing. As the child grows older, his behavior tends to be based on broader principles that make it possible for him to generalize from one situation to another. If these principles have deep roots in his personality, they are likely to control his momentary needs and desires.

Piaget's theory is that a child's moral development begins with obedience to rules superimposed by others, and progresses to acceptance of rules which he himself has a share in making.[14] This theory fits our own observation of children, and accords with children's statements about what "right" and "wrong" mean to them.

Younger children equate "right" with obedience to someone in authority; older children interpret "doing right" as being kind and considerate, and living up to rules that people have agreed on. The most mature youngsters also recognize that each individual must deal with conflicts between the good and the destructive forces or impulses within him.

Adolescents would rather develop their own criteria for judging behavior than accept parental pronouncements about what is right or wrong. Although they understand the need for regulations concerning the use of the family car, being out at night, and watching TV, they often rebel against these if they are imposed by parents. If the parents give them opportunities to think through these troublesome considerations, they will develop their own basis for setting reasonable standards.[15] Understanding the development of one's own moral values strengthens them. If we introduce a child to moral values that he recognizes as authentic, we provide him with a firm foundation or anchorage for his moral life.

Values guide much of our action. They are the steering wheels of conduct. They are "meanings perceived as related to the self." [16]

The values presented to young people today in the mass media of communication are predominantly materialistic. They suggest that life should be easy and entertaining and place little or no emphasis on duties and responsibilities. A glance at any issue of certain teen-age magazines will make clear the kind of shoddy, superficial, indulgent adult life that young people are encouraged to value.

This pleasure-seeking orientation is in marked contrast to the traditional work-success ethic which dominated the moral climate of American homes, churches, and schools during the nineteenth century. It is still further removed from the moral outlook of the Pilgrim Fathers. The modern attitude has been fostered by approving and rewarding social success more than courage, conformity more than critical thinking, mediocrity rather than excellence, and low rather than high moral values.

Fortunately, an opposing point of view is also being expressed. Many compositions written spontaneously by high school students express genuine altruism and idealism. Perhaps these adolescents have caught their basic American values from enthusiasm expressed by teachers, parents, and pastors for the best rather than the worst in human nature. Perhaps they have been inspired by volunteer projects such as the American Friends Service Committee and the Peace Corps.

Bronfenbrenner described five patterns of value systems.[17] These he tentatively designated as "self-oriented, adult-oriented, peer-oriented, collective-oriented, and objectively-principled character structures."

1. The self-oriented child gratifies his own impulses without regard to the desires or expectations of others, or to the dictates of conscience.

2. The adult-oriented child—the oversocialized "good child"— has become subservient to parental authority and accepts parental values without question.

3. The peer-oriented child conforms to group opinions and standards. This is the price he pays for acceptance by the group.

4. The collective-oriented person sets group values and goals above his individual desires and his obligations to family or friends. Competition between groups often motivates teen-agers more strongly than individual competition. They want to do their best for the sake of the group; they work for the achievement and reputation of the group. When rewards are given on a group basis, all members lose or gain from the actions of each individual.

5. The objectively-principled child is guided by the values that he has learned through his experiences in the family and in the peer groups.

Which of these patterns the child follows seems to be a matter of parental influence and cultural emphasis. The parent who always permits a child to have what he wants when he wants it is teaching him to be self-indulgent. The parent who constantly demands that the child submit to his authority and moral standards, or to those of the peer group, is teaching the child to conform at all costs. The child will place the demands of the social group above his own needs and interests if his parents do likewise. The child who lives in a family atmosphere that is both firm and affectionate, where he has many opportunities to learn from experience both in the family and in the peer group, is likely to act according to the values he has built up within himself.

Thinking, feeling, and acting are interrelated. The individual grows in wisdom by getting facts and fitting them into the mental patterns he has already formed. Feeling, or *affect* as the psychologists call it, is involved in this thinking process. "For as a man thinketh in his heart, so is he." [18] True, he learns by doing. But whether he continues to do what he is now doing depends upon the satisfaction the activity brings and the extent to which it is sensible, reasonable, and in line with his concept of the kind of person he wants to be.

GUIDANCE AND EDUCATION IN CHARACTER DEVELOPMENT

The role of the parent in a child's social development varies with the age of the child as well as with the individuality of the parent and the child. It is important that the child identify with a parent who treats people with understanding, affection, and respect. Attitudes toward people are caught. They are acquired first of all through personal relationships and experiences in family living.

A little child, unfamiliar with social standards and expectancies, often wonders whether he is doing the right thing or the wrong thing. He depends on the judgment of others. What they say or do in a new social situation helps him to select the proper responses.

The way people respond to a child's behavior may encourage him to modify a habit or to continue to behave in his accustomed way. It is often a good practice to praise a child for his correct or approved performances and ignore his mistakes. However, ignoring a child's error does not always have a neutral effect. If the child has usually been praised, he may interpret his parents' silence as disapproval. If, on the other hand, his parents have tended to criticize everything he does, he may interpret their silence as acceptance or approval of his behavior. Skillfully given, criticism lets the child know that the adult is disappointed at the moment, but still confident that the child is capable of living up to his ideal.

If it becomes habitual, any parental response to a child's behavior tends to lose some of its potency. Indiscriminate approval comes to mean less and less. Similarly, a child gets used to criticism; it goes in one ear and out the other, without affecting his behavior very much. In either case, he will pay more attention if the parent's comment is unexpected.

The parental pattern that seems to promote the best character development is one in which (a) the standards are realistic and appropriately high for the child, (b) the emphasis is on what the child does right rather than on what he does wrong, and (c) the parent seldom has to resort to force or the assertion of his authority.

Unless parents make clear by their own conduct that certain standards are more desirable than others, how can their children acquire well-conceived long-range goals? If adults are irresponsible, what image of responsibility can children be expected to form? When radio and television commercials are obviously dishonest, what other standards of honesty are presented to children and young people? When violence and murder are presented as entertainment, what sensitivity to human suffering will the viewers develop?

To bring ideals down to earth, the child or adolescent should set specific personal goals. For a preschool child, "Be strong and of a good courage" might be interpreted as trying not to cry when mother leaves the house. For a primary age child, this goal might become not making a fuss at the dentist's. For the "Big Injun" stage, it might be refusing to take dangerous dares. For an adolescent, "to be of a good courage" might mean being kind to a socially unacceptable youngster, even though the group may give him the cold shoulder for championing an isolate.

The Golden Rule, "Do unto others as you would that they would do unto you," may lead an adolescent to the discovery that concern for others makes *him* feel more self-confidence. A nine-year-old may find that asking the lonely child next door to play with him helps him overcome *his* shyness.

To be most appropriate, goals of conduct should be formulated jointly by the child and the adult. The goals of a child or adolescent may be trivial or unreal; the adult's goals may be too general or stereotyped. It takes two heads to set worthwhile goals that can be attained.

The Union College Character Research Project, 10 Nott Terrace, Schenectady 8, New York, has obtained thousands of descriptions of children's moral behavior at different ages, and has studied the positive and negative dynamic forces that produce changes both in individuals and in the family atmosphere.

To obtain specific information on the influence exerted by the father and by the mother, the children were asked, "How does daddy help you most? How does mother help?" The responses to questions showed that the mother handled discipline problems better, while the father had more influence in developing the children's philosophy of life. Each parent has his own unique role: the father should be manly, and the mother womanly. Some excellent suggestions about parental influence came from the children and young people themselves.

Much can also be learned from the "critical incident technique" —asking youngsters to write descriptions of their successful and unsuccessful experiences in carrying out certain principles. Many adolescents, and younger children too, have had the experience of standing up for what they thought was right contrary to popular opinion. Their descriptions of successful and unsuccessful attempts to do this have been helpful to other teen-agers who fear being unpopular or "different."

Parents can be their own investigators. They can apply scientific methods, with love and understanding, to the study of their own children's character development. Their observations will show whether their assumptions about the causes of children's behavior hold true for their own children. They will discover that a child's behavior never—"well, hardly ever"—has a single cause; it almost always involves a cluster of dynamic factors.

In this way parents can sometimes identify conditions that are causing certain behavior tendencies. For example, Sammy's mother wanted to know what to do about his fits of anger. She observed everything about the situations in which these outbursts occurred: What time of day did angry feelings arise? What had Sammy been doing just before the outburst? Who was present? Did he have a cold or some other illness? Had he been staying up late at night, etc.? She discovered that Sammy's temper tantrums were most frequently associated with occasions when adults were paying attention to his baby brother. Aunts and uncles smilingly played with the baby while Sammy stood by quite ignored. Thus, accurate and systematic observation can often uncover the causes of a child's behavior. Although published studies of large numbers of children are useful as a basis for comparison, they are not a substitute for sensitivity to one's own child, and to the family attitudes and pressures that have been, and still are, influencing him.

When a child leaves home to go to school, the teacher becomes an important person in his life. First grade children want to be like their kind and affectionate teacher. One six-year-old urged his mother to buy a certain kind of cereal. Eventually it came out that this was the cereal his teacher had casually mentioned having for breakfast!

The teacher's influence on children's values and behavior diminishes, but does not cease, during the later elementary school years. Although the teacher of "Big Injuns" is no longer the important person that she was to first grade children, she can influence her tribe in many ways. Her decisions must be fair, for children of this age have a strong sense of justice. Her requests must be reasonable, for these children are practical-minded; they lose confidence in adults whose suggestions do not work. Children of this age are also much more likely to accept rules that they themselves make. For example, one group disregarded the "Keep Off the Grass" sign that adults put up, but obeyed the rule made by their own student council, after they had discussed the reasons for it.

A child's school experiences may give him satisfactions and security that he cannot obtain elsewhere. On the other hand, if he experiences failure and rejection, he may become hopeless, bewildered, or anxious.

Different methods of education produce different kinds of child behavior. Emphasis on obedience and submissiveness, strict rules for conduct, a rigid schedule, and reliance on punishment rather than rewards, have generally produced submissive behavior, a low degree of spontaneity, and occasional regression. On the other hand, a warm, supporting relationship, encouragement of self-expression, reasonable permissiveness, and more emphasis on reward and approval than on punishment seem to produce diverse results that range all the way from deep affection to scorn and hostility.

One school, in which all the children, from Kindergarten up, conduct their own activities under the kindly, efficient guidance of the teacher, emphasizes cooperation and service rather than individual competition. Each child helps the others to succeed. The record of the individual child depends upon the efforts of all the members in his group. The results are reported for the group, not for individuals. The group takes charge of discipline and tutoring. Each member has some work responsibilities. This type of education apparently produces children and adolescents who are attentive and mature, and desire to learn. There is little or no juvenile delinquency. They accept discipline by their peers; they do not develop hostility toward adults, since discipline is largely in their own hands. A work-oriented program tends to encourage industry; it also provides an outlet for aggressive feelings.

As the child grows older, wider participation in group experiences contributes to his social growth. Parents can tell their teenagers about discussion groups in churches, "Y" groups, and clubs. If expertly conducted, these groups help young persons to understand and come to terms with their own feelings. In a healthy group, members recognize and accept individual differences. Conformity is not demanded at the price of personal integrity. The ideal leader is not the aggressive, driving, domineering person; but rather, the person who is skillful in releasing the creative energy of all the members of the group. When a decision is made or a task is accomplished, all the members feel that they have done it themselves.

Guiding discussions of values and standards of behavior with children and young people is both an art and a science. The leader does not want to dominate the discussion, yet he does not want the group to arrive at a decision that he knows is unsound. How does he resolve this dilemma? By (a) skillfully bringing up all sides of the question; (b) preventing a few aggressive individuals from dominating the discussion; (c) being sure that the more quiet, thoughtful pupils have a chance to express their points of view; (d) insisting that pupils present facts to support their opinions; (e) clarifying a cloudy statement that confuses most of the group; and (f) translating generalizations into concrete behavior. This—and much more—constitutes skillful leadership in discussion. The techniques of group discussion should be taught to pupil leaders; this, in itself, is a most important responsibility of teachers. The teacher who is skillful in developing pupil leaders will need to take over the leadership only occasionally to demonstrate a new discussion method or to clarify a controversial issue that is causing the group discussion to bog down.

At youth conferences, teen-agers and adult leaders have translated precepts into practice. Going beyond theoretical good intentions, they have set for themselves realistic and achievable goals. For example, the principle of service was made concrete by the boy who set as his learning goal, "helping my father more around the yard and not expecting praise or pay for it." Thus the gap is closed between knowing and doing.

Instead of dealing with our social environment blindly, we should try to obtain as much insight as possible into the reasons why people behave as they do. Children can acquire and use this knowledge without becoming prigs. Dr. Ralph Ojeman, professor at the University of Iowa, has helped pupils, teachers, and parents to understand the forces that are operating in their social environment.[19] He has developed methods and materials for teachers and pupils to use in studying the causes of aggressiveness, jealousy, and other kinds of unsocial behavior in both real and imagined situations. The children attempt to determine why children do certain things, and how parents and teachers should respond. They learn the difference between the judgmental and the causal approach—between passing judgment on a person and trying to understand him.

Education in social understanding should begin in the kindergarten. If children learn the causal approach early, they will not have so much re-learning to do. All during their school years pupils can be learning this way of responding to people. In their social studies, history, or literature classes, they can investigate why certain characters or historic persons acted as they did, why people commit crimes, what underlying forces in human nature lead to wars, why so many people are miserable. They can discuss social situations that arise on the playground, in the classroom, and in the home. Why did the teacher, parent, or child do what he did? Handling situations in this way minimizes conflicts among children, and between children and adults.

In some groups the members not only discuss situations of anxiety or conflict, but also have the opportunity to act them out spontaneously by means of role-playing or sociodrama. For example, one school group presented a convincing scene in which a teen-age girl comes home from a party at two o'clock in the morning and is confronted by her anxious parents. The youngsters who play the parents in such scenes have to view the situation from the parents' point of view and feel with them.

In another session the group read and discussed advertisements in which the love-sex theme was used to sell products. They noted how glamorously the loving couples were portrayed, and then contrasted them with the real people they knew. After discarding the unrealistic stereotypes, they tried to find challenge and "plus values" in their real world.

However, we must remember that a pupil does not develop character or good conduct in any one special course, group activity, or counseling session. Life experiences mold character. A child may develop tenacity of purpose in building a house of blocks or in solving a difficult arithmetic problem. An adolescent may learn to cooperate with others in planning a school dance or making a group report in history. The teacher's guidance in any daily activity—in the classroom or outside it—may help the pupil to think and feel and act in socially desirable ways.

METHODS AND MEANING OF DISCIPLINE

Young children are naturally impulsive. They do whatever gives them pleasure and satisfaction. How do they learn to control their behavior out of consideration for others?

The child who receives affection in the very early years and is allowed reasonable freedom to respond to his impulses is not likely to develop pent-up hostility. Since his own emotional needs are being satisfied, he is more likely to be sensitive to the needs of others; he is less likely to use others for his own purposes. His good feelings toward his parents tend to spread to other people. His parents' affectionate attitude toward him serves as a model for his own behavior.

The methods of discipline to which the child is subjected also affects his ability to control his impulses. Simple explanations of the consequences of certain acts make the child conscious of the disadvantages of uncontrolled behavior. Some comments may relate to the consequences of the act for the child himself: "You'll slip and fall if you walk where it is muddy." "If you run so fast, you may drop the vase and break it; then we'll have to pay for it." "If you don't wash your face before going to bed, you'll get the nice clean sheets dirty."

Another kind of comment points out the possible effect an act may have on other people: "If you make a slide on the sidewalk, someone may slip on it and hurt himself." "If you don't speak to the new boy, he may think you don't like him." "When you call Tommy 'Midget,' you hurt his feelings because he's sensitive about being so little."

Similar comments call the child's attention to other people's needs and feelings: "If Daddy can sleep a little while longer, he will feel better. Try to be quiet." "You can help mother by hanging up your clothes and putting your toys away. She's often very tired." "Be sure to tell Mrs. Smith you enjoyed her dinner. That would please her."

Inviting a child to consider the possible motivations for another person's act is also an important way of helping him control his behavior out of consideration for others. "Don't hit him; he didn't mean to knock over your blocks." "He didn't have any breakfast. Why don't you give him one of your sandwiches and a cookie?" "If you knew what a hard time Betty has to keep clean, you wouldn't mind her dirty clothes."

This kind of "other-oriented discipline" helps the child to understand his parents' values and other people's needs. Since it also makes the parents' discipline seem less arbitrary to the child, it is less likely to arouse his hostility. Moreover, considering the social effects of his behavior may enhance the child's natural capacity to experience the feelings of others. The approval he gets from others for his considerate behavior will further reinforce his habit of acting considerately. If the child habitually acts in accord with the values and standards exemplified by the parents, then parental discipline tends to become increasingly unnecessary as the child grows older. Other-oriented discipline leads to self-motivated consideration of others.

On the other hand, as Hoffman also pointed out, some mothers use "love-withholding discipline"; they withhold love or threaten to withhold it.[20] "I don't like you when you interrupt me when I'm talking to someone." "If you do that any more, Mommy will leave you all by yourself." "If you don't get ready for bed right away, you'll not get your goodnight kiss." Under this method they may express strong disapproval of the child or his behavior: "You ought to be ashamed to hit your little brother." "You are acting just like a baby, not like a boy your age." "Good children don't do things like that." This type of discipline, while it stops certain kinds of behavior and checks hostile impulses, tends to arouse the child's anxiety and to make him dependent on adults for approval.

The child's response to any specific disciplinary technique is influenced by the over-all disciplinary atmosphere in the home, which in turn is influenced by the frequency with which the parent asserts power over the child. The less dominating the parent, the more effective the other-oriented type of discipline is likely to be. Some children of low ability seem to respond to this type of discipline better than do some who have higher ability. Although both types of discipline "get results," the other-oriented discipline is superior from the standpoint of the development of the child's capacity for empathy and active consideration for others.[21]

Discipline is a complicated business. What appears to be the same punishment may not always evoke the same response on the part of the child. In some instances, it may deter him from the forbidden act, but, at the same time, make the act seem more attractive. If, after the child has been punished, parent and child review the whole situation together, the child may come to understand it as the parent understood it. If an activity can be made to appear inherently painful or destructive or wrong, the child is likely to avoid it.

It also makes a difference who does the scolding—Mother or Teacher. Moreover, Mother's scolding is different when she is angry than when she feels sad about the child's behavior. Punishment that carries with it the feeling of personal rejection is different from an exchange of blows by two boys on the playground. The effect of punishment depends a great deal on the relationship between the child and the person who punishes him.

Most of all, the effect of a punishment depends on what the punishment means to the child. It may make him fearful of doing the same thing again. Or it may merely inconvenience or annoy him. The child may perceive a punishment as an expression of personal dislike. Or he may perceive it as a kind parent's attempt to help him do what he knows is right and what he really wants to do. As one boy said, "I'd rather have my parents punish me than not care for me." In some cases, it may be punishment enough if the parent remains silent and does nothing; the child may interpret this as disapproval. In this event, silence may be more effective than scolding or physical punishment in changing a child's behavior.

Under severe and repeated punishment, the child may refuse to respond in any way. We sometimes see this happening when parents put constant psychological pressure on children to make them achieve. These children often unconsciously refuse to try. They have been called "self-sabotagers." They defeat themselves in order to punish their parents. A few older children are stoics; they refuse to be either deterred or moved by pain. To preserve their self-esteem, they "rise above" the influence of either reward or punishment.

COMMUNITY AGENCIES

By far the most important agencies in helping children develop their social, moral, and spiritual potentialities are the home and the school. Both of these institutions have contact with all the children from their early years. In the many ways already suggested in this book, parents and teachers can help boys and girls acquire the knowledge and skills that will give them a sense of competence. They can minimize frustrations by providing suitable tasks. They can help children to tolerate the inevitable frustrations of life and early learn to accept delayed satisfactions. Adults can encourage young people to join groups that have a constructive influence. Many an adolescent has stayed in school despite considerable academic difficulty because he found a friend, or obtained membership in a group in which he experienced acceptance and success.

Children who have been fortunate in their heredity, home conditions, and early childhood experiences have a very real responsibility for the less fortunate. These lucky youngsters are "their brothers' keepers." Able, popular students can set the standards in a school and determine its tone. Their parents, too, to the degree that they are kind and helpful to all children, protect their own children from the delinquent tendencies that are invading the best of our residential communities. Preventive services for delinquents benefit the whole neighborhood.

The role of the school is:

to gain an understanding of all the pupils year after year during their period of growth.

to teach with maximum effectiveness the basic skills of learning.

to prepare young people for the duties of citizenship.

to develop their values and standards.

to supply incentives to right conduct.

to train them for useful work and stimulate them to seek it.

to coordinate other agencies.

The long-established youth groups—Scouts, Camp Fire Girls, Future Farmers of America, Y-teens, and many others have a beneficial influence. They supplement the work of the schools by providing students with opportunities to develop ideals and standards, to experience wholesome leisure-time activities, and to be of service to others.

Industry, too, is meeting its important responsibilities to be concerned about the emotional health of its employees as well as about their technical competence. Incidentally, industry is now offering as many courses and other educational opportunities as are the public schools.

Psychiatric clinics such as The Menninger Foundation apply "milieu therapy" and consider teaching a part of their clinical service. Hospitals such as Jefferson Hospital, Philadelphia, have become concerned about the learning difficulties as well as the social problems of children who are referred for defects in hearing, sight, and other physical functions. These children are studied intensively by the medical students in their six weeks of pediatric training. The hospital staff contacts the schools that referred them, and interviews teachers, counselors, principals, reading teachers, and other specialists.

Local communities have formed coordinating councils for the prevention of juvenile delinquency. These offer parents opportunities to contribute to the solution of the problem. The Niagara Falls Council, headed by three school principals, includes religious leaders, representatives of parent education groups, members of citizens' committees, Board of Education representatives, city directors of public safety and of recreation, the executive secretaries of the Council of Social Agencies and the local boys' clubs, school directors of physical education and of research and guidance, and interested citizens.[22] This council meets once a month with various authorities on delinquency. One of the most interesting and informative meetings was a panel discussion in which teenagers expressed their frank opinions. They were hard on themselves, their parents, and the school curriculum and guidance program. In another enlightening session, a former teen-age inmate of the State Industrial and Agricultural School for Boys described the experiences that led to his commitment to this special school.

Newspapers should feature the socially useful activities of the 95 per cent of teen-agers who are not delinquent, and enlist the cooperation of representative youngsters—potential delinquents, popular boys and girls, and Honor students—in the formation of a council to be focused not on juvenile delinquency, but on developing the potentialities of every child and adolescent in the community.

SPIRITUAL DEVELOPMENT

There is a spiritual element in most of our social and moral behavior. The Old Testament sums it up this way: "What doth the Lord require of thee but to do justly, and to love mercy, and to walk humbly with thy God?" [23] Saint Paul regarded things of the spirit as basic. He put loving-kindness above all other virtues—a loving-kindness that encompasses patience, capacity for suffering, tolerance, a positive approach to life and to people, faith, and hope. Albert Schweitzer places central importance on reverence for life. The disrespect for human beings that we see reflected in the work of some modern playwrights—is it not in part the result of a philosophy that respects neither God nor His creation? Without a spiritual orientation to life, a person is likely to be conscienceless and unconcerned about his fellows.

Moral values are strengthened by religious beliefs as well as by experience and reason. For many people, religion is a powerful ally in the personal struggle against destructive tendencies. Progress in the things of the spirit should promote moral development. The ideal morality might be described as self-realization without detriment to the best development of other people; concern with justice for all, tempered by compassion; and individual action influenced by spiritual forces that are invisible but real in that they produce real results.

"Children are instinctively religious. They believe and trust." [24] They can acquire a sense of reverence early in life. The wonder of the world is very real to the little child. "We can but watch and wonder" was the refrain that a group of pre-school children wrote to their song. In the verses they described the stars, the spring leaves, and other natural things that had aroused their awe and wonder. Many people have had feelings of reverence as they walked out under the brilliant stars, looked up at a bright blue sky set off by autumn leaves, observed a bird singing and swaying on the topmost bough of a tree, or watched the soft new-fallen snow transforming dingy streets and silencing the city's incessant noise.

The church develops the child's spiritual potentialities by a variety of means: the music, the stained glass windows, the mysterious words which open doors to the unknown and the unknowable, the reverent attitude of people worshipping together. These are the quiet, uplifting experiences.

Cultivation of the spirit requires time and silence as well as inspiration. Children today are confused by noise, bewildered by persuasive voices making conflicting claims. Many have become blasé and unreceptive to spiritual influences. They are subtly and invisibly conditioned by the alien thoughts and feelings that are constantly presented to them. There is no time for children and parents to read the Bible and other great books together as in bygone days; no time to think on things of the spirit.

To become acquainted with themselves, children need leisurely, pressure-free hours. When nothing is scheduled for them to do, they are thrown on their own resources. They begin to think about themselves and their destiny. Unless they are emotionally disturbed, their daydreams are likely to be constructive, especially if they have resources of the mind and spirit on which to draw: quotations from great literature, Bible verses, the words of a hymn, an idea from a sermon or a youth leader's talk. The child who is undisturbed by the demands of adults or by the tyranny of television has a chance to develop his spiritual potentialities even in a materialistic culture.

A SUMMING UP

The following quotation from John W. Gardner's *Self-Renewal: The Individual and the Innovative Society* sums up with exceptional clarity, precision, and conviction the theme of this book:

"No one knows why some individuals seem capable of self-renewal while others do not. But we have some important clues to what the self-renewing man is like, and what we might do to foster renewal.

"For the self-renewing man the development of his own potentialities and the process of self-discovery never end. It is a sad but unarguable fact that most human beings go through their lives only partially aware of the full range of their abilities. As a boy in California I spent a good deal of time in the Mother Lode country, and like every boy of my age I listened raptly to the tales told by the old-time prospectors in that area, some of them veterans of the Klondike gold rush. Every one of them had at least one good campfire story of a lost gold mine. The details varied: the original discoverer had died in the mine, or had gone crazy, or had been killed in a shooting scrape, or had just walked off thinking the mine worthless. But the central theme was constant: riches left untapped. I have come to believe that those tales offer a paradigm of education as most of us experience it. The mine is worked for a little while and then abandoned.

"The development of abilities is at least in part a dialogue between the individual and his environment. If he has it to give and the environment demands it, the ability will develop. Any small boy with real ability to wield his fists is likely to discover that ability fairly early. The little girl with the gift for charming grown-ups will have no trouble discovering that talent. But most abilities are not so readily evoked by the common circumstances of life. The 'mute, inglorious Miltons' are more numerous than one might suppose, particularly in an age in which even an articulate Milton might go unnoticed, certainly unrewarded. Most of us have potentialities that have never been developed simply because the circumstances of our lives never called them forth.

"Exploration of the full range of his own potentialities is not something that the self-renewing man leaves to the chances of life. It is something he pursues systematically, or at least avidly, to the end of his days. He looks forward to an endless and unpredictable dialogue between his potentialities and the claims of life—not only the claims he encounters, but the claims he invents. And by potentialities I mean not just skills, but the full range of his capacities for sensing, wondering, learning, understanding, loving and aspiring.

"The ultimate goal of the educational system is to shift to the individual the burden of pursuing his own education. This will not be a widely shared pursuit until we get over our odd conviction that education is what goes on in school buildings and nowhere else. Not only does education continue when schooling ends, but it is not confined to what may be studied in adult education courses. The world is an incomparable classroom, and life is a memorable teacher for those who aren't afraid of her." [25]

If this goal is achieved, your child will never have to say, in the words of Tagore: "The song I came to sing remains unsung."

QUESTIONS AND ANSWERS

1. *What price popularity?*

By pushing children and adolescents into a ceaseless round of activities, are we not depriving them of something very precious—time to think their own thoughts? Dr. Beulah Ephron Wray, in her work as psychotherapist, frequently observed problems caused by this parental practice. In her words:

Parents and teachers seem bent on *keeping children busy*, without recognizing the need for quiet times when the child seems to be doing nothing at all. Any number of adolescents have been brought to me by parents alarmed by a camp or school report that their child "was not as interested in group activities as in projects carried on alone." Was the child being creative and happy in his solitary pursuits? No one had thought to ask; no one had troubled to make the distinction between the fantasy of discontent and the imaginative activity that is essentially social rather than escape from society.

Permitting children to "do nothing" requires a relative absence of anxiety in the adults. It means good relationship between children and their teachers and parents, a relationship of loving proximity without compulsion to direct and teach and interfere. Adults must themselves be strong and trusting, and thus able to give love instead of fearful vigilance.[26]

2. Why do some neglected children develop a strong affection for cruel and abusive parents?

Babies are likely to become attached to any individual or object with which they have been in contact long enough. This fact helps to explain why some neglected children develop so strong an affection for cruel and abusive parents that they want to return to them even if this means leaving a much more favorable environment. This is why social workers consider so carefully any decision to separate a child from his parents and place him in a foster home or institution.

3. How is lack of reading ability related to juvenile delinquency?

For the most part, people gain knowledge by listening and reading. Many or most juvenile delinquents have never learned to enjoy reading. They have not started on the path to life-time learning. Skill in reading leads to knowledge and competency in gaining knowledge. As the individual develops this competency, his self-esteem increases.

4. What conditions give rise to gangs and other self-organized youth groups?

Gangs and other self-organized youth groups are most likely to develop in societies in which parental standards conflict with prevalent adolescent values. When the parental values are in conflict with those of the peer group, adolescents from twelve to eighteen years of age tend to side with the peer group.

5. What are some of the conditions that contribute to a child's sense of security?

Even in spite of the ever-present threat of nuclear war, emotional security can be built day by day through the personal relationships that adults maintain with children, and the responses that they make to children. Dr. Eugene C. McDanald, Jr., psychiatrist and Director of Training for Psychiatric Residents at the Medical Branch, the University of Texas, used the 13th Chapter of I Corinthians as a framework for suggesting specific ways in which mature security can be achieved.[27] He described the following responses that children want from adults:

Listen; don't talk down to children; don't use ridicule; don't talk too much.

Be humble; do not pretend to know everything; be able to laugh at yourself.

Be willing to help—give "information, stimulation, and inspiration"; be considerate.

Do not play favorites, fuss, or make unreasonable demands; be unselfish, not easily provoked, good humored.

Look for the best in people.

Be aware of a higher power that transcends human efforts.

APPENDIX

Pamphlets of Interest to Parents
Published by Different Organizations

Association for Childhood Education International. 3615 Wisconsin Avenue, N.W., Washington 16, D.C. Publish a large number of pamphlets on all aspects of the development of children two to twelve. The titles include: *All Children Have Gifts; Children's Views of Themselves; Creative Dramatics; Discipline; Play—Children's Business;* and several pamphlets on books and reading. Most of these pamphlets cost 75¢.

Child Study Association of America, Inc., 9 East 89th Street, New York 28. A series of practical pamphlets to help parents in fostering the healthy development of children from birth through adolescence. Among the titles are: *What Makes a Good Home? Behavior: the Unspoken Language of Children; The One-Parent Family; The Controversial Problems of Discipline.*

Educational Policies Commission, 1201 Sixteenth St., N. W., Washington, D. C.
A variety of pamphlets that have a bearing on the development of children's potentialities.

Occupational Outlook Quarterly, United States Department of Labor, Bureau of Labor Statistics, Superintendent of Documents, U.S. Government Printing Office, Washington 25, D.C. 20402. Subscription price per year $1.00.

Science Research Associates, 259 East Erie St., Chicago 11, Illinois. Pamphlets on many aspects of child and adolescent development, such as *Emotional Problems of Growing Up,* directed to parents as well as to teachers and counselors.

U.S. Department of Health, Education, and Welfare, Office of Education, U.S. Government Printing Office, Division of Public Documents, Washington 25, D.C. A large number of specialized pamphlets, technical and practical. Among the titles are *Blind Children; Degree of Vision; Mode of Reading; Education of the Severely Retarded Child;* and the familiar bulletins on child care.

References

Chapter One

1 Gregory, John. *A Father's Legacy to His Daughter,* 1775.
2 Rosten, Leo. "The Real Reason for Being Alive," *This Week Magazine* (January 20, 1963), p. 2. Reprinted from *This Week Magazine.* Copyrighted 1963 by the United Newspapers Magazine Corporation.
3 Jones, Howard Mumford. Unpublished speech, Honors Convocation, University of Arizona, Tucson, 1961.
4 Ashton-Warner, Sylvia. *Teacher,* p. 105. New York: Simon and Schuster, 1963.
5 Longan, Robert Coleman (Jr.). "The Social Group," in *The Emotional Climate of the Exceptional Child,* Proceedings of the Spring Conference on Education and the Exceptional Child, Child Research Clinic of the Woods Schools, Langhorne, Pennsylvania, May 1949.
6 Perkins, Hugh V. "Teachers' and Peers' Perceptions of Children's Self-concepts," *Child Development,* Vol. 29: (June 1958), pp. 203–226.
7 Allport, Gordon W. *Becoming.* New Haven: Yale University Press, 1955.
8 Allport, Gordon W. "Psychological Models for Guidance," *Harvard Educational Review,* Vol. 32: (Fall 1962), pp. 373–381.
9 *Ibid.,* p. 379.
10 Cowie, Alexander. *The New York Times Book Review* (September 1, 1963), p. 1.
11 Harris, Dale B. "The Development of Potentiality," *Teachers College Record,* Vol. 61: (May 1960), pp. 423–434.
12 Lecky, P. *Self-consistency: A Theory of Personality.* New York: Island Press, 1945.
13 Gardner, John W. *Self-Renewal: The Individual and the Innovative Society.* New York: Harper and Row, 1964.
14 Strang, Ruth. *The Adolescent Views Himself.* New York: McGraw-Hill, 1957.
15 Cohn, Benjamin, and A. Mead Sniffen. "A School Report on Group Counseling," *The Personnel and Guidance Journal,* Vol. 41: (October 1962), p. 136.

[16] Langdon, Grace, and Irving W. Stout. "Quality in Nursery Schools," *PTA Magazine*, Vol. 57: (January 1963), pp. 18–20.

[17] Barclay, Dorothy. "The Battle of the Ages," *The New York Times Magazine* (February 11, 1962), pp. 59–60.

Chapter Two

[1] Doll, Edgar. In Doris D. Klaussen, "The Physically Different," *Childhood Education*, Vol. 32: (January 1956), p. 211. Reprinted by permission of the Association for Childhood Education International, 3615 Wisconsin Avenue, N.W., Washington, D.C.

[2] Graham, Ray. "Handicapped and Normal Children Are More Alike than Different," *NEA Journal*, Vol. 50: (November 1961), pp. 48–50.

[3] Kanner, Leo. "The Emotional Quandaries of Exceptional Children," in *Helping Parents Understand the Exceptional Child*, p. 23. Proceedings of the Annual Spring Conference on Education and the Exceptional Child, Child Research Clinic of the Woods Schools, Langhorne, Pennsylvania, May 1952.

[4] *Ibid.*, p. 24.

[5] *Ibid.*, pp. 25–28.

[6] Hill, Arthur S. "The Schools Can Help Them," in *Helping Parents Understand the Exceptional Child*, p. 31, Proceedings of the Annual Spring Conference on Education and the Exceptional Child, Child Research Clinic of the Woods Schools, Langhorne, Pennsylvania, May 1952.

[7] Johnson, G. Orville. "Special Education for the Mentally Handicapped —A Paradox," *Exceptional Children*, Vol. 29: (October 1962), pp. 62–69.

[8] Children's Hospital Medical Center, and Child Study Association of America. *Helping Parents of Handicapped Children: Group Approaches*, p. 18. Proceedings of Conference held in Boston, Mass., October 15–16, 1959. New York 28: The Child Study Association of America, 1959.

[9] *Ibid.*, p. 20.

Chapter Three

[1] Craig, Marjorie L. and Frances U. Everett. "Developing Health Potentialities," *Teachers College Record*, Vol. 61: (May 1960), pp. 430–431.

[2] Krogman, Wilton M. "How Your Children Grow," *Saturday Evening Post*, Vol. 235: (July 14–21, 1962), p. 50.

242

242   APPENDIX

3 Hoyman, Howard S. "Our Modern Concept of Health," *Journal of School Health,* Vol. 32: (September 1962), pp. 253–264.

4 Hunsicker, Paul A. *AAHPER YOUTH Fitness Test Manual.* Washington, D.C.: American Association for Health, Physical Education, and Recreation, a Department of the National Education Association, 1961.

5 Metropolitan Life Insurance Company. "Health of the School-age Population," *Statistical Bulletin,* Vol. 42: (August 1961), pp. 1–3.

6 Berryman, George H. "Teen-age Growth and Diet," *GP* American Academy of General Practice, Kansas City, Vol. 25: (March 1962), pp. 98–101.

7 Horn, Daniel, and others. "Cigarette Smoking among High School Students," *American Journal of Public Health,* Vol. 42: (November 1959), pp. 1497–1511.

8 Sallak, V. J. "A Study of Smoking Practices of Selected Groups of Junior and Senior High School Students in Public Schools in Erie County, N.Y. (exclusive of the City of Buffalo)," *Journal of School Health,* Vol. 31: (November 1961), p. 307.

9 Hechinger, Fred M. and Grace Hechinger. "The Teen-age Problem: A Prime Example," *The New York Times Magazine* (September 30, 1962), pp. 15, 73–76.

10 Sullivan, Harry Stack. *The Interpersonal Theory of Psychiatry.* New York: Norton, 1953, pp. 273–274.

11 Baumgarten, Leona. "What Parents Must Know about Teen-agers and VD.", *McCall's,* Vol. 90: (January, 1963), p. 44.

12 Bauer, Frances. "The 'Junior Rat Race,' " *The New York Times Magazine* (December 2, 1962), p. 137.

13 Schoelly, M. L. and A. Fraser. "Emotional Reactions in Muscular Dystrophy," *American Journal of Physical Medicine,* Vol. 34: (February 1955), pp. 119–123.

14 Spencer, Stephen M. "The Untold Story of the Thalidomide Babies," *The Saturday Evening Post,* Vol. 235: (October 20, 1962), pp. 19–27.

15 Metropolitan Life Insurance Company, Health and Welfare Division, School Health Bureau. *Accident Prevention Can Be Learned.* New York: The Company, 1962, 38 pp.

16 Wheatley, George M. and Stephen A. Richardson. "Some Approaches to Research in Childhood Accidents," *Pediatrics,* Vol. 25: (February 1960), pp. 343–347.

17 Rusalem, Herbert. "The Physically Handicapped Student and the College Faculty," *College and University,* Vol. 37: (Winter 1962), pp. 161–167.

[18] Shontz, Franklin C. "Somatic-Psychological Interaction in Physical and Mental Health," *Review of Educational Research*, Vol. 32: (December 1962), p. 535.

[19] Cowen, Emory L. and others. *Adjustment to Visual Disability in Adolescence*. New York: American Foundation for the Blind, 1961.

[20] Carter, Burnham. "The Talented Blind," *Saturday Review*, Vol. 45: (August 18, 1962), pp. 53–54.

[21] Massow, Rosalind. "Because of One Woman," *Parade* (January 20, 1963), pp. 7–8.

[22] Brecher, Ruth and Edward Brecher. "Epilepsy," *Family Circle*, Vol. 63: (July 1963), pp. 54–55.

[23] Baker, A. B., Chairman. *Exploring the Brain of Man*. Minneapolis 14: National Committee for Research in Neurological Disorders, The Medical School, University of Minnesota (n.d.).

Chapter Four

[1] Thurstone, Thelma Gwinn. "What Is Intelligence?" in *A Briefing for Parents: Your Child's Intelligence*. Washington, D.C.: National Education Association (n.d.).

[2] Vernon, Philip E. *The Structure of Human Abilities*, pp. 23–36, 25–36. New York: John Wiley and Sons, Inc., 1951.

[3] Strang, Ruth. "Intellectual Differences," *Childhood Education*, Vol. 32: (January 1956), pp. 211–214; and Murphy, Lois B. "Emotional First Aid." *Childhood Education*, Vol. 32: (January 1956), pp. 205–207. Reprinted by permission of the Association for Childhood Education International, 3615 Wisconsin Avenue, N.W., Washington, D.C.

[4] Harris, Dale. "The Development of Potentiality," *Teachers College Record*, Vol. 61: (May 1960), pp. 423–434.

[5] Moriarity, Alice. "Children's Ways of Coping with the Intelligence Test," *Bulletin of the Menninger Clinic*, Vol. 24: (May 1960), pp. 115–127.

[6] *Ibid.*, p. 126.

[7] Bing, Elizabeth. "Effect of Child-rearing Practices on Development of Differential Cognitive Abilities," *Child Development*, Vol. 34: (September 1963), pp. 631–648.

[8] Moor, Paul. "The Former Prodigy Is Still Prodigious," *The New York Times Magazine* (September 30, 1962), p. 50.

[9] *Ibid.*, p. 52.

[10] *Ibid.*, p. 57.

[11] Kough, Jack and Robert F. DeHaan. *Teachers Guidance Handbook,* Part I, Identifying Children with Special Needs, pp. 76, 82, 88. Chicago: Science Research Associates, 1955.

[12] *Ibid.,* p. 76.

[13] *Ibid.,* p. 82.

[14] Hinds, Gloria Jean. "Adolescents Gifted in the Performing Arts: A Study of Self Reports." Unpublished Doctoral Project, Teachers College, Columbia University, 1963.

[15] *Ibid.,* p. 100.

[16] *Ibid.,* pp. 102–103.

[17] *Ibid.,* p. 96.

[18] Strang, Ruth. "Creative Child," *National Parent Teacher,* Vol. 54: (February 1960), pp. 14–16.

[19] Mead, Margaret. *A Creative Life for Your Children,* Headliner Series Number 1. Washington 25, D.C.: U.S. Government Printing Office, 1962.

[20] Torrance, E. Paul. "Cultural Discontinuities and the Development of Originality of Thinking," *Exceptional Children,* Vol. 29: (September 1962), pp. 2–13.

[21] *Ibid.,* p. 8.

[22] For a much more detailed treatment of this topic, see Ruth Strang, *Helping Your Gifted Child,* New York: E. P. Dutton & Company, Inc., 1960.

[23] Witty, Paul. "The Nature and Needs of Gifted and Superior Adolescents," in *Programs for the Gifted; a Case Book in Secondary Education,* Fifteenth Yearbook of the John Dewey Society, p. 36. New York: Harper and Brothers, 1961.

[24] Terman, Lewis M. and others. *Genetic Studies of Genius, Vol. I: Mental and Physical Traits of a Thousand Gifted Children.* Stanford, California: Stanford University Press, 1925.

[25] Bailard, Virginia and Ruth Strang. *Parent-Teacher Conferences,* Chapter 10. New York: McGraw-Hill Book Company, Inc., 1964.

[26] Strang, Ruth. "Intellectual Differences," *Childhood Education,* Vol. 32: (January 1956), p. 214. Reprinted by permission of the Association for Childhood Education International, 3615 Wisconsin Avenue, N.W., Washington, D.C.

[27] No author. "On Telling Parents about Test Results," *Test Service Bulletin,* No. 54. New York: Psychological Corporation (December 1959), p. 3.

[28] Vernon, Philip E. "Practice and Coaching Effects in Intelligence Tests," *The Educational Forum,* Vol. 18 (March 1954), pp. 278–280.

Chapter Five

1 A percentile is a point on a scale of scores ranging from 0 to 100. If a child scores at the 90 percentile, it means that only 10 per cent of the many pupils who have taken the test scored higher than he; 90 per cent scored lower.

2 Krugman, Morris. "Identification and Preservation of Talent," *Teachers College Record*, Vol. 61: (May 1960), pp. 459–463.

3 Walton, George. "Uncle Sam's Rejects," *Saturday Evening Post*, Vol. 235: (December 8, 1962), p. 10.

4 Barclay, Dorothy. "Following Directions Can Be Fun," *The New York Times Magazine* (March 11, 1962), pp. 95–96.

5 Carlsmith, Lyn. "Effect of Early Father Absence on Scholastic Aptitude," *Harvard Educational Review*, Vol. 34: (Winter 1964), pp. 3–21.

6 Scott, J. P. "Critical Periods in Behavioral Development," *Science*, Vol. 138: (November 1962), pp. 949–958.

7 McGraw, Myrtle B. *Growth: A Study of Johnny and Jimmy*. New York: Appleton-Century, 1935.

8 Scott, *op. cit.*, p. 957.

9 Dale, Edgar. "Learning to Learn," *The News Letter*, Vol. 28: (May 1963), p. 4

10 Riessman, Frank. *The Culturally Deprived Child*. New York: Harper and Brothers, 1962.

11 France, Anatole. *The Crime of Sylvestre Bonnard*, p. 198. New York: Dodd-Mead and Company, 1918.

12 Repplier, Agnes. *Eight Decades*, "The Masterful Puritan," p. 88. Boston: Houghton Mifflin Company, 1937.

13 Greer, Edith S. and Richard M. Harbeck. *What High School Pupils Study*, pp. 25–36. Washington, D.C.: U.S. Government Printing Office, 1962.

14 Pressey, Sidney Leavitt. "Concerning the Nature and Nurture of Genius," *Scientific Monthly*, Vol. 81: (September 1955), pp. 123–139.

15 Coleman, James S. "Teen-agers and Their Crowd," *The PTA Magazine*, Vol. 56: (March 1962), pp. 4–7.

16 *Ibid.*, p. 5.

17 Strodtbeck, Fred L. "Family Interaction, Values, and Achievement," in *Talent and Society*, edited by David C. McClelland, Alfred L. Baldwin, Urie Bronfenbrenner, and Fred L. Strodtbeck, pp. 135–191. New York: Van Nostrand Company, 1958.

18 Warburton, Amber Arthun. *Stimulating Guidance in Rural Secondary*

Schools; Influence of the National Defense Education Act. Title VA on Guidance in Rural Schools, p. 25. Washington, D.C. 20009: American Personnel and Guidance Association, 1964.

[19] Barclay, Dorothy. "Meeting the Test of Testing," *The New York Times Magazine* (January 7, 1962), p. 56.

[20] *Ibid.,* p. 56.

[21] Davids, Anthony and Jack Sidman. "A Pilot Study—Impulsivity, Time Orientation and Delayed Gratification in Future Scientists and in Understanding High School Students, *Exceptional Children,* Vol. 29: (December 1962), pp. 170–174.

[22] Torrance, E. Paul. "Who Is the Underachiever?" *The NEA Journal,* Vol. 51: (November 1962), pp. 15–17.

[23] *Ibid.*

[24] Strang, Ruth. *Helping Your Child Improve His Reading.* New York: E. P. Dutton and Company, Inc., 1962.

[25] Spache, George D. "Estimating Reading Capacity," *Evaluation of Reading.* Conference on Reading, 1958, compiled and edited by Helen M. Robinson, V.20 Supplementary Educational Monographs No. 88. Chicago: University of Chicago Press, 1958. 208 pp.

[26] Dolch Word Games. Champaign, Illinois: Garrard Press.

[27] Vernon, M. D. *Backwardness in Reading, A Study of Its Nature and Origin,* pp. 186–197. London: Cambridge University Press, 1957.

[28] Strang, Ruth, Ethlyne Phelps, and Dorothy Withrow. *Gateways to Readable Books* (Third Edition). New York: The H. W. Wilson Company, 1958.

[29] Ashton-Warner, Sylvia. *Teacher,* pp. 27–62. New York: Simon and Schuster, 1963.

[30] Penty, Ruth C. *Reading Ability and High School Drop-outs,* pp. 43–50. New York: Bureau of Publications, Teachers College, Columbia University, 1956.

[31] Unpublished record by the author.

[32] Krugman, *op. cit.,* pp. 459–463.

[33] Evans, Richard L. "The Time That Is Yet Thine . . . ," *May Peace Be with You,* pp. 87–88. New York: Harper and Brothers, 1961.

[34] Hollister, William G. "Homes That Nurture Intellect," *The PTA Magazine,* Vol. 58: (May 1963), pp. 8–10.

Chapter Six

[1] Field, Frank L., Chris D. Kehas, and David V. Tiedeman. "The Self-concept in Career Development: A Construct in Transition," *The*

Personnel and Guidance Journal, Vol. 41: (May 1963), pp. 767–771.

[2] Barber, Bernard. "Social-class Differences in Educational Life-chances," *Teachers College Record,* Vol. 63: (November 1961), p. 103.

[3] *Ibid.,* p. 107.

[4] Katz, Martin R. *You: Today and Tomorrow* (Third Edition). Co-operative Test Division, Educational Testing Service, Princeton, New Jersey, 1959. (*See also* Strang, Ruth. *Target: Tomorrow.* New York: Dell Publishing Co., 1964.)

[5] Celebrezze, Anthony J. "Aim for the Top Jobs of '67," *This Week Magazine* (June 16, 1963), pp. 6–7.

[6] *Ibid.,* p. 4.

[7] *Ibid.,* p. 4.

[8] Blumenthal, Fred. "Will Your Child Be a National Leader?" *Parade* (January 20, 1963), pp. 4–5.

[9] Lifton, Walter M. "Will College Be Wasted on Your Child?" *Saturday Evening Post,* Vol. 235: (June 2, 1962), p. 6.

[10] Wertz, W. Willard. "When Junior Seeks a Job," *The PTA Magazine,* Vol. 58: (May 1963), pp. 12–14.

[11] Conant, James B. *Slums and Suburbs;* a Commentary on Schools in Metropolitan Areas. New York: McGraw-Hill Book Company, Inc., 1961.

[12] Havighurst, Robert and Lindley J. Stiles. "National Police for Alienated Youth," *Phi Delta Kappa,* Vol. 42: (April 1961), pp. 283–291.

[13] Michael Harrington. "The New Lost Generation: Jobless Youth," *The New York Times Magazine* (May 24, 1964), p. 13.

[14] Harris, Dale B. "Work and the Adolescent Transition to Maturity," *Teachers College Record,* Vol. 63 (November 1961), pp. 146–153.

[15] *News from U.S. Department of Labor,* April 18, 1962, pp. 2–3.

Chapter Seven

[1] Jahoda, Marie. *Current Conceptions of Positive Mental Health.* New York: Basic Books, 1958.

[2] Committee Report. "Strengthening the Behavioral Sciences," *Science,* Vol. 136: (April 1962), pp. 233–241.

[3] Witty, Paul. "Interest and Success—the Antidote to Stress," *Elementary English,* Vol. 32: (December 1955), pp. 507–513.

[4] Spock, Benjamin. "Should Mothers Work?" *Ladies Home Journal*, Vol. 80: (January-February 1963), pp. 16, 18, 21.

[5] Sullivan, Harry Stack. *The Interpersonal Theory of Psychiatry*. New York: Norton, 1953.

[6] Barclay, Dorothy. "How to Succeed as Grandma," *The New York Times Magazine* (June 10, 1962), p. 44.

[7] This section is based on the pamphlet, *Children and the Threat of Nuclear War*, by Sibylle Escalone, Child Study Association of America, Inc., 9 East 89th Street, New York 28, New York, 1962.

[8] *Ibid.*, p. 8.

[9] *Ibid.*, p. 13.

[10] *Ibid.*, p. 19.

[11] *Ibid*, p. 20.

[12] Bower, Eli M. "Mental Health in Education," *Review of Educational Research: Mental and Physical Health*, Vol. 32: (December 1962), pp. 441–454.

[13] Bergen, Mary E. "Trends in Basic Training," *The PTA Magazine*, Vol. 57: (October 1962), pp. 26–29.

[14] Murphy, Lois B. "Emotional First Aid for the Young Child," *Childhood Education*, Vol. 32: (January 1956), p. 206.

[15] Trippe, Matthew F. "Conceptual Problems in Research on Educational Provisions for Disturbed Children," *Exceptional Children*, Vol. 29: (April 1962), pp. 400–406.

[16] Hollister, W. G. and Caroline A. Chandler. "When Feeling Storms Precloud the Learning Process," *NEA Journal*, Vol. 51 (November 1962), pp. 18–20.

[17] See Metropolitan Life Insurance Company film, "If These Were Your Children." Two reels 16 mm. black and white. Part I—28 minutes. Part II—21 minutes. New York: One Madison Avenue.

[18] Ojemann, Ralph H. "Helping Children Understand Why They Feel as They Do, Why They Act as They Do," *NEA Journal*, Vol. 49: (September 1960), pp. 24–26.

[19] Harris, Dale B. "Work and the Adolescent Transition to Maturity," *Teachers College Record*, Vol. 63: (November 1961), pp. 146–153.

[20] Johnson, Orval G. "The Teacher and the Withdrawn Child," *Mental Hygiene*, Vol. 40: (October 1956), pp. 529–534.

[21] Banks, Robin K. and Daniel Cappon. "Developmental Deprivation and Mental Illness: 'A Study of 20 Questions,'" *Child Development*, Vol. 34: (September 1963), pp. 709–718.

[22] Eisenberg, Leon. "Treatment of the Emotionally Disturbed Pre-adolescent Child," in *The Pre-adolescent Exceptional Child*, p. 39,

Proceedings of the 35th Conference of the Child Research Clinic, held in Philadelphia, May 23, 1953, The Woods Schools, Langhorne, Pennsylvania.

23 "The Quiet One," Sound, 16 mm.; 1 hour, 7 minutes. Athena Films, Inc., 165 W. 46th Street, New York.

24 Kanner, Leo. "The Place of the Exceptional Child in the Family Structure," in *The Emotional Climate of the Exceptional Child,* p. 16. Proceedings of the Spring Conference on Education and the Exceptional Child of the Research Clinic of the Woods Schools, Langhorne, Pennsylvania, May 1949.

25 Scott, J. P. "Critical Periods in Behavioral Development," *Science,* Vol. 138: (November 1962), pp. 949–958.

26 Barclay, Dorothy. "A Small Child in the Big City," *The New York Times Magazine* (January 28, 1962), pp. 43–44.

27 Inglis, Brian. "The Aspirin Jungle," *The Nation,* Vol. 197: (August 24, 1963), pp. 83–86.

Chapter Eight

1 Coleman, James. *The Adolescent Society.* Glencoe, Illinois: The Free Press, 1961.

2 Scott, J. P. "Critical Periods in Behavioral Development," *Science,* Vol. 138: (November 1962), pp. 949–958.

3 *Ibid.,* p. 957.

4 *Ibid.,* p. 953.

5 Lynn, David B. "Sex-role and Parental Identification," *Child Development,* Vol. 33: (September 1962), p. 559.

6 The Demonstration Guidance Project, 1957–1962; Pilot Program for Higher Horizons. George Washington High School, Henry T. Tillson, Principal; Florence C. Myers, Administrative Assistant. Board of Education, New York City, May 1963.

7 *Ibid.,* pp. 23–24.

8 Conant, James B. *Slums and Suburbs;* a Commentary on Schools in Metropolitan Areas. New York: McGraw-Hill Book Company, Inc., 1961.

9 "Youth in Search of Identity." Mimeographed report of the Child Study Association of America, 9 East 89th Street, New York 28, New York, 1962.

10 Blanding, Sarah Gibson. "The Day I Spoke Off the Cuff to the Girls of Vassar," *McCall's,* Vol. 90: (November 1962), pp. 91, 162, 1962.

11 Kreppner, Stanley. "Sociopathic Tendencies and Reading Retardation

in Children," *Exceptional Children,* Vol. 29: (February 1963), pp. 258–266.

[12] White, Robert W. "The Dangers of Social Adjustment," *Teachers College Record,* Vol. 62: (January 1961), pp. 288–297.

[13] Symonds, John Addington. *The Life of Michelangelo Buonarroti,* p. 543. New York: Modern Library (n.d.).

[14] Piaget, Jean. *The Moral Judgment of the Child.* New York: Harcourt Brace and Company, 1932.

[15] Jones, Robert L., Jr., and Robert H. Shaffer. "The Ethical Discriminatory Abilities of High School Students," *Personnel and Guidance Journal,* Vol. 41: (February 1963), pp. 518–521.

[16] Allport, Gordon W. "Values and Our Youth," *Teachers College Record,* Vol. 63: (December 1961), pp. 211–219.

[17] Bronfenbrenner, Urie. "Soviet Methods of Character Education: Some Implications for Research," *American Psychologist,* Vol. 17: (August 1962), pp. 550–563. See also Bronfenbrenner, Urie. "Socialization and Social Class through Time and Space," in Eleanor Maccoby, T. M. Newcomb, and E. L. Hartley (eds.), *Readings in Social Psychology* (Third Edition), pp. 400–425. New York: Henry Holt, 1958.

[18] Old Testament: *Proverbs* 23:7.

[19] Ojemann, Ralph H. *Developing a Program for Education in Human Behavior.* Iowa City, Iowa: State University of Iowa, 1959.

[20] Hoffman, Martin L. "Parent Discipline and the Child's Consideration for Others," *Child Development,* Vol. 34: (September 1963), pp. 573–588.

[21] *Ibid.,* p. 587.

[22] Polley, Victoria Z. "Niagara Falls Coordinating Youth Council Makes Another Approach to Juvenile Decency," *New York State Education,* Vol. 48: (February 1961), pp. 26–27.

[23] *Old Testament:* Micah 6:8.

[24] Eby, Kermit. "A Letter to a Young Mother-Teacher," *The Educational Forum,* Vol. 26: (January 1962), p. 219.

[25] Gardner, John W. *Self-Renewal: The Individual and the Innovative Society,* pp. 10–12. New York: Harper & Row, 1964. Reprinted with permission of the author.

[26] Wray, Beulah K. Ephron. "The Good Mother," *Journal of the National Association of Women's Deans and Counselors,* Vol. 24: (January 1961), p. 75.

[27] McDanald, Eugene C., Jr. *Emotional and Spiritual Security.* Austin 12, Texas: The Hogg Foundation for Mental Health, The University of Texas, 1960.

Index

Ability, identifying child with special, 90-97
Accidents, as cause of handicaps, 67-68; information on prevention of, 79
Achievement, effect of, on learning, 118; guidance toward, 141-47; school, and conditions affecting, 121-24
Adolescents, blind, training of, 74; embarrassments common to, 58; emotional development of, 191-92; attitudes of, toward learning, 112; moral development of, 220-22; and nuclear threat, 183; nutrition and, 60; attitude of, toward parental guidance, 30-32; guide to self-appraisal for, 157; self-descriptions of, 18-22; sex and venereal disease among, 63; smoking, drinking, and drug addiction among, 61-63; social development of, 209-11; social values of, 208; as talented students, 97; underachievement of, and peer approval, 119
Aggression, as social problem, 217
Alcohol, addiction and potential, 15
Allport, Gordon W., on "becoming," 25
American Academy of Pediatrics, on sports, 69
American Foundation for the Blind, publications of, 71
American Friends Service Committee, work of, 221
American Medical Association, on child-beating, 69
American Social Health Association, on venereal disease, 63
Anxiety, the adolescent and current, 25; effect of, on emotional health, 183-84; effect of adult, on children, 182; and emotional blocks, 129-30; and the overachiever, 126; and underachievement, 142
Armed Forces Qualification Test, failures in, 109
Arts, the, value of, for the blind, 73, 74; for handicapped children, 44; in the home, 98

Ashton-Warner, Sylvia, methods of, in teaching Maori, 138-39
Automation, effect of, on employment, 50, 160-61
Automobiles, adolescents' use of, 69

Barclay, Dorothy, on alleviating anxiety in learning, 126; on parent-teenage relations, 34
Baumgartner, Leona, on venereal disease, 63
"Becoming," process of, 25-28
"Bilingual" children, special needs of, 137-39
Biochemistry, in mental health, 178
Biological needs, and motivation, 116
Blanding, Sarah, on moral standards, 215-16
Blind child, assets of, 35; understanding and training of, 46, 69-74
Brain damage, and emotional disturbance, 194
Bronfenbrenner, Urie, on value systems, 221-22

Careers; see Vocations
Celebrezze, Anthony J., childhood and career of, 157
Cerebral palsy, training of child with, 77, 78
Child, the, emotional disturbance in, 192-203; emotional health of, 178-82, 184-91, 204; moral development of, 219-20; and nuclear threat, 182-83; and reading retardation, 130-37; social development of, 209-11; development of thinking in, 110-14; see also Gifted child, Handicapped child, Underachiever, etc.
Clubs, school, as aid to gifted child, 104
Cognitive development, defined, 81
Coleman, James S., on school achievement, 123
College, choice of, 175-76; decision to attend, 153; financing, 173-74; planning for, 172, 173-74; and vocational success, 158
College Entrance Examinations, practice for, 107